The
Healing Heart

The
Healing Heart

ANTIDOTES TO

PANIC AND HELPLESSNESS

Norman Cousins

W · W · NORTON & COMPANY NEW YORK · LONDON

Acknowledgment is made to the following for permission to use or adapt the author's material previously published in these journals:

American Health: 2, nos. 3 and 4 (1983).
Archives of Internal Medicine: 142 (1982).
Annual Review of Public Health: 2 (1981).
Creative Living: 12, no. 2 (1983).
International Journal of Cardiology: 3, nos. 1 and 2 (1983).
Journal of the American Medical Association: 248: 2,5 (1982).
The Physician in Literature: W. B. Saunders Co., Philadelphia (1982).

Library of Congress Cataloging in Publication Data
Cousins, Norman.
The healing heart.
Bibliography: p.
1. Heart—Infarction—Patients—California—Biography.
2. Heart—Infarction—Psychological aspects.   3. Will.
4. Healing.   5. Authors, American—California—
Biography.   6. Cousins, Norman.   I. Title.
RC685.I6C7   1983   362.1'96237'0924 [B]   83–11449

ISBN 0-393-01816-4

W. W. Norton & Company, Inc., 500 Fifth Avenue, New York, N. Y. 10110
W. W. Norton & Company Ltd., 37 Great Russell Street, London WC1B 3NU

ACKNOWLEDGMENTS

I am grateful to Dr. John Kastor, editor of the *International Journal of Cardiology,* for prodding me to write the article that led ultimately to this book; to Howard Sandum and Peter Jovanovich for helping me to steer that article into book form; to George Brockway for the continuation of his editorial guidance and friendship, of which I have been the beneficiary for many years and which is reflected in the final form of this book; to Dr. Lawrence D. Grouse, senior editor of the *Journal of the American Medical Association,* for the hospitality he provided in *JAMA* for several articles woven into this book; to the deans and graduating students of the schools of medicine at Baylor College of Medicine, the University of California at Irvine, the University of California at Los Angeles, Case Western Reserve University, Harvard University, Tulane University, the University of Southern California, and George Washington University for their permission to draw from commencement talks at those schools; to T George Harris, editor of *American Health,* for his unconditional support and personal encouragement; to Frances Thompson and Carol Prager, for their research memoranda; to Caroline Blattner, who spent numberless hours in the physical preparation of the manuscript and whose editing suggestions I value highly; and to Ellen Cousins, who makes me possible. It is difficult for me to imagine that any human being can give more to another than my wife has given to me.

Contents

10) CONTENTS

Introduction

Bernard Lown, M.D.

Professor of Cardiology

Harvard University School of Public Health

A merry heart doeth good like a medicine;
but a broken spirit drieth the bones.

King Solomon, Proverbs 17:22

The ongoing scientific and technological revolution in the health field has stimulated a surge of publications raising a theme as ancient as medicine itself, namely, that psychological factors can affect every aspect of human illness. No one has argued the issue more cogently than Norman Cousins, whose impact on a growing public perception stems from his 1979 book, *Anatomy of an Illness as Perceived by the Patient.* His new book is not a compendium of technical information; rather, it is an account of a man who used himself as an experimental laboratory in confronting a major heart attack.

Cousins's message comes at a critical time, when some physicians are increasingly distancing themselves from the bedside, are abandoning the power of the word as a therapeutic tool, and manifesting indifference to the patient's psychological and spiritual needs. In short, contemporary medicine is ever more sharply focused on the disembodied disease, rather than on the afflicted patient. This conventional biomedical model, though giving lip service to the patient as the object of care, largely ignores the subjective dimension and views it as an irrelevant epiphenomenon. The patient's body is the battlefield; when the physician prevails, recovery follows. While psychological processes color the patient's perceptions, they are deemed to have little relevance to the outcome of the case and the regaining of health.

The growth of medical scientific insight during the past half a century has exceeded the accumulation of knowledge during all the preceding millennia of recorded human history. An elegant, ever-burgeoning technology makes it possible to probe recesses of the body and decode the secrets of many pathological processes. The enormous medical accomplishments, the consistency of results, the reproducibility of findings, and the resolution of life-threatening disease all derive from the rigorous application of scientific methods and spur confidence in the biomedical model.

Although most physicians would not deny that many variables, including psychological factors, influence disease, these are regarded as secondary and largely irrelevant once the basic cause is discovered. For example, when streptococcal upper-respiratory infections are controlled, psychological factors in a child's rheumatic fever are not given serious consideration. Without the tubercle bacillus, the soaring imagination of a Thomas Mann might not have produced a *Magic Mountain*. Similarly, some physicians would maintain that once the biology of cancer is comprehended, the psychological factors that may govern its progress or modulate its anxiety and pain become but an irrelevant script on ancient scrolls.

The most immutable fact of life is death. It will never be annulled by artificial organs or scientific progress. The days of a human being will ever be finite, and disease and pain will always stalk life's journey. The patient will always require care, sympathetic judgment, and healing. The physician will never be relieved of the responsibility to assuage pain, promote comfort, and instill hope. But there is an additional aspect, relating to the patient's psychobiological constitution, that has powerful self-regulating and self-healing capacities. In ignoring these intrinsic gifts for self-repair, the physician obstructs the amplification of the efficacy of his own scientific methods and impedes the very process of recovery.

These aspects were already recognized by practitioners of Hippocratic medicine about 2,500 years ago, as Cousins points out. The cure they preached resided within the patient; the function of medicine was merely to activate this process and lend it support. Hippocrates recognized the profound impact on illness which stemmed from the physician-patient relationship. The passage of time has not diminished the validity of his observation that "some patients, though conscious that their condition is perilous, recover their health simply through their contentment with the goodness of the physician."

The Lethal Power of Words

Very early in my career I encountered painfully the adverse impact of psychological factors on disease. The experience still provokes in me a shudder of disbelief. Some 30 years ago I had a postdoctorate fellowship with Dr. S. A. Levine, professor of cardiology at the Harvard Medical School and at the Peter Bent Brigham Hospital. He was a keen observer of the human scene, had an awesome presence, was precise in formulation, and was blessed with a prodigious memory. He was, in effect, the consummate clinician at the bedside. Dr. Levine conducted a weekly outpatient cardiac clinic at the hospital. After we young trainees examined the patient, he would drop in briefly to assess our findings and suggest further diagnostic workup or changes in the therapeutic program. With patients, he was invariably reassuring and convincing, and they venerated his every word. In one of my first clinics, I had as a patient Mrs. S., a well-preserved middle-aged librarian who had a narrowing of one of the valves on the right side of her heart, the tricuspid valve. She had been in low-grade congestive heart failure with modest edema of the ankles, but was able to maintain her job and attend efficiently to household chores. She was receiving digitalis and weekly injections of a mercurial diuretic. Dr. Levine, who had followed her in the clinic for more than a decade, greeted Mrs. S. warmly and then turned to the large entourage of visiting physicians and said, "This woman has TS," and abruptly left.

No sooner was Dr. Levine out of the door than Mrs. S.'s demeanor abruptly changed. She appeared anxious and frightened and was now breathing rapidly, clearly hyperventilating. Her skin was drenched with perspiration, and her pulse had accelerated to more than 150 a minute. In re-examining her, I found it astonishing that the lungs, which a few minutes earlier had been quite clear, now had moist crackles at the bases. This was extraordinary, for with obstruction of the right heart valve, the lungs are spared the accumulation of excess fluid.

I questioned Mrs. S. as to the reasons for her sudden

upset. Her response was that Dr. Levine had said that she had TS, which she knew meant "terminal situation." I was initially amused at this misinterpretation of the medical acronym for "tricuspid stenosis." My amusement, however, rapidly yielded to apprehension, as my words failed to reassure and as her congestion continued to worsen. Shortly thereafter she was in massive pulmonary edema. Heroic measures did not reverse the frothing congestion. I tried to reach Dr. Levine, but he was nowhere to be located. Later that same day she died from intractable heart failure. To this day the recollection of this tragic happening causes me to tremble at the awesome power of the physician's word. This point is emphasized by Norman Cousins.

The Healing Power of Words

Many times since then I have encountered patients whose cardiac congestion, arrhythmia, bronchospasm, or angina pectoris has been aggravated by a physician's maladroit utterances. But words can not only smite but also heal. I recall vividly a critically ill patient with a massive heart attack whose cardiac muscle function was irreparably compromised. While venous pressure was high, blood pressure was maintained only with an intravenous drip of a cardiac stimulant. The lungs were congested, the heart rate was uncontrollably rapid, and the rhythm was at times chaotic. The patient's breathing was labored and required oxygen. We had exhausted all the usual therapeutic means.

At one morning rounds I commented to the attending staff that Mr. B. had a wholesome, very loud third-sound gallop. Everyone dutifully auscultated the heart and nodded assent. Actually, a third-sound gallop is a poor sign and denotes that the heart muscle is straining and usually failing. The patient had an oxygen mask and seemingly was unmindful of the dialogue across the bed, peppered as it was with medical jargon. Slowly and quite unexpectedly he improved and eventually was discharged from the hospital.

Some months later, when I saw him for an office checkup, I marveled at his recovery and asked about the basis for the miraculous improvement. "Doctor, I not only know what got me better," he said, "but even the exact moment when it happened. I was sure the end was near and that you and your staff had given up hope. However, Thursday morning, when you entered with your troops, something happened that changed everything. You listened to my heart; you seemed pleased by the findings and announced to all those standing about my bed that I had a 'wholesome gallop.' I knew that the doctors, in talking to me, might try to soften things. But I knew they wouldn't kid each other. So when I overheard you tell your colleagues I had a wholesome gallop, I figured I still had a lot of kick to my heart and could not be dying. My spirits were for the first time lifted, and I knew I would live and recover."

Such experiences shape the understanding of most physicians. As anecdotes, however, they have little credibility within the profession. Understandably so. Medicine has with difficulty exited from the quagmire of subjectivism, and no one is eager to replace the certain compass of science with the uncertain prediction to be garnered from tea leaves. But how is one to objectivize the power of the word, not as a means of swaying a person's mind—that no one disputes—but as a means of influencing the most intimate of bodily functions? Some years ago I had an opportunity to demonstrate this power.

Visceral Conditioning with Words

The experience I am about to relate occurred 26 years ago. The flow of time, which ordinarily diminishes and dilutes, has in this instance enhanced the relevance of the observations.

A 40-year-old man was first seen in consultation for chest pain. At age 21 he was found to be hypertensive; 11 years later, while working as a meat packer, he experienced the abrupt onset of crushing chest pain due to acute myocardial infarction. Thereafter, he had frequent chest discomfort that he could "walk off." In fact, his avocation was mountaineering. At the beginning of a climb, he experienced soreness behind the breastbone. This forced him to stop and fall behind for several minutes; thereafter, he was able to climb at a sustained pace for several hours without re-experiencing any chest symptoms and was frequently the first to reach the top of Mount Washington in New Hampshire. Although everyone else was winded, he was free of breathlessness. Occasionally, he noted pain in anticipation of a climb while driving to the mountain base. The disparity between symptoms and effort induced several physicians to question the diagnosis of angina, and they urged that he seek psychiatric help.

The family history was pockmarked with heart disease. Both parents died prematurely of coronary attacks, as did his only sister, at age 42. A majority of male members were smitten before their 45th birthday. Mr. A., the patient, was convinced that he was fated to die before he reached 45.

In order to test the efficacy of various antianginal drugs, I had him exercise on a so-called Master two-step test, in which the patient traverses two nine-inch steps for three minutes. Our patient, Mr. A., had to perform 44 such crossings in the allotted time.

The results were consistent. When he crossed the two-step 40 times, he complained about a slight heaviness in the chest. This increased in intensity so that by the time he reached 44 trips, the discomfort was moderate to unbearable and he was compelled to stop. The pain became more severe with recumbency. At this point the electrocardiographic pattern showed profound alterations.

After five such exercise stress tests, the patient observed that each time he was compelled to stop after precisely 44 crossings over the two steps. He commented that the experience reminded him of his dog, who became carsick and vomited in the backseat when taken for a ride. After a while, the vomiting was provoked by the turning on of the ignition key and starting the motor. To obviate the need to clean up, Mr. A. would lead the dog close to the car and then start the engine. The dog would vomit on the sidewalk and then could be taken for a ride without soiling the backseat. I was completely dumbfounded by the relevance of a vomiting dog to Mr. A.'s ability to exercise over a two-step. The meaning of this anecdote eluded me until he explained that the dog, just like himself, had been psychologically conditioned. "Didn't a Russian by the name of Pavlov have something to say about that?" This remarkable question inspired the following study.

On his next weekly visit to the laboratory, he was told that exercise testing would henceforth be conducted without my counting out loud the number of crossings. However, when he was approaching the end of exercise, counting would be resumed out loud, with the 40th trip. Thereafter, the test was performed in the usual manner except that the count was silent. As he reached 28 crossings, I called out 40, then 42, and so forth. He seemed startled at the more rapid approach of the end of exercise, but, after 29 crossings, at a count of 41, he complained of discomfort, and by 32 crossings (the miscount being 44) the pain had increased significantly, forcing him to stop. Most remarkably, the electrocardiographic changes were identical to those occurring when on prior occasions he crossed the two-step 44 times.

In the following week, the same test procedure yielded a similar response. In the third week, exercise was performed in the same fashion, except that the count was out loud throughout the test and that he was stopped at 32 crossings. He felt no pain and exhibited no electrocardiographic changes. Such testing was repeated weekly over six weeks. When the count was silent and the number of crossings was advanced and misstated, pain and electrocardiographic changes resulted. When the count was accurate and Mr. A. was stopped at 32 crossings, he was free of discomfort or objective changes. In the seventh week the test was again carried out, with the miscount at 28 crossings. The patient looked amused and commented, "Doctor, you don't know how to count or else you are finagling—it is only 28." Thereafter, he experienced no pain at 32 crossings and showed no electrocardiographic changes.

By this time we had exhausted the scanty antianginal pharmacopoeia then available, and, regrettably, I did not have the wisdom to carry on with the weekly experiments, which raised his spirits and enabled him to bear the severe angina. The cessation of exercise testing dissipated the hope of finding an effective remedy. About a month later, while driving a truck, he slumped over the wheel and died suddenly in front of the Peter Bent Brigham Hospital, the very hospital where the studies had recently been conducted.

The patient was a high-school dropout, a largely self-taught workingman. An omnivorous reader, he had delved deeply into science. He possessed a profound reverence for life yet was unalterably convinced of his own impending doom. He was pleased with the testing: "If it doesn't help me, it may help someone else." He inspired in his physician a yearning to "do something," although the means then available were woefully meager. So, he underwent exercise testing once weekly, which assuaged the anxiety of both participants. Nine times when the number 44 was called out, the patient was compelled to stop because of disabling pain accompanied by significant electrocardiographic changes. On four occasions, his response was unaltered even though he traversed the two-step in 12 fewer crossings. When during two exercise tests the counting was out loud and the test was stopped at 32 trips across the two-step, there was neither pain nor electrocardiographic deterioration.

This experience made a lasting impression on me. It suggested that a relatively innocuous activity such as counting, in a particular setting, was a sufficient biobehavioral factor to induce angina pectoris. The ability of seemingly neutral signals to serve as symbolic stresses was now demonstrated reproducibly.

That such harmless psychological cues can activate disease mechanisms depends upon the fact that all our bodily organs are connected with and responsive to nerve traffic that reaches them by way of autonomic, neurohumoral, and humoral pathways from the highest integrative centers of the brain. In the clinical setting, there frequently occur unique but unknowable transient linkages between outer experience and the functioning of various organ systems. Wolf has put it appropriately: "It is probable that most adaptive functions of the cardiovascular system are responsive to stimuli that owe their force to their special significance to the individual."

The publication of the above case study was delayed for two decades.* It took much time for me to become convinced of the reality of what I had witnessed, to deem it relevant and deserving of communication. These experiences both shaped my clinical outlook and determined the focus of my research interests.

Psychological Factors and Sudden Cardiac Death

Only in retrospect do I see the links between these early events and my preoccupation over the past two decades with the problem of sudden cardiac death.

Two thousand years ago, Seneca commented that "death is sometimes a punishment, often a gift, and for many a favor." In the case of sudden cardiac death, it is neither gift nor favor, for it extinguishes life at its creative prime. It is the leading cause of fatality in the industrially developed world. In the United States someone dies unexpectedly every 75 seconds, day or night. Sudden cardiac death has been shadowing man's life since the inception of recorded history. The unpredictability of its occurrence burdens our dreams and provides an awesome reminder of the fragility of our biology. While it is recognized that sudden death is due to an electrical derangement of heart rhythm known

*Published as a case study. B. Lown, "The Verbal Conditioning of Angina Pectoris during Exercise Testing," *American Journal of Cardiology* 40 (1977): 630–34.

as ventricular fibrillation, no clear acute morphologic lesions in the heart have been identified which trigger this event.

Sudden cardiac death presents a paradox: A massive unheralded catastrophe, yet in the heart a paucity of acute changes. Extensive coronary artery disease is the rule, but its severity and distribution are not distinctive. The underlying process is known to be caused by atherosclerosis, which evolves over a lifetime, but the trigger for the terminal, nearly instantaneous event remains undefined. A common view, shared by physicians and laymen alike, suggests psychological stress as a trigger for the lethal arrhythmia. This is indeed a curious suggestion, for the patient may experience closure of a major coronary artery, or be afflicted with an extensive myocardial infarction, without these injuries throwing the heart into ventricular fibrillation. Can a painful thought be a more powerful trigger for arrhythmia than extensive injury to the heart itself? These questions are raised by Norman Cousins in connection with his own case.

An individual's ability to handle stress depends on a complex amalgam of factors, including genetic predisposition, experiences in early childhood, a lifelong process of conditioning, as well as an array of social and cultural elements. These factors and many others contribute to the psychological prism that refracts daily events uniquely and individually. Furthermore, the adverse stimulus is rarely singular, overt, and substantial; more frequently, it is either chronic or intermittent and seemingly insignificant. In addition, the response may be temporally remote from the provocative stimulus, thereby obscuring causal connections.

The Acute Heart Attack

While we have learned to cope with many of the organic aspects of cardiac illness, the cardiologist, unfortunately, is growing ever more indifferent to psychological factors. Nowhere is this more evident than in the coronary-care unit, where the tendency is to treat objects instead of human beings. Much grief results from the physician's dealing with patients as if they were things. This is especially likely in the case of a victim of a fresh heart attack.

A patina of common sense is all that is required to appreciate the psychological stress of being well at one minute and seemingly at death's door in the next. The hospital environment imposes indignity and stress even when the patient is not critically ill: lack of privacy, separation from family and friends, encouragement of dependency, disruption of sleep, painfulness of procedures, adverse effects of drugs, fear of bodily harm, loss of control, uncertainty of recovery. All of these factors mobilize diverse emotions such as anxiety, guilt, shame, and rage, which lead to a sense of helplessness, regression, as well as depression. The silent, somber, noncommunicative physician looms terrifyingly large as the patient becomes pitifully Lilliputian.

The paradox pertains to the fact that the physician is not unaware of the adverse effects of psychological stress on the cardiovascular system. The founder of modern heart physiology, William Harvey, comprehended this relationship 300 years ago when he said, "Every affection of the mind that is attendant with either pain or pleasure, hope or fear is the cause of an agitation whose influence extends to the heart."

Norman Cousins takes up this agitation and gently rocks the medical boat. Once again his illness, now a heart attack, provides the text for a sermon on the importance of mobilizing healing emotions. The restoring power of a positive thought, the ability of optimism to halt and reverse a downhill course even when the heart is badly damaged, is not foreign to medicine. The famous 17th-century physician Thomas Sydenham expressed it succinctly: "The arrival of a good clown exercises more beneficial influence upon the health of a town than twenty asses laden with drugs."

Unhappily, modern physicians are largely veering away from Sydenham's view. The patient arriving in a hospital emergency ward with a fresh heart attack is confronted by technically proficient house staff. Their immediate aim is not to still the terror induced by the uncertainty of survival but to insert catheters, obtain measurements, and deliver drugs. Human uniqueness and individuality are washed away under the indifferent onslaught of rehearsed protocol procedures. Anxiety and fear are allayed not by comforting reassurance but by the prescription of Valium around the clock. When the heart rhythm grows chaotic and degenerates to ventricular fibrillation, this is ascribed to the magnitude of the infarction. There is scant appreciation that the kind of ministration and absence of sympathetic communication have cut loose the anchor of the patient's identifiable being. Norman Cousins's point about the need to liberate patients from panic needs to be emphasized again and again.

Instead of sensing uneasiness and answering questions, the staff frequently deluge the patient with unfamiliar and fear-inducing terms. One day while rounding in a coronary-care unit, I was examining a depressed-appearing man. When I asked about the reason for the somber mood,

he responded, "Doc, I don't think I am going to make it."
To the question why not, he replied, "Well the intern told
me that I have a massive anterior wall infarct, the resident
said I had a transmural heart attack, the cardiology fellow
indicated that I experienced an occlusion of a major coronary artery, while the attending physician called it a coronary thrombosis, and the nurse advised me not to ask
questions. How can anyone survive so much heart damage?"

All of the varied jargon had the same meaning. When
the staff was chided for instilling fear, the answer was "But
we meant well." We physicians invariably mean well; not
infrequently we do ill and justify our ill doing by our well
meaning.

How Do Physicians Become This Way?

How have physicians grown to be purveyors of biotech-
nology? As with any other complex social phenomenon,
no single explanation suffices. Medical-school admission
is geared to the very bright, achievement-oriented students who have accumulated top grades in scientific subjects. This necessarily selects qualities of intense
competitiveness, intellectual narrowness—belonging to
young people who often have neglected interpersonal rela-
tions and have not permitted the leavening of their own
sensibilities and their capacities to "reach out."

Norman Cousins has been teaching literature and philosophy to medical students. I can testify to the need. During clinical rounds, my allusions to literary or cultural
figures elicit blank stares from these intelligent, scientifically sparkling physicians. No one has heard of Camus or
Sartre, and Strindberg is identified as a pitcher for the Yan-
kees.

The selection process is only part of the problem, for the medical-school curriculum dehumanizes even those who come with deeply held aspirations to serve. The four-year, intensive indoctrination aims to install scientific competence and train bioscientists to manage massive complex technology. Little time or effort is devoted to the cultivation of caring.

Students usually score higher on psychological testing in empathy measures upon entry to medical school than upon graduation. The weekly medical grand rounds might deal with esoteric disease, but they rarely focus on responding to patient needs, alleviating anxieties, or comforting the family. If the curriculum is deficient, how is the medical aspirant to acquire, in Cousins's words, the ability "to mobilize and release all those forces in a human being that work for regeneration and repair"?

An even more critical factor accounting for the current behavior of physicians has to do with the marketplace. Procedures are richly rewarded especially if they are invasive, while counseling, rendering empathy, or patient advocacy receive meager recompense. A good patient-physician relationship is cemented through the acquisition of a painstaking and unhurried history. It is also the decisive transaction that provides information for a diagnosis in more than 70 percent of the patients. The pay for history taking is picayune compared with that for most procedures, which are generally much less informative. The young, debt-ridden physician rapidly learns the economic facts of life and concentrates his efforts on activities that yield the largest income.

There is an additional dimension to the prism distorting the image of medical values which I would designate the "father-son syndrome." Whereas clinical experience is

slowly acquired over many years and whereas sound judgment is the product of nearly a lifetime of arduous labor,
technology can be rapidly mastered. It is far easier to learn
how to interpret scientific data than to acquire the art of
obtaining a sound history or performing an adequate
physical examination. A skewed cybernetic ensues, wherein
inadequacy of bedside skills increases resort to technical
solutions. The older physician has difficulty keeping up
with the veritable Niagara of new devices, altered methods, novel concepts, and ever-changing vocabulary.

In a competition with the established and experienced
physician, the advantage now accrues to the technically
proficient and to those conversant with the latest scientific
findings. In this struggle the young, inexperienced physician has every advantage; the accent is not on judgment
but on technical skill. Mastery of the latest method now
permits rapid ascent on the academic ladder to the very
top. This process enjoys every encouragement from the
medical-industrial complex.

Current developments have widened the ancient gap
between science and philosophy. Science is constantly
changing; human nature and psychological realities remain
fairly stable. While artistic and literary creativity incorpo-
rates and expands upon the past, scientific truth negates
the past from which it derives. A medical textbook, even
a decade old, is already outdated. The idolatry of the latest
issue of a medical journal reflects restiveness and impa-
tience with yesterday's facts. The modern physician tends
to ignore the past. There are no medical heroes, merely
temporary celebrities. To the artist or writer the main-
spring of creativity is an umbilical cord to the masters of
bygone ages. Aeschylus and Shakespeare are as relevant as
Dostoevski and Hemingway. They all address the same

human condition, exposing the inexhaustible diversity of life and probing the reason for being. As Norman Cousins says, art and literature do not yield answers but do pose questions and provide perspective. The physician, the child of science, is disenchanted with generalities and searches for hard, factual answers. But many of the patient's problems are better comprehended through the realm bequeathed by art and literature than through the facts revealed by science. While science may help explain how a virus multiplies, it leaves unanswered why a tear is shed.

The physician's fervent courtship of science and technology is not to be faulted except for its excess and for its neglect of humanistic traditions. It is unlikely that a reasoned and deeply felt appeal from a single and singular patient will diminish the intense dalliance between medicine and technology.

The importance of *The Healing Heart* is that it will educate future patients to search in themselves for the powers of healing, thereby fostering the self-reliance and optimism necessary to help overcome the travail of illness. For this process to succeed, the physician must become the patient's ally rather than his adversary. Only then can the art and science of medicine be truly conjoined for the promotion of health and well-being.

Barring nuclear war, a historical perspective encourages hope, for self-correcting mechanisms operate in social systems as in human organisms. Sooner or later, medical-school curricula and admissions criteria will change. Economic forces will eventually curtail improper incentives. Paraprofessional competition will compel physicians to be responsive to the expectations of patients. As Peabody counseled half a century ago, the medical profession must relearn that "care of the patient requires caring for the patient."

The
Healing Heart

CHAPTER I

The Reckoning

Statistics, if you happen to know about them, can be morose hospital companions.

Fifty percent of all persons who have heart attacks die during the first 24 hours. It was hard for me to put this figure out of my mind after having been ambulanced on December 22, 1980, into the UCLA Hospital emergency room. The diagnosis was "significant" heart-muscle destruction and congestive heart failure.

As evening approached, I wasn't sure I ought to take a chance on going to sleep. Like a character in a Dostoevski novel, I found myself wondering whether this would be my last night in this world. The thought that kept recurring was that there was something oppressively incidental and bare about coming to the end of the road in a half-lit coronary-care unit. The sense of the perfunctory was not relieved by the electronic bleeps of the heart monitor to which I was attached or by human sounds from nearby rooms. I don't particularly crave ceremonies, but it seemed to me that, just as there are commencement exercises and designated observances at various stages and plateaus of one's life, so there ought to be a final graduation affair, with a diploma, perhaps, and farewells, smiles, and handshakes all around.

I don't know why I should have supposed that death should be any more sentient or eventful to the person about to die than birth is to the person about to be born. Yet the sequences of life would seem to call for a grand culmination and not just discontinuity and paradox. Socrates, only a few minutes away from the hemlock, was at least able to engage in a philosophical dialogue in which he discharged a final obligation. "I owe a cock to Aesculapius," he said, and pledged Crito to the commitment. Those last words may not have been the most illuminating or profound of his lifetime, but they had certain culminating qualities and made possible a debt-free departure.

My own catalogue of debts had mostly to do with inadequately expressed feelings of love for those closest to me. The compulsion to lay bare one's heart is all too easily quieted with the self-reassuring belief that a more propitious moment is not far away. I thought of my visit to my father's hospital room a few hours before he died. His eyes were open but he couldn't see. His lips moved; I came to his side and put my hand on his.

"Norman, is that you?" he had asked.

"Yes, Pop."

"Norman, I just want you to know how much I love you," he had said. "Please give my love to everyone."

So far as I know, those were his last words.

It would be impossible for me to describe the richness of that experience. Pop had never been very demonstrative in his affections. Nor, I fear, had I. And now, only half a dozen or so years later, I lay on my own hospital bed. Even the off-white walls conveyed uncertainty. Would I have a chance to speak to my wife and children, my brother and sisters, and my friends, as my father had spoken to me?

I thought to myself: What else ought I to be thinking about at this particular time? In an essay he wrote for the *Saturday Review,* John Steinbeck said there comes a time when each of us must ask, "Have I lived enough? Have I loved enough?" I had no doubts about the first question. As for the second, the question for me was not whether I had loved enough but whether I had made it known and felt by those I loved.

These Proustian ruminations reverberated with the statistical bleakness of my situation as I understood it. Did I dare close my eyes? Was sleep an exit to be resisted? Then I laughed at myself. I was supposed to be the fellow who wouldn't panic, who knew how to mobilize his confidence and his healing resources. After the publication of my book telling of a recovery from a serious collagen illness, I was supposed to be a walking health exhibit. But here I was, bedded down in a coronary intensive-care unit in a hospital attached to a medical school in which I, a layman, was a professor whose job was to emphasize the need for patients to develop health habits that would help prevent breakdowns. It was all very embarrassing.

I snapped on the TV set and picked up a UCLA basketball game. It was a squeaker, but UCLA won by three points in overtime. The fact that I could put my attention on the game and indeed get caught up in it helped me out of my introspective preoccupations. I drew a deep breath, turned off the TV, and went to sleep. At about 6:00 A.M.,

I awoke, looked around the room, congratulated myself on having made it through the night, reached for some paper, and put down some notes about the events leading up to the heart attack.

As I thought back on the last half of 1980, I realize that I had had very little opportunity to engage in sports or other physical recreation. The main source of stress in my life for some years had been airports and airplanes, necessitated by a heavy speaking and conference schedule. Battling traffic congestion en route to airports, having to run through air terminals carrying my luggage because the sidewalk attendants were too busy and the counter lines overcrowded, having to queue up for boarding passes at the gate and then being turned away because the plane had been overbooked, waiting at baggage carousels for bags that never turned up, time-zone changes, irregular meals, insufficient sleep—these features of airline transportation had been my melancholy burdens for many years and were especially profuse in the latter part of 1980.

Once in the air, I usually relished the journey above the clouds. I had unobstructed access to my books and work papers. Every now and then, however, something would go wrong. In October 1980, on a flight from Los Angeles to San Antonio, the cabin pressure failed at about 35,000 feet. For some reason, the oxygen masks couldn't be activated. The captain struggled for almost an hour to correct the malfunctioning system before deciding to make an emergency landing at El Paso. I had some bleeding from the ears, as did several other passengers, but no discernible chest symptoms.

Sometime in late October or early November, I began to experience shortness of breath, especially in cold weather. I had feelings of pressure low in my throat and heaviness in my right leg. There were faint traces of blood in my sputum. I reported these symptoms to my internist. A cardiograph showed almost no change from two earlier ones, taken over a period of several years. The symptoms receded, and all seemed well again.

I returned from a hectic trip to the East Coast just before Christmas, only to discover that I was due to leave again in a few days for the Southeast. I asked my secretary about the possibility of postponement or cancellation. She carefully reviewed with me the special facts in each case that made it essential to go through with the engagements. It was obvious, on the basis of what she said, that only the most drastic event would get me out of it.

My body was listening. The next day I had my heart attack.

Arnold Hutschnecker, in his book *The Will to Live,* made the point that people who feel locked into obligations that they would rather set aside are candidates for sudden and serious disease. Was my body giving me the perfect excuse for avoiding the airports and the attendant frustrations? I had something to think about.

In any case, I could hardly complain, as Ivan Ilyich had done in Tolstoy's famous story, that I had been inexplicably singled out by the Deity for punishment. In literature, as in life, the patient's persistent and plaintive cry when hit by severe illness has always been "Why me?" The answer to that question in my case was no mystery; I had it coming to me. Too many places. Too little time to get there. Too few opportunities to recoup.

On December 22, I officially became one of 38,000,000 Americans who suffer from heart disease in one form or another. Of these, more than 500,000 have heart attacks each year. No other illness—not even cancer—claims as many lives. The particular label attached to my illness carried the initials CHD—coronary heart disease. What it meant was that the heart was not receiving enough oxygen to perform its functions. The flow of blood carrying the oxygen was being impeded by arteries clogged and narrowed because of the accumulation of fatty substances that had hardened into plaque. Cases in this category carry the risk of SCD—sudden coronary death.

The attack occurred at home. Just after lunch, I was hit by a wave of nausea and weakness. I began to pant. I had none of the massive squeezing pains generally associated with a heart attack, but pressure in my chest and difficulty in breathing left little doubt that my heart was failing.

We keep a small portable oxygen tank in the house for the same precautionary reasons we keep a fire extinguisher. It is a simple device, weighing only a couple of pounds. A plastic transparent cup is placed over the nose. The tank has a capacity of about two hours. I directed my wife, Ellen, in hooking me up.

After being unable to reach Dr. Omar Fareed or Dr. Howard Weinberger, Ellen called Dean Sherman Mellinkoff, my boss at the School of Medicine at UCLA, to report my condition. Dr. Mellinkoff said he would dispatch an ambulance immediately.

All this time, the words I had used in talking to medical students at UCLA kept coming back to me: Free your heart-attack patients of panic. Panic is a killer. One reason so many heart-attack victims never reach the hospital alive is that the heart, already in a precarious condition, has had imposed upon it the additional burden of panic. Panic can destabilize the heart and sometimes even rupture heart muscles. Panic can constrict the blood vessels, forcing the heart to pump blood through narrowed openings. Reassurance is the first order of treatment. The mood of the person or persons attending to the patient should be calm and confident.

When the paramedics arrived, I was able to de-escalate the usual emergency mood and thus was spared their strenuous heroics. The very fact that I was already on a portable oxygen tank helped to moderate the usual routine. They reconnected me to a regular oxygen tank and took my cardiograph. I declined the lidocaine and morphine injections; I had pressure but no sharp pain. The paramedics notifed the hospital, then carried me out to the ambulance in a half-reclining bench chair that facilitated proper respiration.

The ride to the hospital was a comparatively leisurely one. At my request, the driver turned off the siren and drove at ordinary speed. I saw no point in fostering accidents en route, leading to yet more ambulances and more accidents. Moreover, the last thing in the world a patient needs is a shrieking wail and a panicky, hell-for-leather, careening ambulance ride. The paramedics apparently appreciated not having to put other people at risk on the way to the hospital. I experienced no chest pains during the ambulance ride, but I was bringing up blood.

When we arrived at the UCLA emergency room, a battery of medical talent was waiting for me: Dean Sherman Mellinkoff; Dr. David Solomon, chief of UCLA's Department of Medicine; Dr. Howard Weinberger, who, at the suggestion of Dean Mellinkoff, had treated me for a transient health problem some months earlier; and Dr. Kenneth Shine, the eminent cardiologist, who took charge.

I could read the apprehension in their eyes, and I tried to reassure them by telling them that they were looking at what was probably the darnedest healing machine that had ever been wheeled into the hospital. They went into action immediately—blood pressure, oxygen tank, and cardiograph. When I was offered morphine and lidocaine, I explained I had a long record of adverse drug reactions. I reported that I was experiencing some chest pressure but was otherwise without pain; I assured them that if any pain should occur, I would not hesitate to let them know.

Dr. Shine accepted my decision not to take morphine or lidocaine but felt it was important that I take nitroglycerin. He said there were seldom adverse reactions to nitroglycerin, which helps to dilate the arteries and increase the oxygen supply to the heart. This made complete sense to me, and I took my first nitro pellet. The pill is placed under the tongue, producing a tingling sensation. Sometimes it creates a slight stretching feeling on the sides of the head, but it is not painful in any sense.

After taking a cardiograph, which revealed the early signs of a myocardial infarction (destruction of heart muscle), Dr. Shine took my case history. I was 65 on June 24, 1980. No, I had never smoked. No, I didn't drink. Yes, my blood pressure had always been in the fairly low range—about 110 over 60. No, I had never been overweight. Yes, I had been heavily involved in athletics, but my recent sports life had been intermittent and sparse. No, I was not a jogger. Yes, one of my parents, my mother, had had a history of cardiac trouble; she died at the age of 65. My father had had no record of any heart problems; he died at the age of 94. I had been turned down for life insurance at age 39 because of a cardiograph that showed evidence of a "silent coronary." The rating was removed two years later because the cardiograph was stable, and I had no trouble in obtaining additional life insurance. I briefly described my encounter with a serious collagen disorder in 1964.

I was brought to the coronary-care unit, where I was installed in a small but comfortable room and connected to the heart monitors. After about an hour, Dr. Shine came in to discuss my case and to tell me what was expected of me. I was to avoid physical exertion and mental strain. Visitors would be limited. When I asked about my chances, he reviewed the general statistics. I had already come through the first two zones of maximum risk. About 50 percent of the people hit by heart attacks were not able to make it to the hospital. This maximum risk extended to the first 24 hours. After that, the odds would become less intimidating.

"I don't want you to think you're out of the woods yet," he said. "That is why you are in the CCU and have to be especially careful."

He said he had informed Dr. William M. Hitzig, in New York, about my condition. (Dr. Hitzig, an internist and cardiologist, had been our family doctor for 30 years or so before we moved from the East.) Dr. Shine then inquired whether I had any chest pains. Again I reported a little pressure but no pain. He emphasized the importance of informing the nurse immediately if any pain or other symptoms should develop. He asked me to stay on the nitroglycerin; during the night I would wear a nitro paste patch on my arm. The paste was absorbed through the skin. Thus the arteries would be dilated while I slept, reducing the danger of sudden cardiac death at night. I would also have a heparin lock attached to the vein on my arm. This plug-like device facilitated injections to prevent clots and simplified any intravenous infusions that might be necessary. Dr. Shine's stethoscope examination confirmed the existence of congestive heart failure and the presence of chest fluids. I would be given diuretics to reduce the fluid in my lungs.

The time had come for polite negotiations. I told Dr. Shine that two substantial blood specimens had already been drawn from me in the two hours since I arrived in emergency. Was I unreasonable in suggesting that the various departments of the hospital coordinate their demands? Was it really essential that I give more than one blood specimen a day? My hope, indeed, was that the extractions could be confined to one every two days.

He smiled and assured me that he concurred with this request and authorized me to turn away any attendants who exceeded the one-a-day frequency—and that he shared my expectation that before long it could be cut in half. (This contract worked very well during my hospital stay. Only once was it necessary for me to turn back the ubiquitous blood takers.)

I also asked Dr. Shine whether it would be a serious inconvenience to the hospital if its various routines did not take precedence over my slumbers. At the very least I didn't want to be awakened during the night in order to be given medication. He said he found this request completely reasonable and would so instruct the house staff. He reiterated his admonition that I not overdo things.

I told Dr. Shine I would stay well within his guidelines. However, I did have several writing projects on which I was working. The writing conditions at the hospital were ideal. He posed no objections.

Dr. Shine then asked for additional details about the 1954 episode, when the life-insurance doctors had found cardiographic tracings that gave evidence of a "silent" heart attack. What had happened, I said, was that my aunt, who was the insurance agent, reported fully the findings of the insurance doctors. I had insisted on the unvarnished truth. She wept and told me they had given their opinion that my heart was in very poor condition, that I might have 18 months to live, but only if I gave up everything— my job at the *Saturday Review,* my sports activity, my travel—and took to bed.

I had been devastated by this report. Little by little, however, I pulled myself together. I was sure a mistake had been made. My heart had functioned beautifully. Was it possible I could have had a heart condition without knowing it? That night, upon my return home, my four young daughters came running up to me to be thrown high in the air. I told Dr. Shine how, in that instant, I looked down two roads. One road was marked Cardiac Alley, where I would give up everything important to me and try to squeeze out 18 vegetative and melancholy months. The other road was the one I had been traveling. It was one I knew and loved. It might last 18 months or 18 weeks or 18 minutes; but it was my road. In that brief instant, I made up my mind. I caught my daughters and threw them higher in the air than ever before.

That same weekend in 1954, I played my full quota of hard singles and doubles in tennis. Then, on Monday morning, I reported the verdict of the insurance doctors to Dr. Hitzig, who insisted that I accompany him immediately to Mount Sinai Hospital for a complete cardiograph checkup.

The diagnosis of a silent coronary was confirmed. When we returned to Dr. Hitzig's office, he asked what I intended to do. I told him that I had no complaints about my heart and that, indeed, whatever the cardiograph might show, I had to go on the actual evidence of a beautifully function- ing mechanism. I added that I intended to continue giving my heart the exercise I thought it needed.

I also told Dr. Shine how, in 1957, I had met Dr. Paul

Dudley White, the great cardiologist, who told me that I had done exactly what I had to do to save my life and that, if I had become as inactive as I had been advised to become, I would probably have fulfilled the prediction of the doctors. Dr. White said that new findings had discarded the notion of extreme inactivity for heart patients. Moreover, he said, persons who were heavily athletic over many years produced cardiographs that were sometimes mistakenly interpreted. Athletes, he said, tend to have enlarged and heavily muscled hearts that can make precise cardiograph readings somewhat difficult.

Taking this personal history into account, I told Dr. Shine that it was not unnatural for me to have profound confidence in my heart. Instead of carrying me for only 18 inactive months after the grim diagnosis in 1954, my heart had carried me for almost three decades—with more to come. If I was now in trouble, it was because I had punished my heart beyond reason. But, despite all that punishment—despite the severe muscle damage and the blood in the sputum and the fluid in the lungs—my heart was demonstrating remarkable sustaining and recuperative powers.

In fact, as I looked back at the weeks immediately preceding the attack of December 22, 1980, when I had experienced shortness of breath and was coughing up blood, it appeared to me likely that I had had several episodes involving a degree of cardiac failure, yet my heart had stood up under this undiagnosed burden. If I had a glass in my hand, I said, I would propose a toast to a great heart.

Dr. Shine said it was true that, a quarter century ago, misreadings of cardiograph tests were not uncommon; also, that modern cardiology accepted the importance of exercise in cases that had previously been assigned to total bed rest. He was pleased that I had confidence in my heart but cautioned that serious problems now had to be faced. He said that congestive heart failure, superimposed on clogged coronary arteries, is a very dangerous business. We couldn't ignore the need for drastic measures.

He said that the new cardiograph revealed an unequivocal myocardial infarction and showed evolving changes that went with the kind of heart damage I had experienced. The continuing blood in my sputum and fluid in my chest reinforced the requirement for my presence in the coronary-care unit. There was also evidence that the left side of my heart was not functioning properly. He said the primary cause of the attack was atherosclerosis, a disease marked by narrowing or closure of the arteries caused by accumulated fatty substances.

Dr. Shine left. I had a great deal to think about. I was grateful that I had a doctor who was not minimizing the seriousness of my condition; but I was at least equally grateful that I had a heart that could stand up under terrifying pressures and that so far had defied some of the experts. We had all the ingredients of an ideal physician-patient relationship. Dr. Shine would be governed by his concerns, and I would be energized by my confidence. It was a happy prospect.

The world looked brighter when I awoke after my first night in the hospital.

Shortly after breakfast, a portable cardiograph machine was wheeled into my room; its sundry monitors were attached to various parts of my anatomy. When the test was completed, another hospital attendant appeared; his mission was to take a generous blood specimen from my arm. I told him I didn't expect to see him or his colleagues for another day.

At about 9:00 A.M. the hospital put through a call to the

coronary-care unit. Bill Hitzig was on the phone, his voice breaking now and then with concern.

"I had a long talk last night with Dr. Shine. Listen, Norman," he was saying, "this is entirely different from that collagen episode in 1964 you wrote about in your book. Back then, we didn't know exactly what it was at first and it was a good thing for you to be actively involved. But this time, the diagnosis is 100 percent. Norman, you've had an out-and-out heart attack. You can't minimize it. You've got to settle down. I don't want you to do a damn thing. No masterminding. No activity. No writing. Nothing. I'm taking away your general's stars. You're just a buck private and you take orders. You do everything Dr. Shine tells you to do. For God's sake, let him call the shots.

"One more thing," he continued. "No laughing. You yourself have said laughing is a form of internal jogging. You're not up to any jogging right now, especially internal jogging. No spoofing. Stay flat on your back and just be a vegetable. I'll be flying out in a day or two. Meantime, remember, Dr. Shine calls the shots. Do you hear me?"

I told Bill I heard him and not to worry; I had made it through the night and would talk to him on the phone the next morning as well. After ringing off, I reflected on the tension and alarm in Bill's voice. Was the situation even more serious than I had been told?

Shortly thereafter, Ellen came into the room. I told her that I was under orders from Bill Hitzig to do something I had very little practice in doing: that is, not laughing. We both smiled at the severity of the prohibition. Then, at my request, Ellen read to me from the morning newspaper.

One of the items in the *Los Angeles Times* that morning reported a feud between the editor of an area newspaper

and a local councilman. The councilman was protesting
what he regarded as an ethnic slur by the editor, who had
referred to him as a "Greek orator." The councilman
demanded a public apology.

Queried by a reporter from the L.A. *Times* as to whether
he would meet this request, the editor was hardly ambiguous.

"No apologies," the editor was quoted as saying.
"Actually, I was being a little ambiguous. What I should
have said was that he was a loquacious asshole."

I let out a roar of laughter that caused the nurses to come
running from their station. The fact that the L.A. *Times*
would report the conversation verbatim was to me, who
had started out as a newspaper reporter in more decorous
times, an absolute delight.

"You're not supposed to laugh," Ellen said in the midst
of her own mirth.

The laughter hadn't hurt one bit. In fact, I felt warm and
relaxed. Right then, I knew I was going to make it all the
way. Laughter was still a friend. But I decided that I would
wait until I was out of the hospital to tell Dr. Hitzig about
it.

A second hospital experience added to my confidence.
It may or may not have been the consequence of being
wheeled through drafty corridors en route to the X-ray
room or other diagnostic units, or of being on the receiving end of a multitude of cold metal ends of stethoscopes
that obviously had been refrigerated for my benefit; anyway, I came down with a cold. I went through the usual
sequence of nasal flow leading to nasal congestion.

Unable to sleep because of a stuffy nose, I asked the nurse
for a nebulizer, or, if none was obtainable, an old-fash-
ioned kettle with boiling water. She asked whether I had

difficulty in breathing. I said yes, but before I could finish the sentence she was off and running. Seconds later, an entire crew, led by the resident in charge, materialized in my room, primed for instant action. They snapped on the lights and began to move me onto a rolling stretcher. I was told I would be brought to the X-ray room. I also needed a cardiograph.

It was 2:30 A.M. I tried to slow down the emergency drill; I told the resident in charge that my breathing difficulties originated not in the chest but in my nose. Wouldn't they please give me some steam and let me get some sleep?

It seemed apparent that they didn't hear me—or, if they did, that they thought my request was irrelevant. All I wanted to do was to open up my sinuses; yet here they were, buzzing around in the middle of the night, interfering with the kind of rest that I had been told was essential to someone in my condition.

They brushed aside my protests and persisted with their efforts to move me onto the stretcher. After a moment or two of fruitless negotiations, I spun loose from their grasp, sat up straight, and ordered the entire crew out of my room. The precise words I used were more graphic than just indicated.

The resident in charge drew back. "I'm going to call Dr. Shine," he said.

"For heaven's sake, don't wake up the poor man," I said. "It's the middle of the night."

"But we've got to follow the rules!"

"Doctor," I replied, "I don't want to presume to tell you what to do, but one of the first things a doctor has to learn is when the rules don't apply. Now, you had better leave before you create the very situation you think you have to treat."

They did telephone Dr. Shine, who told them that they could safely assume I knew the difference between a stuffy nose and congestive heart failure. Thirty minutes or so later, an attendant brought a nebulizer to my room and I was able to breathe more easily.

I reflected that if I could survive this episode I could survive anything. I dozed off and slept soundly for the next four hours, when the routine of the new day started. After breakfast, I wrote a note to the night resident physician, apologizing for having lost my temper. I thanked him for his concern and said that I hoped he would come by for a chat and that we would get to know each other better. He accepted my invitation, and we became good friends.

One other incident occurred during my stay in the hospital that emphasized in my mind the need to educate medical personnel about the hazards of slavish and unreasoning adherence to the rules. While still in the coronary-care unit I experienced some slight chest pressure during the night. Dr. Shine had stressed the importance of taking a nitroglycerin tablet the moment I felt anything unusual in my chest. I rang for the nurse. She said she couldn't let me have nitroglycerin, because Dr. Shine had said I was not to have medication at night.

I explained that this had been done at my request in order to avoid being awakened. She nodded understandingly but held her ground. Orders were orders. Nitroglycerin was medication, and it was night-time.

I suppose I should have been amused and have allowed the matter to drop, but the persistence of the chest heaviness made me press the point. No use. Finally, out of sheer exasperation, I demanded to see the resident in charge. When he came, he lost no time in providing the nitroglycerin. He also listened to my chest and took my blood

pressure. He stayed a few minutes to make sure the nitroglycerin would produce the desired effect, then left.

I must not allow this particular experience with an over-
zealous nurse obscure the fact that nothing was more
impressive to me during my hospital stay than the major
role played by nurses in my improvement. Their knowledge, their compassionate understanding and care, and their
total support were powerful healing forces. I concur heart-
ily with Lewis Thomas, in his book of autobiographical
essays, *The Youngest Science,* when he says of nurses:
"If they ask for the moon, I am on their side."

Incidentally, I have the same feeling about Lewis Thomas
himself. How does one go about thanking such a man for
all his services to society? I know of no one inside the medical profession today whose writings are more poetic and
cogent. Whether with respect to the limitations or possibilities of medicine, or the complicated but ever-enthrall-
ing enterprise of human healing, he has things of
uncommon value to say and he says them with uncommon grace.

My various hospital experiences helped to convince me
that I was not in such bad shape that I could be toppled by
unusual physical or emotional exertion. Just being able to
pop off as I did produced a surge of energy and the conviction that I had fairly good reserves.

Curiously, I had a growing sense of intellectual adventure about the entire experience. After the publication of
Anatomy of an Illness, I had received any number of letters
from physicians asking whether I thought I would be
capable of more than one titanic effort at recovery from a
major illness in one lifetime. How much regeneration was
within the mustering power of a human body? My heart
attack gave me the opportunity to find out whether the

same approach and technique that had worked so well before might work again. I had a chance to graduate from the anecdotal to the reproducible. The essence of the scientific method is reproducibility.

CHAPTER II

Second Time Around

In *Anatomy of an Illness,* I wrote about my experience with an illness that some of the specialists did not believe to be reversible.

What were the basic ideas involved in that recovery?

The newspaper accounts had made it appear that I had laughed my way out of a serious illness. Careful readers of my book, however, knew that laughter was just a metaphor for the entire range of the positive emotions. Hope, faith, love, will to live, cheerfulness, humor, creativity, playfulness, confidence, great expectations—all these, I believed, had therapeutic value. Since the negative emotions could set the stage for illness, it seemed to me reasonable to believe that the positive emotions might help set the stage for recovery.

I never regarded the positive emotions, however, as a substitute for scientific treatment. I saw them as providing an auspicious environment for medical care, a method of optimizing prospects of recovery. Another misconception about my illness was that it was a venture in self-care or self-cure. In my book I emphasized the patient-physician partnership. Some accounts of my story, however, overlooked the clearly stated context in which the patient's role in the partnership was described. In any case, I had learned enough from my own experience about the importance of such a partnership that I relished the opportunity to try to put it to work again. And I found Dr. Shine a thoroughly willing partner.

During our hospital exchanges, he never gave me the impression that he regarded my questions as presumptuous or incompetent. If he felt that what I said was reasonable, he had no hesitation in telling me. For example, after a diuretic was prescribed to reduce the fluids in my body, I raised the question of nutrients being washed out as a result. He said that I would be provided with potassium supplements. I asked him about all the other nutrients that were essential in the economy of the heart—and indeed, in the entire body. Dr. Shine concurred in my request to be allowed to take comprehensive mineral supplementation.

After four days I was moved out of the CCU and to the 10th floor, where the atmosphere in my room was more like that of a comfortable lounge than of a hospital facility. I luxuriated in the non-medical surroundings. The food tasted as though it had been prepared by a master chef. I started to write—I had been working on a play about Franz Anton Mesmer and the beginnings of hypnotism—and was able to get more writing done in a day than I would sometimes be able to do in a week in the office.

Dr. Hitzig arrived the day after I had been installed in my new quarters. The moment he came into the room, I could see from his eyes that he had been deeply apprehensive about my condition and hardly knew what to expect. (Several months later he admitted that the first report to him from the hospital had described my condition as "touch and go" and "desperate." He had found especially alarming the information about a substantial amount of fluid in my chest.)

I could see his amazement and concern when he looked at the small table next to my bed and saw that it had been converted into a desk spilling over with papers, books, and writing materials. It was necessary to reassure him that I was staying within Dr. Shine's guidelines. He listened to my chest, looked at my chart, then asked my nurse some questions.

Dr. Shine, having been informed in advance about Dr. Hitzig's arrival, came into the room. I was pleased to see their evident mutual respect. Dr. Shine expressed his pleasure with my progress but said to Dr. Hitzig, as he had said to me several days earlier, that I was still "not out of the woods." He reviewed the diagnosis and reported that he had changed my nitroglycerin to Isordil (a longer-lasting variant) and that I was taking a nitro patch on my arm during the night. I was getting regular injections of heparin through the intravenous lock on my arm. I was also on diuretics because they could still pick up "rales" in the stethoscope examination—tiny crinkly sounds indicating fluid in my chest, which fit in with the continuing but sporadic blood in my sputum and the diagnosis of congestive heart failure.

After Dr. Shine left, Dr. Hitzig expressed his concern that I was being too active, especially when he saw me get out of bed to go to the bathroom. He reminded me that he himself had had a heart attack some years earlier. Though it had been less severe than the one that had hit me, he had been hospitalized for several weeks, during which time he had been virtually immobile. He said he recognized that treatment had changed since that time but felt it necessary nonetheless to caution me about the dangers of putting any strain on my heart. He begged me to take my condition seriously, although he was gratified by my progress and my appearance.

Just seeing Bill Hitzig was a tonic for me. I told him I was confident that what had worked so well in my overcoming my collagen illness in 1964 would work again, although I recognized there were basic differences in the nature of the illnesses that called for different timing and different approaches. Meanwhile, some aspects of my "old" program were both accessible and workable: total confidence in my recovery, a strong sense of purpose and even joyousness, an undiminished will to live, a genuine curiosity about and interest in the treatment, a sense of partnership with the physician.

All these elements seemed to me to be yielding dividends. Since I didn't have the physical pain that was such a prominent feature of the previous illness, my need for laughter was not as pronounced as it had been earlier. But I had a generous supply of laughter nevertheless. I swapped stories with the nurses, residents, interns, and visitors. My reputation had preceded me in the hospital, and I suffered no shortage of staff personnel wanting to try out their favorite stories.

When Bill Hitzig left for New York the next day, I could see that he was genuinely encouraged. Before leaving, however, he reiterated his earlier admonitions: I was not to try to run my own case; I was not to undertake any physical activity except as expressly authorized; I was not to set aside any of the medication prescribed, whatever my own prejudices might be in the case. Concerning medications, what I was given was an irreducible minimum: Isordil, a diuretic, and a nitro patch at night, plus heparin by injection for anticlotting.

My progress on the 10th floor was rapid. After six or seven days, in which I enjoyed ideal recovery and writing conditions, Dr. Shine told me I could expect to be released before long. Meantime, I would be hooked up to a portable "Holter" device to test the response of my heart to modest activity. I was fascinated with the Holter monitor, an electronic gadget that recorded my heart activity on a tape, which later could be replayed into a cardiograph machine. My job was to wear the Holter and make detailed notes about everything I did, and the precise time of day or night I did it. This would enable the cardiologists, when replaying the tape into a cardiograph, to see how my heart behaved under varying conditions.

The report the next day on the Holter test was encouraging—so much so, in fact, that Dr. Shine wanted me to take a treadmill exercise test. I confess I was troubled by this suggestion. Was there no risk in subjecting myself to physical exertion of this sort so soon after a myocardial infarction? Moreover, I had always had serious reservations about the treadmill. It seemed to me that it was not without flaws as a diagnostic device. Was there no difference between exercising and being exercised? The patient doesn't really do the walking on the treadmill; the ground moves under his feet. When someone decides to engage in physical activity, the mental and emotional involvement is an integral part of a total process. The "second wind" is not solely the result of an autonomic process but belongs to a totality in which emotions and physical activity are interacting. Has anyone ever gotten a second wind on a treadmill? If one of the physiological manifestations of a second wind is the hormonal cushioning for the heart, would this also hold for treadmill exercise? I wondered.

Even more important, perhaps, are the psychological strain and apprehension produced in some cases by a treadmill. Not all patients are indifferent or immune to the emotional stress produced by strenuous diagnostic procedures. To begin with, the fact of an underlying heart problem is made palpable and dramatic in the presence of a treadmill. The ambience in the treadmill room creates a mood of tension in itself. The running blood-pressure readings; the mysterious markings on the cardiograph; the intensity in the voices of the cardiologist and the nurses— all these are emphatic and omnipresent reminders of a heart problem.

It seemed to me that what is being measured on a treadmill is not just the tolerance to physical stress but also the psychological response to the procedure itself. Complicating the picture is the patient's absence of control. The inability to be in control over one's life is a common characteristic of serious illness. Indeed, it would be difficult to think of a more pervasive or more dismal aspect of chronic disease than loss of control. The treadmill seemed to me to epitomize this problem. Was it barely possible that the absence of control could be a contributing factor in producing erroneous information—so that the treadmill readings could reflect emotional instability and not just cardiac suffiency or insufficiency?

Frankly, I was scared stiff. The treadmill procedure is regarded as routine, but I knew of three episodes when serious problems occurred. Dr. Murray Jarvik, of the UCLA medical school, experienced severe arrhythmia on a treadmill and required emergency procedures. Dr. William Kroger, the well-known psychiatrist and author, also affiliated with UCLA, passed out on a treadmill. Years earlier, Peter Charlton, a close friend, had died on a treadmill. These were isolated incidents, to be sure, and I know how hazardous it is to extrapolate from such a narrow base; but they helped to confirm my belief that the apprehension one carries onto the treadmill could affect the result. I had no heart for the affair, literally.

I shared these reservations with Dr. Shine. He sought to reassure me by saying that thousands of patients in my situation had come through such tests and that he would not prescribe the treadmill if he thought there were any such risks as the ones I described. Besides, he said, he would preside over the test and would be able to spot any trouble before it developed into a problem.

Thirteen days after my heart attack, I went on the treadmill. I tried valiantly to suppress my unreasonable fears. I'm afraid I didn't succeed. I felt slightly dizzy even before the rubberized mat began to move. After only a few minutes on the moving mat, I began to feel woozy, was breathing with difficulty, and asked whether I could step down. I was told to keep going for a little while longer. I did so, then felt somewhat faint and stepped off the treadmill.

I sat down and rested for a few minutes. Dr. Shine, who had been monitoring my blood pressure, waited until my normal breathing was restored and my blood pressure had reverted to its usual level, then interpreted the results of the test for me. He said that, at a very low level of speed and incline, my blood pressure, which began at 116 over 65, had not only not risen in response to the unusual demand, but had dropped severely. My pulse rate, which was 86 before I went on the treadmill, had increased to only 110 at the peak of exercise. He had hoped I might have continued the exercise until a higher pulse rate was reached. The cardiograph, in technical terms, showed an alarming depression of 3 mm in the S-T segment. This meant that the heart was failing at that particular level of exertion.

Under these circumstances, he said, the existence of atherosclerotic blockage was clearly established. The question was not whether blockage existed but where and how much—information that, he explained, could be provided only by an angiogram, a procedure in which a radioactive dye is put into the blood and a catheter is threaded into the heart in order to take an X-ray motion picture of the condition of the arteries and the action of the heart.

Since Dr. Shine had said there was unequivocal evidence of blockage, I recognized that bypass surgery to open up the arteries would be an integral sequel to the angiogram.

I asked Dr. Shine whether, instead of taking the angiogram, it might be useful for me to go back on the Holter monitor, submitting myself to exercise at least as strenuous as the treadmill but under non-stressful circumstances. It seemed to me that the results of the treadmill might have been blurred by the emotional stress, which itself can cause changes in the cardiograph readout.

Dr. Shine had every reason to be annoyed by my amateurish observations. Instead, he was beautifully forebearing. He said he would make the arrangements for the Holter but felt I was procrastinating about an angiogram.

"We're losing time and I can't encourage you to believe that anything the Holter will show will change the basic facts or my basic recommendation," he said.

Three days later, I was hooked up to a 24-hour Holter and released from the hospital. Accompanied by my long-time friend Dr. Omar Fareed, I went out for a walk that I was determined would be at least as strenuous as the treadmill.

Omar and I shared common interests and concerns. We had been deeply involved in athletics in our youth and frequently yearned to break away from our desks for hard sports. Omar had been a star football halfback in college. Even now, in his mid-60's, he was of tournament caliber in tennis. He was also the physician to the U.S. Davis Cup team. Tennis at Omar's was always a treat. Sometimes, if you were lucky, you could play with former stars like Jack Kramer, Tony Trabert, or Charles Pasarell.

On our first outing on the walking track, I experienced a little wooziness after about 60 yards and stopped for three or four minutes. Then I resumed and was able to walk for perhaps 200 yards without stopping. But my body warmed to the challenge and I was able to continue for a quarter mile. I was exhilarated to discover that my fatigue, far from increasing with the exercise, actually receded as I went on. The tolerance to exertion improved. I made the appropriate notation on the Holter chart, as I did all my other activities for a 24-hour period.

The next day, I returned to the UCLA Hospital and turned in the Holter equipment and record. It was run through the requisite equipment and showed none of the adverse signs that had turned up on the treadmill.

Dr. Shine moderated my jubilation over the good showing. He said that the Holter test, while indicative, was not definitive, and that one could not attach the same scientific weight to the kind of Holter procedure I had designed for myself as would be afforded under conditions of replication and professional scrutiny. He urged me to return for another treadmill test—say, in about 10 days.

He again called attention to the need for an angiogram, which I interpreted as the prelude to bypass surgery.

I did go back to the treadmill room, although many of my earlier apprehensions persisted. This time, however, I flunked the test even before I set foot on the machine. Just in the process of walking down the long hospital corridor to the treadmill room, all my foreboding came flooding to the surface. My fear of failure was so great that my wooziness increased in direct proportion to the proximity of the testing room. When I arrived, Dr. Shine took one look at me, sat me down, and took my blood pressure and cardiograph. He canceled the test. The fact of cardiac insufficiency had been clearly established without it.

The experience seemed to underline what appeared to me to be the basic question: Could the results of a treadmill test be skewed by emotional strain? Even more significant, perhaps, were the implications concerning possible surgery. If emotional factors could produce an adverse treadmill result, would they have to be taken in account in assessing the risks of an angiogram and open-heart surgery?

Was it possible that my basic problem was not just atherosclerosis but spasm—a sudden, involuntary constriction or closure that would shut off part of the blood supply? My mother had experienced spasm. Were there additional risks for spasm-prone hearts in angiograms and bypass surgery? Instances of myocardial infarction during bypass surgery had been reported. Or was I allowing my imagination to run away with me?

I got all the materials about bypass surgery I could put my hands on: the Western Electric study, the VA study, the papers in the medical journals. The mortality figures for bypass surgery under ordinary circumstances were low

enough to be reassuring. I realized that the bypass procedure was one of the high points in 20th-century surgery.
For some cardiac patients the bypass was not just a means
of prolonging life but of saving it. But it was also clear
that it was not a universal remedy and that it was contra-
indicated for some patients with myocardial infarctions or
other heart problems. Many physicians did not recommend bypass surgery in the absence of intractable pain or
other pronounced indications. It was also apparent that
some cases were not significantly helped by the bypass;
medical papers reported persistence of angina. Twenty
percent of all bypass cases had to return for additional surgery because of further narrowing or closure of the coronary arteries. Also, postoperative complications had been
reported in a number of cases. Shock to the nervous system, manifesting itself in various forms of instability, was
not a frequent aftermath, but it was serious enough when
it did occur.

What about my own case? I hadn't experienced any of
the classic suffocating chest pains associated with angina
symptoms, either before or after the heart attack. True, I
had had feelings of chest pressure, but these had receded in
the hospital. I had never smoked. I did not have a hypertensive heart. Again, I wondered about spasm. Was there
something about spasm-prone hearts that put them in a
different category of treatment?

Wherever there is muscle, there is the possibility of
spasm. The walls of the coronary arteries—and indeed all
the body's arteries—are lined with muscle fibers. Sudden
spasm can contract the arteries, thus shutting down the
flow of blood. A serious spasm in an artery that serves the
heart, therefore, can knock out heart muscle just as dev-
astatingly as blockage caused by atherosclerosis. The inter-

action of spasm and arterial blockage may be especially potent.

In looking through the medical textbooks, I was surprised to find relatively little material on heart spasm or vasospasm—and almost no discussion of the problems involved in bypass surgery for the spasm-prone heart. *The Merck Manual,* a standard prop for medical students, had nothing on vasospasm. *Blakiston's Gould Medical Dictionary* carried a listing for vasospasm, but the other standard medical dictionaries, *Dorland's* and *Stedman's,* had no such entry. Some years earlier, when I was on the board of editors of the *Encyclopaedia Britannica,* Dr. Thomas H. Killip had contributed an article to the *Encyclopaedia Britannica Annual Review* in which he made the point that spasm-caused heart attacks were far more frequent than was commonly supposed. It appeared from the article that it was not uncommon for spasm to be missed in diagnosis.

When I consulted the periodical literature, I found an impressive number of papers calling attention to spasm as a major cause of heart attacks. These articles attested to the relatively recent nature of extensive research in this field. Among these and later papers are H. R. Hellstrom's "Coronary Artery Vasospasm: The Likely Immediate Cause of Acute Myocardial Infarction," in the *British Heart Journal* 41 (1979): 26–32; R. H. Helfant's "Coronary Spasm," in *American Journal of Cardiology* 44 (1979): 839–41; R. S. Eliot's "What I Learned from My M.I.," in *Modern Medicine* 49 (1981): 62–72; B. Lown and R. A. DeSilva's "Is Coronary Arterial Spasm a Risk Factor for Coronary Atherosclerosis?" in *American Journal of Cardiology* 45 (1980): 901; A. Maseri's (et al.) "Coronary Vasospasm as a Possible Cause of Myocardial Infarction," in *New England Journal of Medicine* 299 (1978): 1271–77; and J. L. Marx's

"Coronary Artery Spasms and Heart Disease," in *Science* 208 (1980): 1127–30.

Also, the journal *Circulation* in 1977 presented evidence that many heart attacks were being caused not by blockage of the coronary arteries but by sudden constrictions that are not uncommonly observed in other parts of the body. The article presented arteriographic evidence to support its thesis. In the following months, I was to find equally impressive materials. The October 23/30, 1981, issue of the *Journal of the American Medical Association* carried a comprehensive account of coronary spasm by Dr. Eugene Braunwald, who pointed out that many myocardial infarctions that had been routinely diagnosed as atherosclerosis were actually the result of spasm. Dr. Braunwald reviewed the work of Dr. M. Prinzmetal, who developed the concept of "variant angina," a condition that doesn't fit the classic signs associated with a heart attack. Dr. Braunwald's research convinced him that Prinzmetal's "variant angina" was sometimes consistent with coronary spasm. (Among other recent papers on heart spasm was an article by Dr. Philip B. Oliva, in *Chest,* December 1981. It provided comprehensive evidence to support the belief that spasm was a verifiable cause of heart attacks. It analyzed the coronary arteriography of a number of patients whose arteries were not clogged by the usual plaque but who suffered myocardial infarction as the result of spasm, or sudden closure.)

Dr. Shine had told me originally that the cause of my attack was atherosclerosis. I wrote to Dr. Shine and asked whether he had ruled out a spasm as the cause of my heart attack. No, he replied, he would not rule it out. Only an angiogram could tell definitively whether or not the problem was atherosclerosis. In the absence of an angiogram, he would have to speculate that my problem might involve a combination of atherosclerosis and spasm.

After receiving Dr. Shine's letter, I telephoned Dr. Killip in Detroit, asking whether, in his opinion, spasm-prone heart patients would benefit from bypass surgery to the same extent as would atherosclerotic heart patients. He said that in his view the bypass had its principal rationale in the treatment of the atherosclerotic and not the spasm-prone heart.

The entire subject of arterial blockage was the basis of exciting new discussions and findings within the medical profession. In April 1981, Dr. Hubert Rubenstein, a Los Angeles physician, who himself had atherosclerosis, came to my house with a tape cassette of a talk he had heard in Los Angeles by Dr. William Castelli, of the National Institutes of Health. Dr. Castelli had been involved in the famous study in Framingham, Massachusetts, in which thousands of case histories were studied for information they might supply on the causes of heart attacks. In the cassette given me by Dr. Rubenstein, Castelli sought to eliminate some of the confusion about atherosclerosis and cholesterol levels as factors in heart attacks. His tape discussed the functions and problems associated with lipids. He questioned the view that plaque-clogged arteries were an irreversible condition.

In an attempt to ascertain whether his ideas were relevant to my own situation, I telephoned Dr. Castelli, who said that much more research was required on the matter of reversibility. He was impressed, however, by the evidence now being assembled at various places indicating that oxygen-deprived hearts could increase their capability through the kind of rehabilitation program developed at places like the Pritikin Longevity Center, in Santa Monica,

California, and the UCLA Center for Health Enhancement, Education and Research (CHEER), under Dr. Charles Kleeman. He said there was a tendency within the medical profession to dismiss or disparage Nathan Pritikin's work, but his own investigation convinced him that Pritikin's system had to be taken seriously.

Dr. Castelli referred to the fact that, contrary to the impression existing in some quarters, every aspect of the Pritikin program was administered by fully accredited physicians. The facilities that were to be found in the nation's best cardiac centers were also present at the Pritikin Longevity Center.

I was pleased that Dr. Castelli had also referred to UCLA's CHEER program. Dr. Kleeman had established, as an adjunct to the UCLA School of Medicine, a cardiac rehabilitation program. In addition to facilities for patients and their spouses who enrolled in the live-in program, he maintained an out-patient service for people in the community who found it necessary to live at home. For a long time, the CHEER program was carried out in what was once a hotel only a block or so from the medical school. As this is being written, ground has just been broken for a new building that will become one of the most up-to-date cardiac centers in the world.

Are there serious points of difference between Pritikin and CHEER? Both systems emphasize diet and exercise. Beef, fats, eggs, butter, salt, cheeses, and shellfish are barred. Pritikin advises against all oils—saturated or polyunsaturated. Kleeman permits unsaturated oils in moderation. Pritikin has a 7 percent limitation on fats in the total diet; Kleeman allows 20 percent. Pritikin's research specialists contend that the 7 percent level is consistent with the need to reduce arterial clogging and that, if one exceeds that figure, significant risks are incurred. Kleeman doesn't go that far. He points to a wide range of medical research showing that the human body requires about 20 percent fat in the diet and that dropping it to 7 percent incurs risks. He also emphasizes that cholesterol, at a modest level, is a normal manifestation of the body's requirements. Kleeman is less restrictive on fish and chicken than Pritikin. Kleeman puts no limitation on fruits; Pritikin has quotas. Both recognize the hazards of sugar, but Kleeman is not absolutist on this point.

Not infrequently, I have encountered people who have the impression that the kind of food required under these diets—and especially the one in force at the Pritikin Longevity Center—is so Spartan and tasteless that they would rather not subject themselves to such culinary bleakness. The impression is mistaken. Prepared according to instructions, the food at both places is quite appealing and even delicious.

If I read the brochures correctly, Kleeman gives more attention to life-style and recreation—music, entertainment, creative activities—than does Pritikin, who gives more attention to diet than does Kleeman. In both systems, regulated exercise is a major feature. Also, the patients live with their spouses in the center for at least three weeks in order to develop new habits, new rhythms, new ways of thinking about life. Integral to both centers are medical lectures about the nature of heart disease, blood pressure, cholesterol, triglycerides, lipids, and so on.

The programs at both CHEER and the Pritikin Longevity Center have produced hundreds of "graduates" who have been able to apply the lessons they learned at those places in their everyday lives. These are persons who had been leading tentative and restricted lives as the result of their heart ailments but who now are active, productive, and free of pain.

Wherever I turned in attempting to find information about heart attacks—how to avoid them or how to overcome them—the culprit most frequently identified was cholesterol, the fatty substance that collects on the lining of the arteries and that eventually becomes solidified into plaque. This condition is what is meant by the term "hardening of the arteries."

The accumulation of these fatty substances is not something that begins in upper middle age. The process begins in early childhood. A 1982–83 study of children in New York City and Los Angeles undertaken by Dr. Ernst L. Wynder, of the American Health Foundation, showed average cholesterol levels of 180 for youngsters in the 10-to-12 range. This is about 50 points above normal for children of this age. Continuing on the same course would lead to cholesterol levels close to or above 300 by the age of 35. The Framingham, Massachusetts, study of the National Institutes of Health, the most comprehensive study yet undertaken of the connection between diet and cardiac disease, indicates that cholesterol levels above 245 are an invitation to a heart attack. Some cardiologists feel that the safety zone is closer to 175 or even 150.

What the Wynder children's study in New York City and Los Angeles tells us is that time bombs are ticking away inside the young people of this country. Little wonder that heart disease is the number-one killer in the United States, accounting for more casualties than we suffered in the Second World War. We are doing our children no favor by giving them foods rich in sugar and animal fats. Some parents who drink decaffeinated coffee as a health measure for themselves think nothing of giving their children cola beverages that contain some of the caffeine extracted from their coffee.

The notion has been advanced in some quarters that the average supermarket shopping basket contains everything required for a balanced diet. One has only to stand at the checkout counter of a supermarket to see how wide of the mark that observation is. Foods loaded with fat, salt, sugar, chemical preservatives, and dyes are predominant in the shopping baskets. We know how to send human beings into space, but we have yet to learn how to feed ourselves properly.

It is a mistake, however, to assume that any level of cholesterol is bad. Cholesterol is a·natural substance produced by the human body. In balance, it serves a useful function. In excess, however, it imposes a strain on the heart because of the extra burden involved in pumping the blood through narrowed openings. This applies to the body's entire arterial system and not just the arteries supplying blood to the heart.

In reading the medical literature, I learned that some persons suffer from high cholesterol levels even though they hold to a diet low in animal fats. Dr. Meyer Friedman and Dr. Ray H. Rosenman, who developed the now-popular ideas about Type A and Type B personalities, have presented the results of research showing that people in Type A have far higher cholesterol counts than people in Type B, regardless of diet. Being edgy, tense, and worrisome, therefore, can have its physiological penalties. Even here, however, qualifications are important. If stress is converted into stimulating challenge that has a useful outcome, the physiological effect can be salutary. We are not likely to get through this lifetime without stress—any more than we are likely to get through it without serious illness—but if we are lucky we will be able to develop techniques for dealing with our problems.

I have a long way to go before I can presume to advise others on how to deal with stress, but I can at least call their attention to experts who are superbly qualified to give advice. Prominent among them is Dr. Herbert Benson, of the Harvard Medical School, author of *The Relaxation Response* and *The Mind-Body Effect*. Dr. Benson provides solid scientific evidence on the erosive effects of tension and stress on the body's vital organs, and on the connection between emotional factors and disease. He does not, however, content himself with cataloguing the downside effects of the negative emotions; he is equally illuminating about the benefits of stress-control techniques. I can testify that I have found his ideas genuinely helpful and constructive. I commend his books both to those who have stress-related problems and to those who would like to avoid them.

Dr. Benson makes correlations between the ability to lower high cholesterol levels, and patterns of thought and action. He presents strong evidence to show that it is not enough to reduce one's intake of animal fats; it is also important to reduce the tensions in one's life, as well as to develop techniques for creating a balance between exposure to stress and control of stress.

Other approaches that seek not just to lower the cholesterol count but to augment health in general deserve special emphasis: Dean Ornish's system, for example. Dr. Ornish, then affiliated with the Baylor College of Medicine, in Houston, Texas, came to see me at UCLA sometime early in 1980. We quickly discovered that we were philosophically well attuned. He had read some of the things I had written in the medical journals about the need for a shift in public-health education from the preoccupation with pain to the fundamental issues involved in pursuing health and combating disease. Dr. Ornish enthusiastically described his project at Baylor, which was designed to treat heart disease largely through stress management, diet, and exercise.

Under stress management, Dr. Ornish included relaxation techniques, among them stretching exercises, meditation, and breathing techniques. The diet was uncomplicated; it was high in complex carbohydrates and low in fat and cholesterol. People were taught how to prepare food without salt: onion, tomatoes, and garlic were used to enhance taste. Grains and beans were basic parts of the diet. Brown rice, couscous, and soybeans and flakes were favored. So were fresh fruits and vegetables.

In most respects, the diet was very similar to the ones used at CHEER and the Pritikin Longevity Center. Dramatic improvement in the condition of the heart patients participating in Dr. Ornish's program occurred after only a few weeks. Dr. Ornish may not have proved that atherosclerosis is reversible, but he was able to demonstrate that the symptoms of the disease can be significantly reduced and, in some cases, eliminated altogether.

Perhaps the most dramatic proof of the importance of systematic exercise in the recovery program of heart-attack sufferers is furnished by Dr. Terence Kavanagh, of the Toronto Rehabilitation Centre, Toronto, Canada. Dr. Kavanagh regards exercise not just as basic therapy for persons who have had myocardial infarctions but as a major part of a program for people who want to prevent heart attacks.

The attention-grabber in Dr. Kavanagh's evidence is the fact that each year a group of his patients run in Boston's

famed 26-mile marathon. These patients have suffered heart
attacks, some as recently as one year earlier. In one marathon, for example, seven heart-attack patients not only
entered but completed the full run.

Leading up to this endurance feat, of course, is a period
of rigorous training in the post-coronary program of the
Toronto Rehabilitation Centre. The central feature of that
program is exercise, beginning with walking and pro-
gressing steadily to long-distance jogging.

"In our experience," says Dr. Kavanagh, "this is the best
way to attain endurance fitness, which is the only form of
fitness of benefit to the heart."

Then he adds, "But endurance fitness cannot be stored.
You must work zealously to maintain it. Otherwise it will
deteriorate inexorably and become reduced by inactivity
until finally it is all gone, and your ultimate state will be
no better than your first—or maybe even worse, according
to some studies. This means, for our cardiacs, staying on
a jogging program for the rest of their lives—which we
anticipate will be lengthy."

For those who would like to learn more about Dr.
Kavanagh's ideas, I suggest reading his book, *The Healthy
Heart Program,* published by Van Nostrand Reinhold.

Finally, there is the work of Dr. Lester Morrison, a cardiologist affiliated for many years with the Loma Linda
(California) School of Medicine. Dr. Morrison is convinced that a diet high in lecithin (a natural substance found
in the human body and in a variety of foods, especially soy
beans) could reduce the level of cholesterol in the blood
and promote arterial flow. On this basis, he believes that
many cases of atherosclerosis are reversible.

Dr. Morrison's contentions have been questioned by
those who argue that his basic data do not conform to

established methods for the development of scientific proof. Far from being resentful of these criticisms, Dr. Morrison continues to accumulate data supporting his theories, confident that his basic ideas about reversibility will ultimately be vindicated. He recognizes that various factors—stern dietary management, exercise, and life-style—are involved in the vital process of overcoming coronary artery disease, but he holds fast to the contributing role that can be played by lecithin.

Here, then, are six separate programs—Pritikin's, Kleeman's, Ornish's, Kavanagh's, Benson's, and Morrison's. They have a great deal in common but put varying degrees of emphasis on diet, exercise, mind control, life-style. There was no reason, it seemed to me, why I could not be the beneficiary of whatever aspects of these programs best fitted my own needs. I also possessed a prodigious asset— a wife who could be a partner in the total enterprise.

CHAPTER III

Counterattack

The description of the *Saturday Review* that pleased me most during the years of my editorship was that it never tried to gloss over the seriousness of the issues it discussed but that at the same time it never wavered in its belief that solutions were within reach.

These same generalities are characteristic of my wife. Ellen is a born cheerleader—not the rah-rah, handstand variety but a person deeply committed to the proposition that extra effort wedded to confidence often produces good results. When we lived in Connecticut, for example, I had to commute by train to my office in New York City. Ellen would drive me to the railroad station. Sometimes, because of the traffic congestion, we would arrive at the Norwalk station just as the train was leaving.

"Don't worry," she would exclaim, "we'll catch it at Darien."

At Darien, we came closer to getting it than we did at

Norwalk, but the train was already in motion and the steps were up.

"On to Greenwich," she would sing out.

The turnpike to Greenwich would be clogged, and we didn't even have the privilege of seeing the rear red lights of the train mocking at us as it left the station.

"We don't have too far to go to drive to New York," she would say, without the slightest trace of defeat. "Besides, the train's probably overcrowded anyway."

Ellen never ran out of options.

The business of implementing the kind of rehabilitation program that was laid out was a joyous affair to Ellen.

"Isn't it wonderful," she said to one of our daughters. "Daddy doesn't have to go to the office and I can give him three meals a day."

Ellen's expertise in nutrition was a major asset. When we embarked on the rehabilitation program early in 1981, she figured out ways of cooking without butter and the usual oils. She did research on foods that counteract cholesterol. She invented what I believe is the world's finest salad; she would use cabbage instead of lettuce as the base and have it fairly popping with all sorts of goodies—radishes, peppers, red onion, jicama, parsley, bean sprouts, and other raw vegetables I had never heard of from far-off places. Lemon juice was the main dressing. The totality was a king's delight. We had the salad twice a day.

Soups were a prime feature at lunch or dinner. So were the steamed vegetables. We eliminated beef but had fish or chicken two or three times a week.

What about salt?

The fact that salt is an enemy is clear enough because of its role in increasing the blood pressure. Some people, however, may be making a mistake in attempting to eliminate salt altogether. Under some circumstances, a total prohibition can be harmful.

What circumstances?

In warm weather, people perspire. If they are engaged in physical labor or effort, they perspire. If they play tennis or handball or engage in other active sports, they perspire. If they do any of these things on a hot day, they perspire all the more. When they perspire, their bodies lose minerals—sodium (salt) and potassium among them.

Sodium and potassium are essential for the functioning of the heart. The heart, like a fuel cell, requires chemical and electrical interactions. Sodium and potassium interact to produce the electrical impulses required not just by the heart but by the body as a whole.

When there is a sharp drop in the level of the sodium or potassium, or both, the electrical current is weakened or disrupted. Heart attacks can occur in people with otherwise normal hearts when the electrical supply is too low to meet a particular level of activity. Perhaps the best example is that of the person who plays tennis on a very hot day, perspiring profusely and reaching the point where the loss of sodium is so great that the electrical impulses to the heart are too weak to energize normal actions.

Such heart attacks are often mystifying because the person affected has had no previous history of cardiac abnormalities.

This is why the principle of vital balance and the proportion is all-important with respect to salt. Certainly it is true that the American diet contains far too much salt. Cutting down sharply on salt, therefore, is important. The amount of salt existing naturally in foods is usually enough to maintain the biochemical balance. But if we push the prohibition too far, trying to eliminate salt altogether despite individual requirements and special circumstances, we can get into trouble.

How do we know how much is enough? We have to take into account the kind of lives we lead, the work we do, the exercise we take, the time of the year, and the area in which we live. A simple blood test, which ought to be taken anyway to determine cholesterol levels and triglycerides, can establish where we stand with respect to normal limits. Our physician can help us interpret all these correlations in terms of our own life-style and help us to decide how far to go in cutting down on salt.

Dr. Fareed kept close tabs on my blood tests. It developed that my physical activity not only permitted but actually required a certain amount of salt in my daily diet.

As I say, Ellen was masterly in presiding over the nutritional part of the program. Its other parts were governed according to common sense. I modified my life-style. I was already on a leave of absence from the university and was prepared to extend it or modify it as circumstances required. I cleared the decks for more writing, reading, music, and photography. I continued to do all the things that had worked so well for me earlier in overcoming the illness I had written about in *Anatomy of an Illness,* things that nourished the spirit and were joyous. I knew I had to give full weight and scope to love, laughter, hope, faith, and the will to live.

Ellen made sure we stayed fairly close to a daily schedule. The essentials of that schedule:

8:30–10:00 A.M. After breakfast, my secretary at UCLA comes to my house for work on office matters and correspondence. (Breakfast generally consists of fresh orange juice, cooked unpolished rice, yogurt, home-made bread, and a coffee substitute such as Pero.)

10:30–11:30 A.M. Morning walking exercise. Begin at 1 mph and gradually increase to 2½ or 3 mph.

12:30–4:00 P.M. Lunch, rest, writing, reading, music, photography, etc. (Lunch generally consisted of Ellen's special salad and steamed fresh vegetables.)

4:30–5:30 P.M. Afternoon walking exercise.

6:30–7:30 P.M. Dinner. (Generally the same as lunch, plus fish or chicken once or twice a week.)

8:30–10:30 P.M. Friends, reading, music, chess, etc.

Because of all the hills and the absence of sidewalks in our neighborhood, we found it practicable to do our walking on a jogger's track a couple of miles from the house. In mid-morning and mid-afternoon the jogging traffic on the circular track was not so heavy that it interfered with walking. Walking had become quite fashionable, and we were not without company. We discovered to our delight that the track had become something of a community social center, akin to the old country store with its Franklin stove and cracker-barrel conversations. The focus of talk on the track was on nutrition, life-styles, health, friendships, reading, family.

All age groups were represented. The walkers and runners had chipped in to install metal stretching-bars and stands. This was where the congregants would meet, not only for their pre-running or post-running stretching routines but for the pleasures of social exchange. I doubt that any singles bar had more animation, which ran the gamut from restrained and dignified conversation to earnest negotiations. The skimpy costumes helped create a mood of friendly intimacy.

On Saturday and Sunday mornings, the open field encircled by the track was used for a touch football game, a local institution that had started some 15 years earlier. A veteran touch-footballer, I longed to get into the games. As it was, I enjoyed watching the action from my perimeter view while walking. Some of the players were quite good, having played in college or even professionally. Very frequently, they would get into fierce arguments over whether a player had caught the football or trapped it, whether the man with the ball had stepped out of bounds, or whether a team had actually covered the 10 yards necessary for a first down. The absence of an umpire didn't shorten the altercations or lower the decibels. We didn't want for excitement.

My own activity at the track afforded a good measure of my progress. The first time I had tried it, I was able to walk for only a minute or so and then felt slightly dizzy. Day by day and week by week, however, my capacity increased until I could keep going for an hour or so.

My wife accompanied me on all these excursions. We played word games, some of which we invented ourselves, in order to counteract the monotonous effect of unchanging scenery. We also had long and pleasant discussions about our children.

Dr. Fareed, who insisted on joining us during some of these early excursions, would keep track of my pulse and blood pressure. I found that my threshold of exertion was a pulse rate of 94 per minute; that is, so long as I stayed under that figure, I had no feelings of fatigue. With each passing day, however, I discovered that my endurance improved. By the end of January 1981, I could walk half a mile without stopping and without sending my pulse above 94. At first, when Dr. Fareed took my blood pressure, it would be in the range of 110 to 118 systolic and 65 to 68 diastolic before by starting out and would be around 112 to 120 systolic and 65 to 70 diastolic just after exercise. My aim was to improve on these figures by bringing up the pressure somewhat. In that way, we would know that the heart muscle was responding to the increased demand.

By the end of February, I was up to almost 4 miles a day, divided evenly between morning and afternoon, at a rate of 2 mph. I was making the interesting discovery that my pulse rate was coming down—slowly to be sure, but down nonetheless. I was also able to walk at a rate of 2 mph with a pulse rate of 88—a gain of only 6 units but evidence that my capacity for physical exertion was improving. Blood pressure during exercise was in the vicinity of 135 over 70.

Dr. Fareed was enthusiastic about my progress and felt that, whatever the severity of the initial heart attack, I was probably opening up new blood vessels. He encouraged me to believe that the new regime was working. Meanwhile, I was holding to the diet and to the things that gave me deep enjoyment. When Dr. Fareed sent a sample of my blood in for laboratory analysis, it showed that my cholesterol level had dropped from the hospital high of 285 to 190. There was a similar improvement in the triglycerides.

Something else was happening on my walks besides physical regeneration. I found all my senses becoming sharper, more attuned. I became aware of delicate shadings of light, the way trees and leaves changed their colors at different times of the day, the way barks of trees, viewed close up, were like abstract murals, distinct as the trees themselves. Even ferns had exotic shapes I had never seen before. Some of them looked like wind-swept designs in sand.

My camera had never been busier. I experimented with the ability of the lens, controlled by speed and light settings and its changes of focus, to produce soft-shaded and blurred backgrounds that would give added prominence to the objects being photographed. Just in my own backyard I found a thousand different subjects I had never seen before waiting to be photographed—the variations in the colors and shapes of small stones and pebbles; the deep crimson powder-puff formations of the "bottle brush" plants; the delicate hues of gazanias and marguerites; the majestic plumes of pampas grass; the crisscrossing effect of bamboo shoots. By using a telescopic "zoom" lens up close, I was able to penetrate the inner world of small flowers and see deeply into their textures.

What especially fascinated me about photography was that a camera could be made to "squint." As children, we would squint at the clouds and change their shapes in our minds to large animals. We can make the camera "squint" along with us by combining its speed, light, and depth-of-field capabilities.

This sense of sharpened focus in life under conditions of serious illness was beautifully described by the late Dr. Lauran Eugene Trombley, of the University of Oklahoma. Following the diagnosis of a terminal illness while still in his internship, Dr. Trombley was able to transcend his initial emotional devastation. He wrote in the journal *Life-Threatening Behavior* that he "became increasingly aware of a new sensitivity that had gradually developed in my interpersonal relationships. . . . I found that all of my senses seemed more acute, though I believe that I simply paid more attention to what was going on around me and, in a way, I found myself hungering for every sensory experience that I could absorb. In many ways the world seemed to offer more beauty, and there was a heightened awareness of sounds and sights which in the past I may have only casually observed or simply not have paid much

attention to at all. . . . Aside from the sensory and affec-
tive sensitivity that I had seemed to acquire, there appeared
to me to be a culmination of all the learning experiences
that I had in my professional career which, in a com-
pressed space of time, became the foundation for practically a new way of life."*

*I am grateful to Eugene Pumpian-Mindlin, a colleague in the UCLA Depart-
ment of Psychiatry and Biobehavioral Sciences, for calling this article to my
attention.

CHAPTER IV

Reassessment

Sometime around March 20, I received a telephone call from Dr. Shine.

"We've got to have a serious talk," he said. "No office telephones or other interruptions. Let's do it away from the office."

A few days later, he delayed his dinner in order to come up to the house. We sat in the living room.

"I'm not sure you're facing up to the realities," he began. "Let me go over my records and the hospital charts with you."

Armed with these materials, Dr. Shine underlined key facts. He reminded me that the enzyme studies made the day after I was brought to the hospital showed substantial heart-muscle loss.

"The CPK enzyme test gives us a precise measurement of the amount of heart muscle that was destroyed and went into the bloodstream," he said. "You had a reading of

2600—a great deal higher than the average heart attack. This was confirmed by supplementary enzyme tests. There is a reference here in your hospital record to severe left-ventricular dysfunction. This means that the most important part of the heart pump is not working as it should.

"The report also refers to congestive heart failure. Your lungs were filling up with fluid, and you had blood in your sputum throughout your hospital stay. I know how you feel about treadmill tests. You look at it in terms of your own reactions—and I respect your feelings. You are right when you say that psychological factors can affect the result. But I look at the results of the treadmill test just as additional evidence that there is a serious underlying condition and you really ought to go back to the hospital—say, not later than Tuesday. Let's get the angiogram over with and find out exactly how much blockage you have and how best to deal with it."

By this time—seven weeks after my hospital stay—the reconditioning program was showing good results. My symptoms were diminishing. The heart rate was slowing, the beat was steady, I felt increasing strength and endurance. How much significance should we attach to the improvement?

"You've got to take two things into account," he said. "The first is that—as I said a moment ago—you had severe left-ventricular dysfunction. Even if you can improve that function, you've got the second hurdle to contend with. That has to do with the arteries to the heart. Once they are clogged, you have coronary artery disease. That doesn't go away."

I observed Dr. Shine. He was sitting forward, speaking slowly and earnestly. I was deeply moved. He had delayed his dinner in order to come to my home for the purpose of persuading me to a course of action that was in my own interest. Yet I couldn't deny the evidence of my improvement, especially the fact that I was able to sustain increasing amounts of physical effort.

"What would you like me to do?" I asked.

"I think you ought to go back to the hospital and have an angiogram. That way we can determine exactly where the blockage is, how serious it is, and how best to correct it."

I realized that this meant bypass surgery. Since the blockage was also established, the angiogram would serve as a road map for the surgeon.

"Isn't it possible that the condition of my arteries has improved along with the general improvement of everything else?" I asked.

"The heart itself has been undergoing a healing experience," he said, "but that process does not extend to the coronary arteries. When the walls of the arteries are lined by accumulated plaque, you have to contend with ongoing coronary disease."

"Hasn't there been some research," I asked, "showing that, when the level of cholesterol in the blood is reduced and stays reduced over a period of time, the arteries widen? What about the work of Lester Morrison? How about the evidence assembled by Dr. Castelli, of NIH?"

"The most comprehensive studies on the subject have been carried out by David Blankenhorn, of USC," Dr. Shine replied. "These studies showed that the femoral artery in human beings could be freed of blockage to some extent, but there was no corresponding improvement in the coronary arteries. The evidence you cite is interesting but not yet conclusive."

"Then you don't think the program I am on will have

the effect of bringing more oxygen to the heart?"

"I wish I could encourage you to believe you have reversed the problem in your coronary arteries," he said, "but this is not what accumulated experience says will happen."

As Dr. Shine spoke, I thought to myself, "Here we go again." I felt a surge of energy and couldn't suppress a smile.

Dr. Shine asked whether he had said anything funny. I replied that he hadn't; it was just that the notion of irreversibility had touched off something deep inside me. That was the concept that had been used to describe the condition, 17 years earlier, that I wrote about in *Anatomy of an Illness*.

"You must understand," said Dr. Shine, "that I am not going to experiment with your life. It is quite possible that you can get away with what you want to do; but since I have the responsibility for steering you in the right direction, I've got to play it safe. It's only been three months since your heart attack. Your treadmill tests showed serious blockage. Cases such as yours tend to produce recurrences, and you don't have that much reserve."

I didn't know whether he thought my upbeat mood meant that I had missed the seriousness of his diagnosis. It occurred to me that he thought I was practicing "denial"— a term used by physicians to describe the failure of seriously ill patients to face up to their problems. I thought it might be pertinent, therefore, to tell him why I thought I had a magnificent heart and how well it had served me over the years. I reminded him of the diagnosis in 1954, when my cardiologist showed evidence of a silent coronary, and how I had been told if I gave up all activity and took to my bed, I might have 18 months to live.

Dr. Shine said a great deal of new knowledge had been accumulated in the past 25 years. Looking back, he could identify outmoded ideas about diagnosis and treatment.

"Is it at all possible," I asked, "that 25 years from now, they might be saying the same things about the present period?"

"Quite possibly," he replied. "But we can't assume that everything we know is wrong just because so much has changed in theory and practice. We've got to go with the best we know."

I recognized the responsible nature of this comment. But there were some questions that seemed to me to be relevant.

Granted that heart surgery was required in my case because of an unacceptably high risk of sudden cardiac death, in what respect and to what extent did the statistical averages about risks apply in my case?

Dr. Shine was very helpful, in response to my requests, in exploring these issues with me, and in sending me material. I also had detailed discussions with Dr. Weinberger, Dr. Fareed, Dr. Hitzig, and specialists in the Los Angeles area like Dr. Eliot Corday and Dr. Robert Kositchek, whom I knew in non-medical circumstances. I also talked to Dr. Michael DeBakey, of Houston, a good friend, who was kind enough to send me his new book on heart attacks. All of these materials and discussions threw considerable light on the issues just mentioned.

With respect to the statistical risks, for example, I saw abundant evidence supporting the figures cited by Dr. Shine—0.3 percent mortality for the angiogram and less than 5 percent for the surgery. Five percent of the patients experienced heart attacks or other complications, including blood clots, while being angiogrammed. The special dyes used to enable the X-ray machine to peer into the heart and its arteries created very little risk for most patients but specific risks for others. It was also clear that these statistical risks did not apply uniformly. For the overwhelming majority of individuals, the risk was negligible. But for a very small minority, the risk was 100 percent. Was there some way of determining what category I belonged to? Did my documented difficulty in tolerating medications place me in the extra-risk category because of the dyes used in the angiogram? So far as surgery was concerned, would the use of anesthesia present a problem both because of a recent myocardial infarction and because of the anesthesia itself? If in fact vasospasm had figured in my myocardial infarction, would open-heart surgery incur an increased risk of touching off another spasm and another MI? There were documented cases of people who had heart attacks or MI's under bypass surgery.

With respect to rehabilitation: since there was a strong possibility that my life-style—frequent long-distance travel and pressures of close scheduling—had figured in the heart attack, it seemed obvious that any attempt at recovery had to begin with a stark change in that life-style. I knew I would have to impose firm restrictions on airport and associated encounters. I would try to control my cholesterol level through a combination of diet, exercise, and life-style change. I would sharply reduce the intake of foods like meat, eggs, cheeses, sugars, desserts, and saturated oils.

And, to return to my favorite theme, I would give adequate scope to the things that I believed were the patient's own responsibility: hope, faith, love, laughter, and a strong will to live.

In the light of all these factors, I found myself strengthened in the belief that I could make it all the way without surgery. I thought it important, nonetheless, to accept Dr.

Shine's urgent recommendation that I obtain a second opinion. But whose? Dr. Shine had himself said that many of the local cardiologists had either studied under him or worked with him and that they tended to view medical matters the same way. But good fortune was to come my way. In correspondence with Dr. Siegfried Kra, of Yale University, I learned that one of Dr. Kra's colleagues, Dr. David Cannom, a cardiologist, had just moved from Connecticut to San Pedro, some 40 miles away from our own home. I telephoned Dr. Cannom and arranged an appointment. I sent him my charts in advance of our meeting, early in April 1981.

Dr. Cannom was young; I judged him to be in his late 30's or early 40's. He was slender and ruddy faced, with a shock of curly blond hair and a wide smile. Before he took my pulse or put a stethoscope to my chest, he spoke with me for about an hour, drawing me out on my own perceptions as to the cause of the heart attack and asking me about the treatment to date. I reported that, with Dr. Shine's knowledge, I had discontinued all my medication a month after leaving the hospital. There was no longer evidence of fluid in my chest, so diuretics were not necessary. I was off digitalis because of adverse reactions. Regular Isordil was no longer indicated, but I carried a small bottle of nitroglycerin pellets around at all times, just in case of an emergency or even feelings of discomfort.

Dr. Cannom asked me how I felt about bypass surgery. I replied that I was prepared to go through with the surgery if I really needed it but that I wanted to see whether significant improvement was possible without it. I also told him of my sense of growing strength, week by week, and of the drop in my cholesterol and low-density lipoproteins.

I asked Dr. Cannom whether it made sense to continue

the course I was on and to see how far the improvement might carry me. The surgery option was always there if the improvement didn't hold.

Dr. Cannom said he was glad I hadn't minimized the seriousness of my situation and that it was hard for him to quarrel with the notion of close surveillance during this phase of any recovery program. By and large, he said, he emphatically agreed that we could defer surgery so long as the improvement in my condition was consistent and verifiable.

Dr. Cannom asked me how I dealt with the depression that almost universally affects people who have had heart attacks—generally in the hospital, when the realization hits that life is in serious jeopardy, and again during the recovery period, when the invalid psychology takes hold.

I had had no such feelings. Depressions are frequently an integral part of the panic cycle. Being free of panic at the start helped to free me of its usual aftermath of uncertainty and dread. I told Dr. Cannom that the dominant emotion, not just at the time of the attack but during the critical period, was curiosity, a sense of challenge, and confidence. Every cubit of progress since the heart attack occurred served as exhilarating evidence that we were en route to recovery. As I had told Dr. Shine, I thought that I had a great heart and that it was doing everything—and more—that anyone could ask of it. Life has many prizes, not the least of which is having confidence in one's physiological endowments and their responsiveness to one's deepest needs.

I said that what was perhaps most fortunate of all was that I was not freighted with feelings of invalidism. I didn't feel that I was living on the edge of a cliff or that I had to govern my every move according to its effects on my heart.

I had cut down on the activities I happened not to like—chasing after planes, for example—and I was relishing the enlarged opportunities for more reading, more photography, more time at the organ, and more time with family and friends. As for my sports life, I knew that I would be able, before very long, to be back on the golf course and the tennis court. The anticipations were a feast in themselves.

Exercise was no enemy. I told Dr. Cannom how, the day after my release from the hospital, Dr. Robert Kositchek, a good friend and golfing companion who had been highly supportive throughout, had come to visit me. I was in the backyard at the time, lazily swinging a nine-iron golf club. Consternation was written all over his face, and he implored me to drop the club at once. I assured him that I was not being monstrously irresponsible, that I was staying within my limits, and that it felt very good to give my body the modest exercise that the pendulum motion offered. Exercise is a powerful antidote to the psychology of invalidism, which tends to foster feelings of doom.

Dr. Cannom said he concurred fully with the idea that proper attitudes are an integral part of any recovery program. He then proceeded to the usual heart examination, taking my blood pressure and cardiograph, listening to my heart, and probing for any evidence of residual congestion. He said it might be useful for me to have a 2-D echogram—one of the new marvels of technology, which, by sending sound waves through the heart, could construct a moving picture, radar-like, of the action of the heart. He was especially eager to obtain information about the adequacy of my left ventricle. The UCLA Hospital examination had diagnosed "severe left-ventricular dysfunction," which was a serious condition indeed.

I left Dr. Cannom's office that day in a mood of high expectations. I was elated that he felt we were justified in proceeding with the present program; I was encouraged by our meeting to see how far it would carry us. He felt that my improvement since leaving the hospital three months earlier had been significant and that everything ought to be done to maintain it.

That afternoon, just after returning from Dr. Cannom's office in San Pedro, Ellen and I went to the track and walked a mile farther than we had done previously. Good news is energizing. I had the confirmation that the increased strength I felt was not illusory and that I was, literally, on the right track.

CHAPTER V

Mind, Moods, and Machines

Early in May 1981, I went in for Dr. Cannom's 2-D echogram. The procedure itself was very simple. I lay on a hospital table and was hooked up to various devices that sent sound waves through my heart. On the monitor I could see a television-type picture, albeit quite blurred, of the squeezing movement of my heart.

Two days later, Dr. Cannom telephoned to report the results of the test. He said that they were able to get a fairly good idea of the amount of heart-muscle destruction, which he estimated at about 75 percent, or so I thought.

I thanked Dr. Cannom and then telephoned Dr. Fareed to relay the report. About half an hour later, however, Dr. Fareed was back on the phone, telling me I got the numbers twisted. He had called Dr. Cannom. The correct figures were 75 percent functional and 25 percent destroyed. It was a big difference. He asked whether I had been apprehensive over the initial report as I understood it. I could honestly tell him I had not. Even if I had only 25 percent of heart muscle left, I had all the evidence I needed that it had been working beautifully; that was all that counted. Now that I knew I had three times as much capacity, I had a lot more to be thankful for. When Dr. Fareed joined me on the track the next morning, we could laugh about my mistake in reversing the figures.

When next I saw Dr. Cannom, he was no less interested in my state of mind than he had been the first time we met. He asked, for example, what significance I attached to the results of the early treadmill tests, which had been interpreted as providing incontrovertible evidence that my heart was incapable of sustaining even a low level of exercise.

I replied that I could only deduce from my negative experiences that treadmills were bad for my health and that I had better stay off them. Physical exertion by itself was no problem. I was not being entirely facetious. On the walking track, for example, as the Holter had proved, I had had no problems. I had no difficulty in climbing stairs two steps at a time. But with much less exercise on a treadmill, I had experienced coronary insufficiency. The critical difference seemed to me to be represented by my emotional response to the treadmill.

Dr. Cannom pointed out that the evidence of coronary insufficiency on the treadmill was genuine enough, whether caused by emotional or physical factors or both. The hospital report on all the elements of my problem couldn't be discounted. What my early treadmill record said to him was that my heart was vulnerable to emotional stress, especially when combined with physical exertion.

I had no difficulty in recognizing these facts. I felt they corroborated our rehabilitation program, which was not confined to diet and exercise but extended to my entire life-style and, indeed, to habits of thought.

In thinking about this conversation with Dr. Cannom, I tried to sort out the many factors involved—clogging of the arteries caused by fatty deposits or other substances; blockage caused by spasm; the possibility that clogging and spasm could interact; the limits of the heart's endurance to physical or emotional exertion or both; and all these factors in varying combinations.

It was logical enough to draw connections between high-cholesterol diets and fatty deposits in the arteries. But I was also aware of the studies, mentioned earlier, showing that some persons whose diets were largely free of eggs, butter, cheeses, and fatty meats were nonetheless found to have high cholesterol levels in their blood. Did lack of exercise figure in this condition? Not necessarily. The studies showed that stress was a key factor. People who are unable to cope with stress tend to manufacture high cholesterol levels. Dr. Rosenman and Dr. Friedman, the authors of the Type A–Type B classifications, discovered that, as federal-income-tax deadlines approach, the cholesterol levels of accountants zoom skyward. The same is true of medical students on the eve of their examinations.

This does not mean that a proper diet is irrelevant or that physical exercise is a waste of effort. What it does mean is that stress can be predominant in many cases. Tension, exasperation, frustration, fears, unremitting pressures, deadlines—all these are no less involved than fatty foods in narrowing the coronary arteries.

Recent research, Dr. Cannom said, tended to underline the importance of combined causes. Spasm is just as likely to hit arteries that are already clogged as arteries that are not clogged. This, of course, added to the danger. Minor spasm could combine with a fairly substantial level of clogging to produce a shutdown of oxygen to the heart, with resultant destruction of heart muscle. Similarly, a minor amount of clogging could combine with a strong spasm to produce a major episode. It was like an equation in which two variables combined to produce a certain number.

Dr. Cannom said that not enough is known about spasm. It can occur in different parts of the body and is manifested by sudden, involuntary contractions. One can speculate that something in the nervous system sets off the contractions, or that abnormalities in the endocrine system may be responsible, or a combination of both. The entire field is being studied by medical researchers. Meanwhile, we must deal with the effects as best we can. So far as heart problems are concerned, however, it seemed reasonable to believe that it is helpful to distinguish between conditions caused by spasm and those caused by arterial abnormalities.

Dr. Cannom told me about the growing interest on the part of cardiologists in the phenomenon of spasm. He gave me a number of references to augment the papers I had already seen and that I have referred to in an earlier chapter.

Dr. Cannom reviewed my progress. He said I had reason to be encouraged, but it was important nonetheless to be mindful of the fact that my tolerance of certain forms of stress, especially airports or frustration or argumentation or unmet deadlines, was not as high as it was to physical exertion. I could readily accept the validity of this observation. The circumstances of physical effort, I had learned, were often more important than the effort itself. For example, if I was late for an important appointment, I might experience chest pressure or even breathlessness, even though I might be walking on even ground. But if I was free of anxiety and, equally important, if I was doing something I liked, I could sustain perhaps ten times as much exertion. I could play fairly strenuous tennis, requiring bursts of hard running, but walking through a crowded airport under heavy time pressure produced severe chest discomfort. If ever I needed evidence that emotional stress—whether caused by anxiety or apprehension or remorse—was the prime enemy, I found it in my own experience in the months following the heart attack.

What biochemistry was involved? In ordinary exercise undertaken in a mood of pleasure, the epinephrine (adrenalin) sent to the heart can have a cushioning effect. But under circumstances of extreme anxiety of panic, the amount of the hormone and the suddenness of the infusion, combined with other hormones known as catecholamines, can disrupt the rhythm and even rupture the muscle fibers. Secretions that are benevolent under auspicious circumstances can become hostile and dangerous under stressful circumstances. Endorphins, morphine-like secretions produced by the brain, are associated with well-being, but they can also cause problems when they are overworked. As in other aspects of life, too much of a good thing can be bad.

By early June, almost six months after the heart attack, I decided that my progress was strong enough for me to go back on Dr. Shine's treadmill. I wanted to be able to satisfy him on his own terms. The poor results of the early treadmill test had indicated to him the existence of a serious cardiac condition, manifested by blocked arteries, but I was hopeful that a good showing on a new treadmill test would be free of abnormalities and thus provide no evidence of serious arterial disease.

What about my earlier point concerning my own attitude toward treadmill testing and the importance of psychological factors in affecting the results of the test? I had thought about this aspect of the problem and figured out a way of unblocking myself psychologically for the test. If I could operate the treadmill myself, I reasoned, I would have an increased sense of control. As I said earlier, one of the depressing characteristics of serious illness is the loss of control felt by the patient. What I had objected to, basically, in the previous tests, was that the machine had been running me; I wanted to run the machine. Would the change make a difference?

I telephoned Dr. Shine and proposed that I go back on the treadmill, suggesting the new protocol. He readily agreed to having me operate the machine myself and said he saw no technical difficulties in the way. I was delighted with his response. A date was fixed.

I turned up in the UCLA treadmill room in advance of Dr. Shine. I brought with me a Woody Allen cassette and some Bach and Beethoven recordings. It had seemed to me, on my earlier visit, that the mood of the treadmill room was altogether too grim and businesslike. The patient is hooked up to a machine that records the condition of the heart in the form of portentous squiggles. The cardiologist has to concentrate on several calibrations at the same time—the markings on the cardiograph, the pulse rate, and changes in blood pressure in response to different levels of exertion. The cardiologist calls out the changes to the attendant. I thought a change in atmosphere might be salutary for all concerned.

The attendant in charge of the treadmill room shaved my chest and attached the suction cups with wires connected to the cardiograph. He attached similar cups to the pulses in my ankles and elbows. These hookups would provide readings, or "leads," of different aspects of heart action in a pre-treadmill cardiograph. These readings would then be compared with the ones produced on the treadmill.

Dr. Shine arrived in the middle of Albert Schweitzer's recording of Bach's Toccata and Fugue in D Minor on the great organ in the Strasbourg Cathedral. He was very amiable about the new sounds in the treadmill room and proceeded to instruct me in the operation of the treadmill. It couldn't have been simpler: one button for start, another for stop; one button for speedup, another for slowdown; one button for increasing the incline of the moving mat, another for decreasing the incline.

Dr. Shine took the pre-test vital signs: pulse 78; blood pressure 116 systolic, 68 diastolic.

I stepped on the machine and pressed the start button, giving the treadmill an initial speed of 1 mph. After a minute or so, I increased the speed to 1½ mph. Dr. Shine was calling out the readings. Pulse increased to 94. The telltale measurement I was waiting for was the blood-pressure reading. On my first test, blood pressure had fallen in response to exercise, even at a low level, indicating cardiac insufficiency. Five months of special effort were now on the line.

The Bach recording was now over. I asked the nurse to put on Woody Allen. Within a matter of seconds his offhand, mordant monologue, reinforced with audience laughter, transformed the atmosphere in the treadmill room. Dr. Shine was smiling broadly.

Soon we would have the blood-pressure reading. I felt as though I were involved in one of those old black-and-white movies about a submarine trying to raise itself from the bottom. The crew is working manfully to increase the pressure. The captain and his lieutenants are grouped around the control panel, their eyes fixed on the depth-level indicator. Finally, in response to the heroic efforts of the crew, the pressure begins to mount and the gauge, after wavering, records an upward climb. Since I couldn't see the blood-pressure indicator, my only gauge was Dr. Shine's expression, at this moment impassive and non-committal.

Dr. Shine asked whether I was all right. I nodded. Then he asked whether I felt comfortable in increasing the speed and incline. I stepped up the speed to 2 mph with the moving mat angled at 10 percent. Dr. Shine called out the blood pressure—124 over 71. I looked at Dr. Shine. His eyes were wide open as he shifted his concentrated gaze from the blood-pressure gauge to the cardiograph.

"How are we doing?" I asked.

"Super," he said.

My heart jumped with joy. I increased the speed to 2½ mph and, after a minute or so, adjusted the incline to 15 percent. The pulse was now 117. Dr. Shine called out a new blood-pressure reading: 138 over 71. My heart was responding beautifully to the challenge of exertion. All the effort and emotional investment of many months were being vindicated.

It was now about 12 minutes since the start of the test. It seemed to me the test was successful and had served its purpose. I pressed the stop button and stepped down.

Dr. Shine asked why I stopped.

"I'm all right," I said. "I just want to quit while I'm ahead."

"Are you tired or short of breath?" he asked. "Your pulse rate is only 117. I'd like to see you extend the exercise and get it up to 150. That way we would have a better idea of how your heart can take a higher level of exertion."

I said that at this point in the healing process, I felt we probably had whatever information was necessary to indicate we were on the right track. I was reluctant to press for my outermost limits. At a later stage in my recovery, I said, I would be happy to return to test my further progress. My assumption was that the healing process was still an ongoing affair.

Dr. Shine said he respected my decision to step down. He congratulated me on my showing and said the treadmill test indicated that my heart was undergoing a remarkable reconditioning. However, while the repair of the heart itself was clearly evident, the condition of the coronary arteries was a matter of continuing concern to him. This disease, Dr. Shine said, does not clear up by itself.

I asked whether under the circumstances he still felt that the angiogram-surgery route was indicated. He reminded me that we were only half a year beyond the original attack; he could only repeat his earlier warning that the first-year risk was unacceptably high. He said he was pleased that I would continue to see Dr. Cannom. Since Dr. Shine had just been appointed head of the Department of Medicine at UCLA, he would not be able to spend as much time as he liked with his private patients. But he assured me that he would always be there if I needed him, and he made sure I had his home telephone number.

I reported the results of the treadmill test, and my conversation with Dr. Shine, to Dr. Cannom on my next regular visit. Dr. Cannom was delighted with the treadmill showing. His own examination and cardiograph confirmed my progress, and he expressed his full confidence in the course I had been following.

By September, nine months after my heart attack, I was up to six miles a day of walking exercise, divided between morning and afternoon. I was now able to walk very briskly with a pulse rate of about 86 to 88—some six to eight efficient beats under what it had been several months earlier under conditions of similar physical exertion. My cholesterol level continued to drop and was now in the 170's, well below the threshold of danger, 245, defined by the Framingham study. There was similar improvement with my triglycerides.

With the fall 1981 school term, the time had come, I felt, to resume part of my work at UCLA. Some half a dozen lectures, at UCLA and in the general vicinity, were on the fall schedule. I was able to perform my school tasks without difficulty. My first long trip came in early fall; I went to Washington for a meeting of the Special Medical Advisory Group of the Veterans Administration hospitals, an appointment I had accepted just prior to my illness. I found the trip stimulating. The VA headquarters were less than half a mile from the hotel, and the route was slightly uphill. I went back and forth on foot. Once or twice I experienced a little tightness in the chest, rested for several minutes until the feeling passed, then resumed my journey.

Back home again, I ventured onto the golf course and tennis courts. I can't pretend that I didn't get winded much sooner than I had before the attack, but it was clear to me, as the weeks passed, that my endurance and speed were improving.

It was now close to the end of the year and the first anniversary of my heart attack. I was back full-time at the university and was surprised to see how quickly the daily correspondence and telephone calls had swelled to their old dimensions, and how many visitors had to be seen. Part of my old daily schedule had been devoted to patients at the hospital or elsewhere who needed a morale boost. Their physicians or relatives believed it might be useful if, on the basis of my own experience, I could help mobilize their will to live. Many of these cases were heartbreakingly poignant; not infrequently, after doing what I could to encourage patients by talking to them about their own resources, I would leave with my own spirits sagging so badly that I was in need of emotional reinforcement myself.

I had an enlarged appreciation for the constant strain on doctors and nurses who put their all into a case and are encouraged when they see a patient improve, only to see the patient later slip back beyond reach. Considering the circumstances of such unremitting emotional and physical strain on physicians, it was little wonder to me that they should have such a high suicide rate or that so many of them sought relief in the drugs available to them.

CHAPTER VI

Spoof and Stress

On December 21, 1981, the day before the first anniversary of my heart attack, I accidentally discovered that my wife was planning a surprise party to celebrate the completion of the first year that some of the specialists thought I might not make. She secretly invited some of my associates at the medical school, my golfing and tennis companions, and members of the family who lived in California.

In possession of this information 24 hours before the party was to begin, I decided it might be fun to expand the surprise somewhat. All my instincts as a spoofer began to throb. I telephoned my close friend Devery Freeman, the author, who had many associates in the motion-picture industry, and asked him to try to arrange for me to have a professional disguise.

On my way home from the office to the "surprise"

party, I stopped off at Universal Studios, where, thanks to Dev Freeman, the head of the makeup department was ready for me. Less than an hour later, I left Universal with a disguise that even I had difficulty in penetrating when I looked in the mirror. I had a rust-colored beard; the shape of my eyes was completely changed. Over my thinning hair I had a wig so authentic-looking that I was tempted not to return it.

I stopped at Dev and Adele Freeman's on my way home and was unrecognized when they came to the door. After I identified myself, we proceeded to the party. My wife and my daughter Candis answered Dev's doorbell ring. Dev introduced me as "Professor Morton, from London," a friend who was staying with him. Ellen held out her hand and greeted me; so did my daughter. I felt like a character from *Our Town* who had returned from the dead and was walking unrecognized through the lives of those who had once known him intimately. To have my wife look at me as though I were a stranger was a shock, to say the least.

I entered the living room, already filled with people, and was introduced as "Dr. Morton" to my friends. In a cracked voice and with an English accent, I said that I understood that people in Los Angeles were inclined to be very affectionate, and accordingly embraced each of the women, patting them as I did so. The women were extremely restrained and forebearing, except for a former nun, a close friend, who jumped back three feet.

Dr. "Jolly" West came over and asked whether he could get me something to drink or eat. Pretending to be hard of hearing, I cupped my hand to my ear and looked at Dr. West blankly. Jolly raised his voice and repeated the question.

"Ah, yes," I replied. "I was there years ago. Dreadful place."

"No, no," said Dr. West, "I was asking if I could get you something to eat."

"You are quite right," I said. "I would never go back."

Dr. West looked at me blankly, accepted defeat, and turned away.

After about half an hour of similar discontinuities, I decided that apocrypha had to give way to revelation, went over to the organ, and started to play one of my signature pieces.

I could hear my daughter Candis cry out from the kitchen over the sound of the organ, "Daddy is home!"

And that was the way Dr. Morton was unmasked. We all had a good laugh, and the rest of the evening was very joyous indeed. What better way to give authenticity to the celebration of recovery than through the enjoyment of laughter?

In March 1982, I telephoned Dr. Shine—one year after he had urged me to take an angiogram. I told him I wouldn't feel I had achieved my goals until he believed, on the basis of his own examination, that I was en route to a full recovery. He readily assented to an examination, and we arranged a date. Afterwards, Dr. Shine sat me down and talked as straight as he could.

"You've come through the past 15 months in fine style," he said, "and I congratulate you on holding to your program. But I can only repeat what I've told you many times before. The damage to your heart was extensive. According to our experience, there may be reconditioning of the heart, but the arteries are never really healed or unblocked. I can't say that you are not at risk. I think the risk can be reduced by following the course I suggested from the very start. I don't want to disappoint you, but neither do I want to mislead you."

"Dr. Shine," I asked, "would you say that I am in better shape than I was a year ago?"

"Infinitely better," he said.

"Would you say, on the basis of progress to date, that further progress is impossible?"

"Certainly not," he said.

"Is it also possible that one year from now I could return again with evidence that I will be as much improved over today as I am today over a year ago?"

"Certainly."

"Who could ask for anything more?" I asked. "We've got a date one year from today."

I held out my hand, which he warmly grasped, and we sealed the contract.

I knew it was still too early to say that, in Dr. Shine's phrase, I was fully "out of the woods." I did know that all the non-invasive tests indicated my heart was getting enough oxygen to meet its needs. Even if the underlying problem was not reversed, then at least there were substantial signs that compensating mechanisms were at work. The arrhythmias of the first six months or so after my leaving the hospital had practically disappeared, so far as I could tell. Average pulse rate slowed steadily and was in the low 60's. Blood pressure at rest ran in the vicinity of 120 over 60. Exercise consisted mostly of tennis and golf, which I played without strain or shortness of breath, and sometimes I did both on the same day. I resumed my full workload at the university, and I was doing increased battle with the airports, albeit on a schedule considerably reduced from what it had been before December 1980.

I can't pretend that my decision to reduce the stress in

my life has been uniformly successful. Sometimes circumstances take over. Early in December 1982, for example, I went to a suburb of Los Angeles to give a community lecture. I had barely acknowledged the introduction and was no more than a sentence into my lecture when the lights went out. So did the amplifying system. It was a fairly large auditorium and the acoustics were less than ideal. Raising one's voice can be a strain, especially when prolonged for an hour or more. I made what I hoped was a humorous reference to the blackout and continued my talk for the full hour sans microphone. At the same time, I was resolved to discontinue the talk if any adverse symptoms became manifest. I declined the question period.

On the way home, I felt a slight pressure in my chest and took a nitro tablet. The next morning, I went down to the walking track. I have discovered that exercise, at least in my case, is a potent corrective. Immediate bed rest—again, in my case—is not necessarily the best response to adverse symptoms. Some hearts dislike cramped experiences or emotional stress but dote on physical action. It is like a bicycle, which needs forward motion in order to retain balance.

What about the actual condition of my heart? Dr. Shine and Dr. Cannom have encouraged me by saying that "recanalization" of my heart has taken place and that a new network of small blood vessels has come into being and is meeting the heart's oxygen demands. Dr. Fareed feels fully vindicated in the early support he gave me in my decision to see whether substantial improvement was possible without surgery.

Has the fact of differing professional advice resulted in confusion? Not at all. The treatment of any serious condition is an equation involving many variables. Dr. Shine's emphasis was on hard facts relating to clinical examination and expectations based on statistical experience. Dr. Cannom was strictly empirical; he was ready to step in at any time if there was any regression in my week-to-week progress. Dr. Fareed and Dr. Hitzig were influenced most of all by what they knew about me over a period of years. They knew that I was not altogether imprudent, and they believed that what had worked for me before—namely, confidence, purpose, a deep will to live, joyousness, and a rigorous rehabilitation program—was worth being put to the test again. Bill Hitzig had begun by directing me to follow Dr. Shine's orders in every respect but eventually agreed that my progress was such that surgery was unnecessary and probably undesirable.

It would be a mistake, I believe, to elevate any single factor above the others in the continuing progress toward recovery. Certainly, emotional and psychological factors, which figure so largely in bringing on heart disease, are vital in any recovery program. Equally important, however, is a regime emphasizing family support, proper nutrition, proportionate exercise, and a way of life that makes it exciting to start a new day.

My convictions about the role of attitudes in intensifying or alleviating illness were reinforced for me in March 1982. A close personal friend telephoned me to say that his son, whom I shall call Larry, was emotionally devastated as a result of a medical checkup showing he had experienced a silent coronary. He said his son feared he was going to die.

Less than a week earlier, Larry had gone to a physician for a regular checkup. After taking a cardiograph, the physician asked Larry when his heart attack had occurred.

Stunned, Larry said he knew nothing about having had a heart attack. The physician pointed to some markings on the cardiograph, which he said never lied. Then he asked Larry whether he recalled ever having had chest pains or other unusual pains. Again Larry, now panicky, said no.

The physician explained to Larry that the markings on the cardiograph had probably been caused by a silent coronary. Larry's panic deepened. Then the physician asked Larry whether he was experiencing any angina or chest pains at that moment. Larry replied in the negative.

That night Larry had chest pains for the first time.

The next three days, during which he lost 17 pounds, were a nightmare. He suffered with uncertainty over whether to sell his business. Every time he looked at his wife and children, he had to turn away so that they wouldn't see his tears. He was put on a treadmill, which showed an S-T segment depression of more than 2 mm and a severe drop in blood pressure. Next came the angiogram, revealing an arterial lesion, on the basis of which prompt bypass surgery was mandated.

It was at this point that Dr. Charles Kleeman, a friend of Larry's father and the head of the CHEER program, came into the picture as consultant. Dr. Kleeman advised that the surgery be delayed pending further investigation and examination. Larry's father asked me to talk to Larry for the purpose of calming him down and bolstering his spirits.

Larry came to my home. He had the physique of a well-trained athlete. His expression, however, clearly showed something was wrong. He was pale and drawn. Every now and then he would put his hand to his heart. His first words, after sitting down, said it all: "I don't want to die."

There was nothing feigned or obscure about the fact that

he was in the tight grip of panic. I could readily understand Dr. Kleeman's apprehension about allowing a man in this panicky condition to undergo serious surgery.

We talked for about 15 minutes about things other than the immediate situation—his family, his business, his athletic activity, and the things that gave him joy in life. Then he reverted to his problem.

"I've got too much to live for," he said; "my wife, my children, my parents. I love my business. There is so much I want to do."

I told Larry that the very fact he had pursued an athletic life for so long was proof that he had a splendid heart. He had experienced no symptoms until he was told there were negative tracings on his cardiograph. Such tracings were not necessarily conclusive. I told him about my own experience in 1954, when Dr. Paul Dudley White informed me of false indications of heart damage that turned up on the cardiograph tracings of persons who had been heavily involved in athletics. I said I had no way of knowing whether this was true in his case but that I was certain Dr. Kleeman, for whom I had the highest regard, would not have suggested that the surgery be delayed for a single minute unless he felt there might be special factors which ought to be more fully explored.

I also reported my own experience on the treadmill. Larry confessed he had been so terrified of the machine that the moment the mat began to move under his feet he thought he was going to pass out. I spoke of Dr. Shine's concurrence in my request that I be allowed to operate the machine myself and how the knowledge that I could stop it at any time had fortified me psychologically.

Larry asked whether he could do the same thing. I told him I would be glad to put the question to Dr. Kleeman.

Larry took his hand down from over his chest. His breathing seemed a little less labored.

The next morning, I reported the conversation to Larry's father, who said he would relay the information to Dr. Kleeman. The doctor readily assented to Larry's return to the treadmill under the suggested new protocol. Before he went into the treadmill room, however, he needed some psychological reconditioning. I accompanied Larry to the treadmill room early enough to try to put him at his ease. Since there were three machines in the room and since they were not being used, we could have a dry run. I went on the machine next to Larry. We had a good time operating the controls.

Larry was in a good mood. Color came into his cheeks. He was convinced, he said, that he could now knock the spots off the monster. We laughed and told stories to each other.

Larry knew that the controls were in his own hands. He asked for a little more practice, then indicated that all signs were go.

The rest of the story is almost anticlimactic. For 15 minutes, Larry stayed on the treadmill, working it up to 3 mph at an incline of 15 degrees. He experienced no discomfort or breathlessness. His heart rate was up to 145 The cardiograph showed no S-T segment abnormality. Blood pressure, which began at 130 over 82, increased to 148 over 88, a good sign of cardiac sufficiency.

I watched Larry carefully. He seemed to be enjoying the experience, although I couldn't help noticing he was mumbling to himself.

The cardiologist stopped the machine. Larry stepped down, grinning. He said he knew he didn't have to ask the cardiologist how he had done; he could feel his victory all over.

After the cardiologist left, I asked Larry why he had been mumbling during the test.

"I kept telling myself," he said, "that I had a great heart and I wanted my heart to know it."

Dr. Kleeman had a meeting with Larry's father and advised against surgery, despite the contrary view of the specialists. Larry and his wife entered the CHEER program. They learned a great deal about proper nutrition and about the care of the heart in general. Larry also embarked on a daily exercise program, most of it in the form of systematic walking. A month later, he began to jog. Within a few weeks he was up to seven or eight miles a day. He revamped his life-style in order to put more emphasis on the things that deeply interested him and gave him genuine pleasure. He stayed close to Dr. Kleeman, who reported he was in excellent shape.

The consulting cardiologists at Cedars-Sinai Medical Center, in Los Angles, who had performed the angiogram on Larry and had diagnosed the arterial lesion were troubled about Dr. Kleeman's decision to cancel the surgery. They felt that Larry was a candidate for sudden cardiac death, and they pursued the matter with Dr. Kleeman. Six months after Larry's reconditioning program began, Dr. Kleeman told his colleagues at Cedars-Sinai that he would be glad to recommend to Larry that he submit himself to another angiogram.

Larry agreed. The test revealed that the lesion had disappeared. There was no longer evidence of arterial blockage. Dr. Kleeman is doing a detailed history for the medical journals. The Cedars-Sinai cardiologists frankly confess their amazement and are at a loss to account for the change. Larry, however, does not share in the general mystification. He worked hard for six months to achieve precisely this result.

Needless to say, Larry's experience was further confirmation that, under certain circumstances, the human heart can make its own bypass. Also, blockage in the coronary arteries need not be regarded as irreversible in every case. Though a single instance, Larry's experience is too significant to be dismissed as anecdotal. It emphasizes the importance of psychological factors in the diagnosis and treatment of heart abnormalities and disease. I don't know whether a different method of communication by the physician during Larry's initial examination would have produced a drastic change in the course of events. The evidence of a silent coronary on his cardiograph was real enough. The cardiologist had the obligation to make known what he had seen. It is fair to ask, however, whether informing a patient about a silent coronary calls for delicate handling. Most patients are unfamiliar with the hierarchy of cardiac diseases; it is necessary to cushion the shock of information that may have a lethal ring to it. Cardiographic evidence of an old silent coronary is not necessarily a catastrophic event, even though it can be made to sound like the end of the world.

What the doctor says, how he says it, can determine life or death, Dr. Thomas P. Hackett told a psychiatric convention in Montreal in 1961.

Words are weapons or building blocks, especially when used by a physician. They can set the stage for auspicious treatment or they can complicate and retard it.

Every patient is, to the physician, a challenge in panic reduction. In heart cases especially, the patient presents two diseases. In addition to the diagnosed disease there is the disease of stark fear, with its disastrous effects of catecholamine flooding and consequent cardiac destabilization and constricted blood vessels. To treat the first disease and not the second is to risk robbing treatment of its intended benefits.

One wonders, indeed, whether the entire philosophy and apparatus of providing emergency care for heart-attack patients need to be reconsidered. So much emphasis has been placed on emergency procedures that we tend to overlook the fact that the large majority of people who have heart attacks are not in need of mouth-to-mouth resuscitation. Very little public education has been directed to the needs of heart-attack victims who are fully conscious. What heart-attack sufferers need most of all, as mentioned earlier, is to be liberated from their panic. They need to be assured that expert help is on the way and that they will be all right. It is quite possible that paramedics themselves have been overly influenced by the kind of muscular heroics attributed to them in TV and movie dramas. In addition to their emergency kits, they might be given instructions in the techniques of persuasion and reassurance.

Inside the hospital, too, the patient's state of mind should be regarded as an integral part of any treatment process. Before sending a patient to an intensive-care unit with its ingenious monitoring systems; it might be a good idea to explain the unit and the reason for it in a way that reduces the strangeness of the experience and therefore the fear.

I recognize that Larry's case and my own constitute too frail a basis for programmatic conclusions. But, as I said earlier, they confirm long-held medical knowledge about the importance of psychological factors in the onset and treatment of serious illness. I refer here, of course, not just to cardiac disease but to disease in general. The writings of René Dubos, Karl Menninger, Walter Cannon, Bernard Lown, Robert S. Eliot, Hans Selye, and Franz Alexander in this area are only a few reference points in a vast and growing literature on the role of the emotions and stress in opening the human body to breakdown and disease.

One of the most comprehensive studies in this field is *Psychoneuroimmunology,* a compendium edited by Robert Ader, of the School of Medicine, University of Rochester. The interrelationship between psychosocial factors and infectious disease is discussed by S. Michael Plaut and Stanford Friedman. They point out that a vast complex of forces and influences is at work and that far more study is required, especially in terms of the beneficial effects of psychological factors on recovery; but they believe that the germ theory of infectious diseases is giving way to knowledge on the downward pull of wear and tear on the total human organism.

Also in this book, Bernard Fox writes that there is good reason to believe that psychological factors "affect the probability of a person getting cancer." George Freeman Solomon writes about emotional and personality factors in bringing on rheumatoid arthritis. Similarly, he says that the course of the disease is "related to the integrity of psychological defenses." Robert A. Good speaks of "the amazing relationship of brain function to the immunity processes." He refers to significant biochemical changes produced in the body as the result of the power of suggestion, as in hypnosis. "Yes," he writes, "I am absolutely convinced that the interaction of mind, endocrines, and immunity is real. Of this there can be no doubt."

CHAPTER VII

Adventure
in Regeneration

The human heart is not sealed off from countless processes that take place within the human body. It is a point of culmination, a collection center for all the malfunctions or deficiencies that exist in the body as a whole. It is a zone of infinite vulnerability to all the anguishes and insults and provocations of mind, soul, and body.

The artistry or inartistry of the physician in communicating with the patient on these matters is hardly less relevant than the specific therapy the physician may invoke. This does not mean that the physician has to lie in order to avoid crippling a patient emotionally. The truth can be told in a way that can lead to challenge instead of collapse. Dr. Shine never trifled with the truth in telling me about my condition, but he was able to communicate with me in a way that did not crush but indeed bolstered my will to live. As for Dr. Cannom, what was most striking about our relationship was that I never left his office with less hope than I had when I arrived.

It may be said, in the light of my personal history, that no physician alive could leave me with a total sense of defeat. This is probably true; still, it meant a great deal to me that Dr. Shine never got angry, never characterized my opinions as frivolous or unworthy, and never threatened to pull out of the case if I did not accept his advice. He made it clear he would be there when I needed him. This to me was vital nourishment. Moreover, I had in Dr. Cannom, Dr. Fareed, and Dr. Hitzig the steady support I required in proceeding step by step on a course of action they believed had the merit of not being irreversible.

It will probably be asked at this point whether the wide array of medical advice at my disposal gave me an advantage not available to most other heart patients. I recognize how fortunate I was in this respect, yet I believe that what was most significant was not the number of doctors involved but the fact that each of them, in his own way, enabled me to keep my hopes high. Dr. Shine held firmly to his position that my coronary arteries were beyond "healing" even though the heart itself showed evidence of strong reconditioning. He therefore never changed his recommendation about the need for an angiogram and bypass surgery. At the same time, he was very careful not to discourage or deflect me from my determination to proceed on my own course, so long as I was in possession of all the facts. Dr. Cannom and Dr. Fareed provided outright support for my belief that it was possible for my heart to create its own bypass through the kind of rigorous rehabilitation program on which I was embarked. The fuel for this effort came from my conviction that it was possible.

I should emphasize here that we have to be careful not to allow ourselves to be crushed by diagnostic technology.

Even the most sophisticated diagnostic procedures can be misleading at times. Valuable and essential though they are in most respects, they cannot be regarded as absolutely sovereign indicators of an underlying condition. The circumstances under which a test is taken can affect the results. Blood-pressure readings are the most obvious example. It is not uncommon for a physician to obtain systolic levels from the same person that will vary as much as 20 points within a few minutes, according to the changing psychological mood of the patient. The results of treadmill tests can be severely skewed by the patient's response to the procedure itself.

Similarly, as I suggested earlier, the ability of the heart to sustain exertion is related not just to the severity of the exertion but to surrounding psychological conditions.

Of all the wonders of the human heart, none seems more remarkable to me than the way it is able, under certain circumstances, to compensate for its deficiencies. There are times, of course, when the damage is so extensive that only surgical intervention or other heroic procedures can save life. It is equally true, however, that there is a tendency to underestimate human regenerative capabilities. Just as the surgical bypass seeks to enlarge the flow of blood to the heart under circumstances of arterial blockage, so the heart has the ability to build a whole new network of small blood vessels to compensate for the clogged or blocked arteries.

Obviously, this regenerative drive comes into play only under special circumstances. A reconditioning program involves key elements—the most important of which are changes in life-style, a rigorous nutritional regime, systematic exercise, and affirmative attitudes and emotions. This program cannot be introduced all at once. In the period immediately following a heart attack, for example, the ability of the heart to sustain a workload is severely limited. But even during that recuperative period, it is important to exercise up to those limits. Total avoidance of exercise can often be as dangerous as too much. One of the most important findings in recent years in the treatment of heart attacks is that complete and prolonged rest can retard recovery. Even damaged hearts need a certain amount of work.

Many times since my original heart attack, on December 22, 1980, I have found myself pondering the question raised earlier in these pages: Why should a heart that is unable to sustain a low level of exercise on a treadmill be able to sustain at least ten times as much exertion on a tennis court? Why would my entire body have a tonic response to many hours of hard exercise that enabled me to breathe deeply and freely and to feel strong and relaxed? Contrariwise, why would I feel depleted and tense after much less exertion under circumstances of emotional strain or even indifference? Why should an interest in what one is doing have such a profound effect on the body's capability?

What are the implications of the fact that a heart can sometimes safely exceed scientifically defined limits when the mind accepts and indeed relishes the experience? How is our understanding of heart disease affected by the fact that the human mind, and not just the condition of the arteries, can play a powerful role in determining the capacity of the body's most vital organ?

I didn't need my personal experience to tell me that these are not transient or incidental questions but are matters having a profound bearing on the way people think about their hearts, and, indeed, on the strategy for dealing with many kinds of heart problems. Isn't it likely, when these implications are better understood, that the prescriptions for treating heart disease will give at least as much weight to qualities of mind as to medicines? Is it possible that irregularities of heart rhythm and even problems of blood pressure should be treated not just chemically but also emotionally and spiritually? Attitudes may be just as important in repairing the heart as they are in combating other assaults on human health.

In retrospect, I am mindful of the serendipitous fact that my heart attack occurred at a time and in a place where I was engaged in research on the role of attitudes in effecting biochemical changes, especially in response to illness. I was able to serve as my own experimental laboratory and could connect my interest in healing to the repair of my own heart.

At this point, perhaps, a question that has been implicit from the first page of this book needs to be answered. How did it happen that someone who had spent all his professional life in journalism, education, and public affairs should find himself on the faculty of a medical school, trying to learn as much as possible about the biochemistry of the emotions? The transition is a story in itself.

CHAPTER VIII

Life Begins at 63

One day in the early spring of 1978, I received a letter from Dr. Sherman Mellinkoff, dean of the School of Medicine at the University of California, Los Angeles (UCLA), inviting me to join the faculty of his school. Several days later, I spoke to Dean Mellinkoff on the telephone.

"Franklin Murphy and Bernard Towers tell me you've been considering an invitation to start a new career at Columbia's College of Physicians and Surgeons," he said. (Franklin D. Murphy, M.D., had been chancellor of UCLA, prior to which he had been president of Kansas State University. After leaving UCLA, he became chairman of the board of the Los Angeles Times Mirror Company. I had known Dr. Murphy in a number of connections, one of which was as trustee of the Kress Foundation, of which he was president. Dr. Towers, an eminent English physician and philosopher, was now a member of the UCLA medical faculty and was directing a series of medical forums in which I had been invited to participate.)

I told Dr. Mellinkoff there was a strong chance I would move in that direction. He asked why I wanted to leave the world of public affairs. What was there about the faculty of a medical school that appealed to me?

I told the dean that I was not giving up my concerns in public affairs. The need to be absorbed in the struggle to find a way out of the nuclear horror was as strong in my mind as ever, and I would continue to work in that direction. But the time had come, I felt, to leave the *Saturday Review*, now that it was in good hands, and to pursue my other interests. Specifically, my interest in physician-patient relationships, as the result of my own experience, as well as my interest in the biochemistry of the emotions, were powerful lures toward accepting a connection with a medical school at this stage in my life.

As for teaching, I thought it might be fun to try to teach literature and philosophy to medical students. As Dr. Bernard Lown points out, young people going into medicine tend to bypass the liberal arts. In their undergraduate education they concentrate on the sciences in an attempt to present impressive credentials to the admissions committees of medical schools. Once having been admitted, they become even more preoccupied with the sciences. They find even less scope for liberal education than in undergraduate school.

The result is that many medical students are superbly trained but poorly educated. One of the frequent observations made in this connection is that, when they become physicians, they know more about disease than about people. Technology dominates the stage.

Dr. Mellinkoff said that some medical schools, UCLA

included, were attempting to stress the importance of the humanities in the medical curriculum.

Again, I wondered whether a course on the physician in world literature might fit in with this new emphasis. The impact of serious illness on people was a recurrent theme in many novels. The physicians in these novels usually had important roles. What was the perception of the physician by the great writers? These attitudes had much to say to young people starting out on a career in medicine. How the great writers saw doctors might be both interesting and instructive.

The dean spoke of the profound impression made on him by writers like Flaubert, Dostoevski, Tolstoy, and Sinclair Lewis. He liked the idea of a course on physicians and writers. Then he asked what it would take to get me to come to UCLA.

It is here that the story becomes apocryphal. According to one version going the rounds in Los Angeles, I am supposed to have said that I had three conditions. The first was a blue parking card. (In the hierarchy of faculty privileges, a blue parking card is akin to a key to all the kingdoms on earth.) The dean is supposed to have been rocked by this condition, but recovered and said he thought it might be arranged. Then he is supposed to have asked, "What are the other two?" And I am supposed to have replied, "I forget."

Actually, what the dean said was that he hoped that, before I decided to stay in the East, I might visit UCLA and get to meet some members of the medical-school faculty. He wanted to introduce me to the various department heads and to acquaint me with some of the exciting research being done in the School of Medicine.

Three weeks later, I turned up in Dean Mellinkoff's office. I took an instant liking to the man. He was soft-spoken and had wide-ranging intellectual interests. He was an expert in the art of creative human relationships. It developed that we shared mutual enthusiasms for a number of medical figures whose contributions to an understanding of human beings was at least as great as their contribution to medical science. We discussed books by physicians we especially liked: Walter Cannon's *The Wisdom of the Body*, Karl Menninger's *The Vital Balance*, Jerome Frank's *Persuasion and Healing*, Hans Selye's *From Dream to Discovery*, and Hans Zinsser's *As I Remember Him.*

It transpired that Dr. Mellinkoff had known or worked alongside some of these men. He had been on the faculty of the Johns Hopkins School of Medicine with Jerome Frank for some years. Zinsser's book was one of his favorites. He had the highest regard for Karl Menninger, whose friendship over the years was a treasure in my own life. We also discovered we had mutual admiration for the late Lawrence Henderson, of Harvard, one of the major philosophers of medicine in the 20th century.

The meeting with Dr. Mellinkoff led to an exchange of ideas with other members of the faculty. I met L. Jolyon ("Jolly") West, M.D., head of the Department of Psychiatry and Biobehavioral Sciences. Actually, I had met Dr. West several years earlier, at a convention of the American Psychiatric Association in San Diego, where I was asked to react as a layman to the major presentations. We had had a good talk at the time. In my written account of the convention, I had singled out Dr. West because his knowledge of psychiatry was only one of the rich intellectual resources he brought to the discussions. He spoke and wrote from a strong background in politics, philosophy, music, literature, and sociology. He had flair, bounce, and profound curiosity about the human situation.

When I talked to Jolly West again in 1978, I learned other

things about him. He was the government consultant in the Jack Ruby case (Ruby was the assassin of Lee Harvey Oswald, the assassin of President Kennedy); in the Patty Hearst kidnapping and bank-robbing case; and in a number of other major episodes over the years. He was also a consulting expert on civil-rights affairs. He lectured on Rachmaninoff and other musical giants. Nothing gave him greater pride, though, than the extraordinary faculty he had assembled in the Department of Psychiatry. The high status enjoyed by the medical school is the direct outgrowth of this fact.

In his physical appearance, Jolly looked like the leader of a Viking expedition. He was about six feet three inches tall and had the facial cast and ruddiness of someone who had spent his life in the outer reaches of Norway. Either that, or a former all-pro tackle on the Minnesota football team. What was even more striking than the appearance of the man was his gentleness as a person.

I also met Dr. Towers, the English physician-philosopher whose concern for human issues had won him a wide reputation and who had proposed to Dean Mellinkoff that I be brought to UCLA. Dr. Towers had appeared on forums with some of England's most prominent scholars, including Sir Peter Medawar. He organized a series of forums on social and ethical issues at UCLA. The programs are videotaped and made available to students throughout the University of California campuses. Dr. Towers was to become a close associate and friend at UCLA.

I met one of the major figures in American psychiatry, Dr. Fritz Redlich, with whom I felt a certain rapport because of our Connecticut backgrounds. Dr. Redlich, after coming from Vienna, taught at Yale University. It turned out that we had many friends in common.

Dr. Mellinkoff, knowing of my interest in the biochemistry of the emotions, said that, if I came to UCLA, I would
be attached to both the Department of Psychiatry and
Biobehavioral Sciences and the Brain Research Institute.
He arranged for me to meet Dr. Carmine Clemente, the
head of the BRI. If I had any doubts about coming to Los
Angeles, I put them aside after talking to Dr. Clemente. It
became immediately clear that the BRI was pioneering in
precisely the areas of my deepest interest—namely, how
the human brain processes the emotions: not just the negative emotions, such as panic or frustration or rage, but
the positive emotions as well. I knew right then that Dr.
Mellinkoff's invitation was like a gift from the gods.

Dr. Clemente had had a wide-ranging career in medicine before being appointed head of the BRI. He had specialized in anatomy and was the author of a leading
textbook on the subject. He had published papers on
research he had undertaken in endocrinology in general and
brain chemistry in particular. I was fascinated by his discussion of the vast number of secretions produced by the
human brain.

I was given an office in Slichter Hall, where the Brain
Research Institute maintains laboratory facilities, alongside
space occupied by the Program in Medicine, Law and
Human Values, headed by Dr. Towers and Dr. William
Winslade, a lawyer and psychoanalyst who had a special
interest in making the intellectual resources of UCLA's
professional schools available to undergraduates. They were
educators in the finest sense, concerned with the interrelationship of the arts and sciences. I accepted their invitation
to be associated with their program.

The process of getting acquainted with a great university can be both exhilarating and exhausting. The UCLA

Center for the Health Sciences is a world unto itself, with a dozen or so units and 73 miles of corridors, supposedly second in length only to those of the Pentagon. Among its units, in addition to the School of Medicine, is the UCLA Hospital and Clinics, to which patients are referred by physicians from all over the world. Among the specialized centers that receive them are the Neuropsychiatric Institute, the Cardiology Clinic, the Oncology Medical Clinic, the Jules Stein Eye Institute, the Pain Management Clinic, the Radiology Clinic, the Marion Davies Children's Clinic, the Reed Neurological Clinic, and the Jonsson Cancer Center.

There are also the research facilities. In addition to the ones attached to the various units mentioned above are the Molecular Biology Institute, the Parvin Institute for Cancer Research, and the Brain Research Institute. Obviously, facilities are important only as they are operated by people who understand that the main purpose of the facilities is to improve the human condition.

Each of these divisions offered endless possibilities for intellectual exploration. I spent many hours with physicians and researchers attached to the specialized centers, trying to learn as much as I could about their functions and goals. The sense of intellectual excitement rose higher with each encounter.

Indeed, just wandering around the campus of the university as a whole gave me an impression of throbbing and creative growth. Fifty years ago, UCLA was a spindly creature on the west side of Los Angeles. Today, it is one of the world's great universities, with distinction in many fields, most notably in the quality of its graduate schools. It is also one of the most attractive campuses I have seen anywhere, with botanical gardens and congenial areas for sitting or strolling. The Franklin D. Murphy Sculpture Gardens, named after the former UCLA chancellor, has one of the finest outdoor collections in the country.

The period of the university's greatest growth came under Dr. Murphy, a physician–educator who was determined to strike a vital balance between the arts and the sciences. By the time Dr. Murphy left, in 1968, most of the major units of the university were in place. The challenge confronting his successor, Dr. Charles E. Young, was to consolidate, refine, and achieve even greater excellence in public education.

Was it difficult to adjust to California after so many years in the East? My friends in New York and Connecticut scratched their heads in provincial dismay, finding it inconceivable that anyone would voluntarily forsake the vast array of cultural wealth so readily available on the East Coast for the "California wasteland." In California, I was to find people who were equally baffled by the willingness of New Yorkers to put up with congestion, noise, and punitive extremes of cold and heat when, on the same continent, they could find such a congenial habitat for both mind and body.

What both groups fail to perceive is that New York and Los Angeles are extensions of each other. One finds the same level and range of conversation, the same intellectual fare. Only cities that are so much alike could show so much distaste for each other. Beyond the tilting and the teasing is the fact that both cities are great metropolitan and indeed world centers. It is unfortunate that the surface disadvantages of both places are allowed to obscure their genuinely attractive offerings.

The first course I taught at the medical school was "The Physician in Literature," a subject enabling me to build a natural bridge between running a magazine that began as a review of literature and my new career in a medical school. Dean Mellinkoff had decided to open my course to non-registrants. The course was held in one of the large lecture halls. The audience consisted of medical students, undergraduates, faculty members, and townspeople, in almost equal numbers.

I don't know how the audience felt, but I found the experience profoundly rewarding. My role was a relatively minor one. The students themselves led the discussion, talking about their reactions to the way doctors were perceived by writers and other doctors. Their minds were attracted, for example, to Hans Selye's exploration of the nature of serendipity. The essence of serendipity is the unexpected, but conditions can foster or favor serendipitous events. The students responded enthusiastically, too, to the ideas of writers like Somerset Maugham, Anton Chekhov, and Arthur Conan Doyle, themselves physicians.

Out of this exchange came my book *The Physician in Literature*. Working on this book was a marvelous learning experience for me. It strengthened my conviction about the extent to which people could elevate themselves to higher plateaus of response and achievement when confronted by serious problems, whether illness or other challenges.

The rationale for the course was clear enough. Almost every novelist or dramatist of any consequence—from Aeschylus to Walker Percy—has had something to say about doctors. The writer deals with the universals of human experience and with the struggle not just to stay alive but to get the most out of life.

To the writer, the physician is not just a prescriber of medicaments but a symbol of all that is transferable from one human being to another short of immortality. We may not be able to live forever, but we persist in the notion that the physician possesses the science and the artistry that will provide us with endless deferrals. He seems to be in command of those fastnesses where the secrets of life are stored. To be able to listen to the human heart and draw meaning from its slightest vibrations or whispers, to be able to take a tiny droplet of blood and perceive its vital balances, to convert electric markings into precise knowledge of the body's chemical complexities—all these may represent science to the doctor, but to the patient they are powers that come from the gods.

Human beings are never really able to shatter their loneliness, but physicians are at least capable of providing them with limited rescues and interim triumphs. Prolongation of life is an attainable prize and a sustaining reality.

Literature helps the medical student to analogize the patient, to make connections between the experiences of the race and the condition of the individual, and to fit the individual into a world that is less congenial than it ought to be for people who are more fragile than they ought to be. What the world's great literature tells us about medicine is that few things are more important than the psychological management of the patient. Hippocrates and Galen and the other early greats of medicine may not have known about endorphins, encephalins, gamma globulin, epinephrine, interferon, and the entire range of neurotransmitters. But they knew a great deal about the totality of the human organism and the interaction of all its parts. Galen made the observation that, not infrequently, breast malignancies occurred in women who were suffering from melancholia. A person's outlook on life, especially one's attitude toward illness, can be a vital factor in the onset and course of a disease. The wise physician, when making a prognosis, does not confine himself or herself to the virulence of the particular micro-organism involved or the nature of an abnormal growth; the wise physician makes a careful estimate of the patient's will to live and the ability to put to work all the resources of spirit that can be translated into beneficial biochemical changes.

Recent medical research has developed information about a wide array of secretions produced by the brain—secretions that have a role in maintaining health and overcoming illness. Richard Bergland, of the Harvard University School of Medicine, has resurrected the French view from a century or more ago that the human brain is not just the seat of consciousness but a gland; indeed, the most prolific gland in the human body. Dr. Bergland has presented mind-boggling evidence that the brain can combine these secretions in an almost infinite number of combinations as part of its ability in "writing prescriptions" to meet the body's varied needs.

Dr. Bergland's research finds verification in the work of UCLA's Brain Research Institute. Dr. Carmine Clemente has estimated that the number of combined secretions in the brain is almost beyond calculation. Not all these secretions are locked into the autonomic nervous system. A substantial number of them are activated by thought processes and by the emotions. It is not necessary, for example, to run a race in order to stimulate the production of epinephrine. Merely the contemplation of a challenge or a danger can cause the mind to trigger the production of chemical changes.

This concept of the human brain as a gland provided an exciting setting for my interest in the biochemistry of the emotions—especially the emotions that play a large part in human uniqueness. UCLA was a major center for such studies.

CHAPTER IX

The Physician
as Communicator

In joining the faculty of a
medical school, I thought I
would have to brace myself for all the shocks that go with
a new career, but I quickly discovered that the physician,
like the writer, is dependent on communications skills. In
journalism, you live or die by your ability to use words.
In health care, the words used by the physician have a profound effect on the well-being of the patient.

Words, when used by the doctor, can be gate-openers
or gate-slammers. They can open the way to recovery, or
they can make a patient dependent, tremulous, fearful,
resistant. The right words can potentiate a patient, mobilize the will to live, and provide a cogenial environment
for heroic response. The wrong words can produce despair
and defeat or hinder the usefulness of whatever treatment
is prescribed. The wrong words can complicate the healing environment, which is no less central in the care of
patients than the factual knowledge that goes into the physician's treatment.

Being able to diagnose correctly is a good test of medical competence. Being able to tell the patient what he or she has to know is a good test of medical artistry. I recognize the problems involved for the physician in proper communication. There is not only the problem of language itself—how to use words that will not confuse or mislead. There are also the professional problems: the obligation of the physician to inform the patient; the difficulties caused by the fact that patients vary in their ability to deal with the truth; the ease with which poor communication with the patient can spill over into tangled relationships and even malpractice suits.

Let me linger over some of these problems.

First of all, proper communication is one of the most difficult undertakings on earth. The older I get, the more I am forced to recognize that many breakdowns and tragedies have their origin in faulty communications. Whether we are talking about the predicaments of human beings or the confrontations of nations, the inability of people to convey intentions and meaning has been one of the prime causes of confusion and violence over the centuries. In the medical world, you need go no further than the administration of hospital affairs to see how many errors, some of them serious, proceed from faulty communications. Consider the wrong medications in the intravenous bottle or the wrong pills or the wrong quantities, or the hospital attendant who mistakenly interprets instructions. Not infrequently, that attendant can point to ambiguous communications. The orders just weren't clear enough.

In my own contacts with patients, I have been made aware of the frequency with which they seem frightened, confused, or immobilized as the result of their medical encounters. I allow for the possibility that their reactions may be the effect of their own failures in understanding, but I am struck nevertheless with the fact that the relationship between patient and physician is often impaired because of careless communication.

Now we come to an entirely different problem. Even when the physician's message *is* clearly delivered and clearly understood, its effect may run counter to the well-being of the patient. Not all patients are equally adept in their ability to handle the truth. With some of them, there may even be physician-induced hazards resulting from being confronted at point-blank range with the fact of extreme illness.

It may be said that the physician has no choice but to convey the facts flat out, that the danger of malpractice suits is such that the physician is forced to tell the patient the worst in unmistakable terms. At least, if the worst should happen, the physician cannot be accused of having failed to prepare the patient—a failure for which he could be held legally accountable.

The essential question, perhaps, is whether the hard facts and nothing but the hard facts are always necessary or useful. If the reason for them is the doctor's fear of legal reprisals, then we have to ask ourselves whether a conflict of interests exists between the patient's need for treatment and the physician's need for legal protection. Consider the case of the San Francisco patient who had a biopsy of a lump in her breast and who telephoned the oncologist three days later asking about the result. She was told that such serious matters were never discussed over the telephone but that she would be informed in due course. She was. She was informed by *certified letter*. The letter was completely unambiguous. It said in the tersest language that she had a malignancy. There was certainly no failure here in communication. But there was certainly little regard for the effect that communication in this form would produce. With a registered receipt in his possession, the physician could protect himself against any possible accusation later that he had failed to make an accurate diagnosis. The woman was not so much told as notified, not so much instructed as sentenced.

Is it reasonable to ask whether some references to the worst help to bring on the worst? To what extent does the unembellished recital of a negative prognosis have the effect of a hex? Physicians are obligated to use all the science at their command—chemotherapy, radiation, surgery—in an attempt to reverse or slow down a malignancy. For the same reason, the wise physician will employ all his artistry to potentiate and motivate the patient. The mood and attitude of the patient are potent factors in effecting treatment. For that reason alone, the physician will try to avoid a situation in which a patient leaves his office in a mood of sheer terror and defeat.

As with heart-attack cases, the treatment of cancer calls for attention to the disease of panic, recognized or unrecognized, conscious or subconscious. If we treat one disease and not the other, we may be treating only half the patient. Panic intensifies underlying health problems. As stated earlier, panic can constrict the blood vessels, disrupt normal heart rhythms, and even cause myocardial infarction. Many people with heart attacks never reach the hospital alive because of their panic and its effect on the heart.

Medical professors have given their students a clear picture of how panic and stress can throw the entire endocrine system into disarray. It is no accident that, not infrequently, disease becomes suddenly intensified, concurrent with the diagnosis being made. The way a patient receives a diagnosis can have a profound effect on the course of the disease.

This does not mean that truth must be deferred or denied. It is a matter of attaching as much importance to the manner and style of communication as to any other aspect of medical care.

We are accustomed to thinking of iatrogenic problems in terms of the wrong medication, of mistaken surgery, or of harm done in diagnostic procedure. But there are also psychological iatrogenic situations: what happens after a patient is sent into an emotional tailspin with physiological consequences as the result of the exchange with a physician.

Everything we have said so far points to this question: Is it possible to communicate negative information in such a way that it is received by the patient as a challenge rather than as a death sentence?

I believe it is. I believe that most physicians, out of their direct knowledge of how patients are affected by diagnoses of serious illness, have developed techniques for communicating without crippling.

First of all, they set a stage conducive to treatment and recovery. They do not minimize the seriousness of the patient's condition. What they do, instead, is put their emphasis on the strategy of combat. They propose a partnership. They describe what modern medical science has to offer, and then describe what the patient has to offer. They talk about the patient's own resources. They make it clear that there are no guarantees of success; but, whenever it is appropriate to do so, they document actual cases where people have overcome similar ordeals. When they mention statistics, they put the accent not on the negative figures but on the positive ones. For a patient to be told that two out of every five persons with a certain illness do not last out the year is not as motivating as to be told that three out of five patients *do* survive their ordeal. The basic purpose here is *not to destroy the hope* that provides an essential environment for healing.

Some physicians I know have a list of cancer survivors at hand and make it standard procedure to involve these survivors in the psychological therapy of anyone who is about to undergo treatment.

During the past four years, I have had the opportunity to talk to hundreds of patients suffering from serious illness. I doubt that it is just a coincidence that so many of the patients who seem to be getting the most out of their treatment are the ones who say they have been inspired by their physicians.

There are qualities beyond pure medical competence that patients need and look for in their doctors. They want reassurance. They want to be looked after and not just looked over. They want to be listened to. They want to feel that it makes a difference to the physician, a very big difference, whether they live or die. They want to feel that they are in the doctor's thoughts. In short, patients are a vast collection of emotional needs. Yes, psychological counselors are very helpful in this connection—and so are the family and clergy. But the patient turns most of all and first of all to the physician. It is the physician who has most to offer in terms of those emotional needs. It is the person of the doctor and the presence of the doctor—just as much as, and frequently more than, what the doctor does—that create an environment for healing. The physician represents restoration. The physician holds the lifeline. The physician's words and not just his prescriptions are attached to that lifeline.

This aspect of medicine has not changed in thousands of years. Not all the king's horses and all the king's men—not all the tomography and thallium scanners and 2-D echograms and medicinal mood modifiers—can pre-empt the physician's primary role as the keeper of the keys to the body's own healing system.

I pray that medical students will never allow their knowledge to get in the way of their relationship with their patients. I pray that all the technological marvels at their command will not prevent them from practicing medicine out of a little black bag if they have to. I pray that when they go into a patient's room they will recognize that the main distance is not from the door to the bed but from the patient's eyes to their own, and that the shortest distance between those two points is a horizontal straight line—the kind of straight line that means most when the physician bends low to the patient's loneliness, fear, pain, and the overwhelming sense of mortality that comes flooding up out of the unknown, and when the physician's hand on the patient's shoulder or arm is a shelter against darkness.

Even as medical students attach the highest value to their science, they should never forget that it works best when combined with their art, and that their art is what is most enduring in their profession. Ultimately, it is the physician's respect for the human soul that determines the worth of his science.

CHAPTER X

Souls and Statistics

How do writers and physicians mix? Does their way of looking at life turn them in different directions?

Physicians and writers both deal with disease, the physician with the ills of the individual, the writer with the ills of society. The physician's function is to identify and classify the malaises that prevent people from functioning properly. The writer deals with collective disorders, especially those that involve injustice, that keep people from developing and using their full potential, and that turn human beings against one another and impair their self-respect. The writer has always wanted to change the world because it has always needed changing. Evolution means change; progress requires change; civilization is the product of change.

The collective unconscious as perceived by Jung has its parallel, perhaps, in collective desires, collective fears, collective anguish, and collective breakdown. All these characteristics of society leave their mark on human beings, sometimes in the form of disease. The pressures and the strains of the surrounding world are key factors in the balance of forces known as health.

The writer and the physician are both involved in the arena of health; both are caught up in the multiplicity of causes and effects that influence the direction of society. And both have substantial power. The physician exercises power directly over people because illness is a melancholy interruption of life, and the physician sometimes has the power to banish the interruption—or is believed to have that power, which comes to the same thing.

The writer has the power to create people. The fact that the people are fictitious does not rob them of reality. For readers are no less affected by the characters they read about in novels than by people in the everyday world. They see themselves in the human beings they read about. The novelist presides over life, fashioning the circumstances of triumph or defeat, elation or despair. And the novelist confers a species of immortality on readers by enabling them to connect other lives to their own. The process is carried on in the imagination but does not disturb the connection.

The fact that physicians and writers have power over life does not mean that they see things the same way. It became apparent to me in the medical school that there were important differences in the way doctors and writers look at the world. Doctors reason from the general to the particular. Their notions of what illness is, and how patients are to be treated, are drawn from a large accumulation of cases. Behind this approach is the belief that it is necessary to know what ought to be expected, from repeated encounters with like sets of circumstances. Similarly, their belief holds that it is irresponsible to treat people except on the basis of verifiable results, meticulously scrutinized. Individual experiences, especially in cases of recovery or cure, are suspect. The adjective used to describe these experiences is "anecdotal." Few words in the medical vocabulary carry more connotations of scorn and even contempt than the term "anecdotal."

Not to the writer. The writer makes his living by anecdotes. He searches them out and craves them as the raw materials of his profession. No hunter stalking his prey is more alert to the presence of his quarry than a writer looking for small incidents that cast a strong light on human behavior. If nothing is valid to the physician except as it proceeds from masses of data, very little has meaning to the writer except as it is tied to the reality of a single person, and except as that reality can illustrate a larger lesson or principle.

A single case may be suspect to the medical scientist. To the writer, the universe itself begins with a single case, a single emotion, a single encounter—in short, a single person.

Statistics are essential to the physician for plotting a course or for comprehending an outcome. Writers, however, shun statistics. Statistics obscure souls, and the writer can never allow himself to wander very far from the internal and ultimate mysteries. Many scientists find the word "soul" imprecise and conjectural. It is this very mystery that excites the writer, who deals with the reality of doubt and wondering, what T. S. Eliot called "the world of shuffling hopes and desires."

It is this inner world, for the most part unreachable by statistics and remote from ready labels, that is the domain of the writer. His workshop is the inner person. For the writer, the wild dream is the first step to reality. Civilization to the writer begins in the imagination.

Physicians and writers also tend to reflect their training in the way they evaluate the materials of education. In the medical curriculum, for example, medical students tend to attach more importance to courses that lend themselves to quantification or to practical instruction than to courses that have to do with values or ways of thinking about things.

The writer moves in an opposite direction. The writer is apt to feel cramped by things that are readily quantifiable. I mustn't carry this too far, of course, for the right numbers on a royalty statement are among life's greatest satisfactions to the writer. On a less subjective basis, however, a writer finds not safety but weakness in numbers.

Tolstoy once said that the most profound question he could think of was "What is Art?"—a question to which he addressed himself with much soul-searching and to which he offered no absolute answers. The UCLA Program in Medicine, Law and Human Values, with which I am affiliated, helps to give students an enlarged respect for those questions for which there may be no absolutely correct answers but which nonetheless have to be confronted almost daily and which affect the patient-physician relationship as profoundly as any diagnosis the most exotic technology can provide.

The words "hard" and "soft" are generally used by medical students to describe the contrasting nature of such courses. Courses like biochemistry, physics, pharmacology, anatomy, and pathology are anointed with the benediction of "hard," whereas subjects like medical ethics, philosophy, history, and patient-physician relationships tend to labor under the far less auspicious label "soft."

The reason it is important to rescue medical education from casual notions of "hard" and "soft" is that a decade or two after graduation there tends to be an inversion. That which was supposed to be hard turns out to be soft, and vice versa. The knowledge base of medicine is constantly changing, and no physician's knowledge is more vulnerable or fragile than that which remains intact. But the soft subjects—especially those that have to do with the intangibles—turn out in the end to be of enduring value. Being able to win the confidence of the patient; being able to mobilize and release all those forces in a human being that work for regeneration and repair; being able to evaluate the patient against the background of all the multiple factors that figure somewhere in breakdowns that lead to disease—all these supposedly soft matters are actually the hard foundations of a profession that may not be the oldest in the world but one that will continue so long as human beings have to cope with their mortality.

Lives can be profoundly affected or even lost because of the way information is conveyed. Admittedly, patients vary in their ability to live with the truth, and sometimes the truth can complicate and impair treatment. Truth, misplaced or poorly conveyed, can crush two vital ingredients in treatment—hope and the will to live. Since everyone in this post-Watergate world wants to avoid the stigma attached to lying, I feel compelled to say that the issue here is not *whether* to tell the truth but *how* to tell the truth. Dr. Oliver Wendell Holmes summed it up when he told his medical students that successful medical practice requires not lying but an ability by the physician to "round the sharp corners of truth." Truth can be told in a way that can potentiate a patient or devastate him. It can lead to challenge or set the stage for shattering defeat.

Sir William Osler, who, like Dr. Holmes, was both a physician and a writer, knew that in most situations the physician's greatest strength is his artistry, for medicine is the interaction of tangibles with intangibles, with things that don't lend themselves easily to measurements. Medical science, Osler believed, works best not when it is positioned against faith but when physicians recognize that their science does not have all the answers. Faith, to Osler, was a manifestation of the intangible that reduces the odds in the patient's favor.

In looking back over my experiences in the medical school, I have come to the conclusion that C. P. Snow's two cultures may not be so unbridgeable after all. In the end, the writer and the physician deal with the uniqueness of human beings and with the need to protect the human condition. Moreover, the physician and the writer need one another: the writer because he can profit from the discipline of testing his facts and slowing down the rush to judgment, and the physician because language is connected to the therapeutic power of attitudes and belief.

Writers believe that what makes human beings unique is their ability to do something for the first time. And physicians know that what makes the science of medicine so compelling is that more remains to be known than is now known, for the process of healing is not yet fully understood. What gives medicine its greatest excitement and energy is that it is still a frontier profession. And, if we are lucky, it will remain that way.

Oliver Wendell Holmes once proposed some perennial questions for doctors:

> How does your knowledge stand today? What must you expect to forget? What remains for you to learn?

Winds of change now blow throughout American medicine, and one of the most promising zephyrs is the growing recognition that a good medical education involves
more than science. The questions Dr. Holmes posed are
essentially philosophical, for they cannot be answered
without reference to the history of man's intellectual and
scientific development, without relating one's learning and
occupation to the needs of society, without retrospective
and prospective compass points. In short, they cannot be
adequately answered without some exposure to the cluster
of intellectual disciplines that come under the heading of
the humanities, by which is meant not just the general range
of human experience but also the creative arts and the way
people come to terms with life.

Science puts its emphasis on research and verifiable fact.
Art and philosophy put the emphasis on creativity and values—values that have something to do with the importance of being human. Among the oldest discoveries in the
practice of medicine is the fact that human beings come
equipped with resources for healing that are best mobilized
not by detached scientific efficiency but by communication and supportive human outreach.

Basic to medical education—or any branch of education,
for that matter—is one unchanging reality: facts do not
stand still. A great deal of what medical students are now
learning in their formal scientific education will become
outdated within a decade or two after their graduation. It
is obviously and remorselessly true that the factual base of
medicine has steadily changed in response to new findings
about the nature and treatment of disease.

The system for teaching scientific knowledge, however,
is hardly less important than what is taught. The *way* new
facts are discovered and developed; the *way* they are scru-

tinized and put to the test; in short, the *way* theory is translated into practice—this is what endures and what gives science its essential character. Respect for the scientific method is a vital ingredient in any medical education.

The separate paths that the sciences and humanities have taken in search of truth are now converging in the wake of new findings. Human survival may depend upon man's ability to work within nature rather than in opposition to it, as well as upon the ability of human beings to control the proliferation of knowledge that threatens to overwhelm us. The convergence is bringing about a new unity that cuts across disciplines. We are seeing a new breed of scientific humanists and humanistic scientists. The separation of the two intellectual worlds is yielding to the recognition that they are both dependent on the conditions of creativity and on the need to accept responsibility for their work.

The division between the two cultures described by C. P. Snow is giving way to a division between those who attach primary importance to human life and those who view their own discipline as sovereign.

The explosive proliferation of scientific knowledge in the past few decades has left members of the human species feeling unsettled, uncertain, even out of control. Young people have good reason to question the adequacy of an education that has separated them from the questions that bear on their own future, the future of mankind, and the quality of life—which, incidentally, has a bearing on health.

Common to the sciences and the humanities is the human urge to understand the universe and man's connection to it. The failures that have pockmarked history have come at times of philosophical poverty. Man may enlarge his objective techniques and even his knowledge, but he cannot change the basic fact that his position in contemplating the great questions is inherently subjective.

The science and art of medicine converge at the point where physicians become basically concerned—as poets traditionally have been—with the whole of the human condition. "I feel convinced," wrote Claude Bernard, "that there will come a day when physiologists, poets, and philosophers will all speak the same language."

CHAPTER XI

We Can Do

New commitments at UCLA developed so rapidly and in such profusion that I had little time to think about my old life in publishing and public affairs. Of all the new involvements, however, two were especially engrossing and gratifying. One was the project named We Can Do. The other was the work with the Veterans Administration hospitals.

Let me begin with We Can Do. One morning in February 1980, a tall, attractive, fair-haired lady named Barbara Coleman came to see me in my office in UCLA's Slichter Hall.

"I was at your lecture two nights ago," she said. "You were talking about the fact that people who are seriously ill also have strong emotional needs. You did say that, didn't you?"

I nodded.

"You are right about that," she said. "I am a cancer survivor. Malignant brain tumor. I've been through surgery twice. It came back after the first surgery. The second time they said they got it all. It's ten years since that second surgery. You said you were lucky in overcoming your illness. I'm lucky, too. What are we going to do about it?"

"Do about what?"

"The emotional needs of people who've just been told they have cancer. You said that if these needs are not met, treatment can be made more difficult, much more difficult."

I told Barbara Coleman that, since coming to the UCLA School of Medicine, I had seen a large number of cancer survivors, almost all of them at the request of their physicians. In fact, eight or nine were doctors themselves who had cancer and recognized that their problems transcended medical and surgical treatment. Very little in their training had taught them how to help patients think about cancer. Now that they had cancer themselves, they were groping for intellectual and spiritual underpinnings. They knew how they were supposed to be treated medically; they didn't know how they were supposed to handle it emotionally. During the long nights when they were alone with their thoughts, they were confronted with more questions than answers. They were not exempt from the inner turmoil that afflicted their seriously ill patients.

"What we are going to do about it?" she repeated.

I looked at Mrs. Coleman carefully. She sat tall in her chair. Her eyes were clear; her voice was strong; nothing about her appearance suggested invalidism. I asked, even before we discussed what might be done, whether she would tell me her story.

She said that in 1968 she first began to develop symptoms. Two of her fingers failed to respond to her directions. On Christmas Eve, she dropped her cigarette into her drink. In the next few days, she began to experience numbness in her left arm. Then her left foot began to turn inward. One night, during her sleep, her left knee involuntarily jolted her chin.

"It was a time of terror and panic," she said. "My doctor put me through all the tests—electroencephalogram, brain scan, myelogram, angiogram. They found a dark spot in the right motor area of my brain. There could be no doubt about it, they said; it was a brain tumor. Technically, it was called a glioblastoma multiform astrocytoma, the kind of brain tumor that carries a poor prognosis.

"Naturally, I went into surgery. My husband was told the chances of success were not very high. I was in surgery for nine and a half hours. The tumor they removed was the size of a lemon. Tentacles from the tumor spiraled across my brain.

"Then they gave me cobalt—31 treatments. That cobalt is strong stuff. The first time I took it, the radiologist laid it on the line for me. He said, 'You will go in a room with concrete walls and you will be bald for the rest of your life.'

"I went into that concrete room. I was alone. Everything is operated by remote control. They transmit orders to you through an intercom. It was depersonalization at its zenith. I could understand it, of course; the cobalt is so powerful that the doctors and the nurses don't want to be anywhere near it. And when that big tube with its cobalt ray came down at me I realized that everything was for real.

"After 10 months, they wanted me to go into surgery again. The tumor had grown back. I was puzzled because I had none of the symptoms I experienced the first time. It was terribly demoralizing. I went back to the hospital. The night before the surgery, fire broke out in my room. Faulty TV wiring. I didn't want to scream because of the panic it might cause, so I walked to the nurse's station. The moment I told the nurse about the fire she started screaming, so we had the panic on the floor anyway.

"After the fire was put out, an intern came to my room. He was terribly clumsy, and he dropped his black bag. All the medicines and instruments clattered on the floor. That was the breaking point. I ordered him out. The next morning they wheeled me into surgery. This time, I was in there 10 hours. When I came to, I asked for the results. One doctor told me there was still the possibility of recurrence; another said he thought I would be all right. Finally, I got the definitive report. 'It's okay,' they told me, 'it's now all clear.'

"It's now 10 years since that report. On February 9, I celebrated the anniversary of my freedom. Yes, I've gone back regularly for other scans. No recurrence.

"I've learned a lot during this experience. And I think I can help cancer patients. I think I know what to say to them that can keep them from becoming emotionally devastated when they are given the diagnosis of cancer. They've got to keep their hopes alive. If they don't, they're going to slide very fast. Will you help me?"

Of course, I wanted to help. What did she want me to do?

Mrs. Coleman said she wanted to start an organization that would make it possible for cancer survivors to meet regularly with people who had recently received a cancer diagnosis. She would also operate a telephone hot line for people and their relatives who didn't know what to do or where to turn.

That was the beginning of We Can Do. Barbara Coleman asked me to be chairman. She said she would attend to all the organizing and promised that my duties would not cut into my work at UCLA.

Barbara kept her word. She turned out to be an organizing genius. She knew how to work both inside and outside the medical world. She recruited oncologists and clinical psychologists who would participate in the undertaking. She sought and obtained the advice of the American Cancer Society. She enlisted the cooperation of the hospitals in arranging for patients to be part of the program. Money raising was very difficult, but she held down the costs by converting her home into an office.

Within a few months, Barbara had chapters started throughout the far-flung Los Angeles area, meeting in hospitals, churches, and other volunteered meeting rooms. Each group would have its own team of medical personnel and lay leaders trained by Barbara.

Today, there are nine chapters, including one in Washington, D.C. I should have known that Barbara would find a way of going national.

In my role as chairman of the board, I've participated in most of the organizing and public meetings. It has been profoundly stirring to me to see the way the quality of life of the cancer sufferers has improved as the result of We Can Do. Obviously, not every patient is able, like Barbara, to experience remission or recovery, but life has been prolonged in many cases by two or three years. And almost all of the members have undergone a transformation of attitudes. They now have a place where they can discuss their needs without awkwardness. Their fears are no longer bottled up inside; they know how to get the most out of whatever is possible. And their physicians report that treatment is enhanced as the result of the group experience.

Each We Can Do session begins with each member of the group reporting on his or her own life since the last meeting. We Can Do meetings are where one can bring things into the open. It helps to be able to identify oneself with a group that has a collective personality and a life of its own, to which each member can make a positive contribution.

Psychologists attending the meetings are a valuable resource for the many problems that occur with family and friends. (Relatives of members are urged to join in the sessions and to raise questions of their own.) But most of the talk is among the members themselves. Being genuinely helpful to other persons is a vital form of therapy in itself. And it means a great deal to cancer survivors or sufferers to be able to draw upon their own experience in helping others. In this way, the terror of things not known but feared loses much of its sting.

Some of these persons have become very close to me. When their medical checkups produce good reports, we hold celebrations. And when some of them start to go downhill and the tests point the wrong way, feelings of desolation are inescapable. At such times Barbara is magnificent. She helps the patients feel a sense of achievement in having done far better than some of the physicians thought possible. In the process, they create a quality of life for themselves and their families that does them great credit. "It's all right to die," she says. "Letting go is a form of art in itself."

The experience with We Can Do was helpful to me in my work at the Veterans Administration hospitals. The UCLA School of Medicine is affiliated with the local VA hospitals. This gave me valuable access to Veterans Administration patients. So did my appointment to the national Special Medical Advisory Group of the Veterans Administration. In this way, I became acquainted with Alex Andres, a retired gentleman who belongs to the amazing army of volunteers involved in public service in this country.

Alex takes a special interest in cancer patients at the Sepulveda, California, VA hospital. He has helped to set up a program to educate patients and hospital personnel about health problems connected to cigarette tobacco. He telephoned me at UCLA to say he had heard about my interest in positive emotions as a factor in enhancing medical treatment. He said he was authorized by the physicians and the cancer patients themselves to invite me to visit the cancer section. In particular, he hoped I might develop a laughter program at the VA to brighten the mood of the patients. I readily accepted the invitation.

A couple of weeks later, Alex escorted me to a special room in the cancer section of the Sepulveda VA hospital. We went into a room used for reading and social functions. The room had been specially rearranged for this meeting, with about six or seven rows of chairs to accommodate the 40 or 50 patients. Alex introduced me, describing my experience with laughter as reported in *Anatomy of an Illness*. I was amused but became somewhat uncomfortable when he said I had come to "make them laugh." Fortunately, their applause indicated that they were not averse to the idea.

First I spoke about studies showing that attitudes played an important part in efforts to combat illness. I referred to the work of the Brain Research Institute at UCLA and to Dr. Richard Bergland's work at Harvard University on the glandular activity of the brain. I identified some of the principal secretions of the brain that helped the human body cope with pain, and noted how confidence and robust spirits helped people get the most out of whatever the brain and body had to offer in creating an environment congenial to treatment.

I emphasized that laughter was only one of the positive emotions, along with hope, faith, love, will to live, creativity, playfulness. All were important. Then I referred to the articles written by Dr. William F. Fry, Jr., of the Stanford University School of Medicine, in which he detailed the physiological benefits of laughter, including improved respiration.

"Even if laughter produces no specific biochemical changes," I said, "it accomplishes one very essential purpose. It tends to block deep feelings of apprehension and even panic that all too frequently accompany serious illness. It helps free the body of the constricting effects of the negative emotions that in turn may impair the healing system."

I then asked whether they would like to take part in a little laughter experiment for which I had obtained the approval of their doctors. The patients enthusiastically supported the idea. I asked for a volunteer, someone who enjoyed hearty laughter and who, in fact, could laugh on cue. A tall, sandy-haired man named Bill, in the front row, stepped forward. I then told some of my favorite stories. The response of the patients was reinforced by Bill's thunderous guffaws, a rich source of laughter in itself.

Then I played a cassette laughter track I had brought with me. The effect on the patients was that of being on a toboggan that had reached the steepest part of the hill and continued to accelerate. They were on a runaway laughter course and couldn't stop. Some of them couldn't stay in their chairs. The contagion of all the laughter was such that I was rolling along with the rest.

After about 10 minutes the laughter subsided. The doctors and nurses who had taken part in the laughfest were sitting back and smiling. Alex Andres was wiping away the tears and couldn't help from breaking out in laughter all over again.

I asked how they felt. Some said their pain had receded—confirmation, perhaps, of the speculations of some medical researchers that hearty laughter could activate the endorphins with their morphine-like effects.

The suggestion I put before the group was that the members develop a program for creating an upbeat atmosphere among themselves. Members could take turns in accepting responsibility for staging one-act plays. Or they might obtain cassettes of stand-up comics. Videotapes of the funniest motion pictures of all time were obtainable. I also referred to the practice of the We Can Do groups in starting every meeting with each person reporting what good things had happened to them since the last meeting.

When I returned to the Sepulveda VA hospital some weeks later, I was fascinated and heartened by the way the patients had arranged their own programs. This time, they were not seated in rows but in a large circle, the doctors and nurses among them. The effect was sharply different from what it had been on my previous visit. The mere fact that the patients were linked to one another gave them a sense of connection and unity that was a happy departure from previous meetings.

The most significant feature of the new format was the report by each person concerning auspicious personal happenings. It was apparent that the dependence of the entire group on having something good happen to each of its members was so great that no person wanted to turn up empty-handed. They all contrived between meetings to make sure that they had some experience worth sharing with the others.

"Let me read a letter to you from my nephew who has just been admitted to medical school," one of the patients said. "My nephew wanted me to know that when he completes his medical education, he's going into cancer research. 'I'm going to come up with answers,' he said. 'Just hang in there.' "

Cheers all around.

Another patient reported he had heard from a friend he hadn't seen in 20 years and how much it meant to them both to be reunited.

Applause.

Then came a report from a patient who said he had been having difficulties with his physician and that he had decided to talk it out frankly. The result was even more successful than he had dared hope.

More applause.

Now it was the turn of one of the doctors.

"I've been up for an income-tax audit. It took several days and it troubled me. Yesterday, I got a letter from Internal Revenue. The letter said the audit had been completed and that the government owed me money. A check was enclosed."

Cheers and applause both.

Suddenly it was my turn. I hadn't realized that I was expected to talk about something good that had happened to me. Fortunately, I was not without material.

"Something happened to me last Thursday that was indescribably wonderful," I said. "Never again, as long as

I live, do I expect it to happen again. It was unforgettable. What happened was that when I arrived at the Los Angeles airport from Chicago, my suitcase was the first one off the baggage carousel."

An ovation.

"That was not all," I said. "I went to the telephone to call the office and promptly lost a dime when an operator came on and asked for a quarter. It was a recording. I put in another dime, got a live operator, told her what happened, and she said the phone company would be glad to send me the dime if I would give her my name and address. It seemed absurd that the phone company would spend 20 cents in stamps, to say nothing of personnel expense, just to refund a dime—and I said so. I also pressed the coin-return lever.

"At that point, all the innards of the machine opened up and quarters and dimes tumbled out in magnificent and overflowing profusion.

" 'Operator,' I asked, 'are you still there?'

" 'Yes.'

" 'Operator, something quite remarkable has just happened. All I did was press the coin-return lever and the machine is giving me all its earnings. There must be more than three dollars in coins here and the flow hasn't stopped.'

" 'Sir,' she said, 'will you please put the money back in the box?'

" 'Operator,' I said, 'if you will give me your name and address I'll be glad to mail it to you.' "

Cheers, applause, standing ovation.

The patients at the Sepulveda VA hospital have kept up their meetings. The staff physicians are impressed with the change in the general mood and the average improvement in the condition of their patients. I have the pleasure, every few months, of returning. As I put down these notes, we are arranging with Bill Dana, the comedian and co-author with Laurence J. Peter of *The Laughter Prescription,* to come with me to the next meeting.

Alex Andres has asked me how I react to the fact that the description I gave in *Anatomy of an Illness* of the beneficial effects of laughter has had such a favorable response. At least half a dozen medical conferences on the therapeutic effects of laughter have been held. Editorials and newspaper columns have referred to the laughter connection. Medical journals have discussed it. Half a dozen hospitals have introduced laughter programs.

I told Alex that I was of course heartened by all these developments but that I was afraid the laughter matter had been overplayed. I didn't want people to think that getting over a serious illness was no more complicated than having a good laugh. I had used laughter to illustrate the importance of all the positive emotions, as I had pointed out on my visit to the VA hospital. Laughter was perhaps the most vigorous of the positive emotions, and it was the one that most readily captured popular attention. But it was a mistake to talk about its role in combating illness to the exclusion of all the other key factors, most notably the physician-patient relationship. Certainly the last thing in the world I wanted to do was to give people the idea that they could hah-hah their way out of all their problems.

CHAPTER XII

Consumerism
Reaches Medicine

Working at a school of medicine has brought me into close touch with hundreds of patients. I was able to travel to many parts of the United States, meeting with different sectors of the public that have personal, professional, and community interests in addressing themselves to the health problems of the American people.

It is apparent to me that the most important thing that has been happening in health care today is that medicine has been caught up in the burgeoning movement of consumerism. It is not necessary for me to detail here the causes, composition, or manifestations of the general revolution in consumerism. It makes little difference whether its high priests go by the names of Ralph Nader or John Gardner or Sylvia Porter or any other. What matters is that people no longer take products and services for granted. They accept and assert a new responsibility for looking into the value of things and have developed yardsticks for appraising not only products but also performance.

The most widespread expression of consumerism in the field of medicine marches under the banner of holistic advocacy. The term is imprecise. It is difficult, in fact, to obtain or apply a definition that will sit still long enough to satisfy lexicographers who are updating their dictionaries. Serious advocates of holistic approaches in medicine are not being well served by those who make it appear that those approaches should include astrology, palmistry, numerology, graphology, and various other exotic or marginal forms of appraisal and therapy.

Another failure of some holistic advocates is that they tend to position holistic medicine against traditional medicine. Hippocrates, 2,400 years ago, emphasized to his students that the good physician takes everything into account in diagnosing and treating an illness. The dictum most frequently associated with Hippocrates is "First of all, do no harm." But Hippocrates also taught students to give full weight to the fact that "the human body is the physician of its own illnesses." No advocate of holistic medicine has ever said it better. Wise medical teachers over the centuries have underlined this Hippocratic advice.

Holistic medicine is an expression of, not a substitute for, the best in traditional medical practice. It is true, however, that the trend toward specialization in medicine, combined with the advent of a ubiquitous technology, has increased the distance between the dispenser and the user of medical help. Many patients have a sense of growing impersonalization and fragmentation resulting from multiple exposures—different faces, different machines, different atmospheres. They go to their doctors' offices seeking refuge from their fears and loneliness and do not adjust easily to new encounters, either with those who preside over separate domains in medical science or with highly sophisticated marvels of diagnostic technology.

The emergence of a new consumerism in medicine is turning against the system of elaborate referrals and the promiscuous use of medical technology. It is felt that the massive costs of medical care—costs that are burdensome whether paid by individuals, government, or insurance companies—can be significantly reduced by better matching, that is, by better matching of genuine needs to suitable medical personnel and technological aids. The emphasis, of course, is on the word "genuine."

Consumers in medicine are now aware of things that happen in a doctor's office that only a few years ago would have had little significance. It says something to a patient today, for example, if a doctor smokes, especially during the interview with the patient. Similarly, if the physician is noticeably overweight, his advice about the need to keep low-density lipoproteins and cholesterol within reasonable limits may seem more theoretical than it should.

It may be said that the personal habits of the physician are none of the consumer's business, and I suppose they wouldn't be if the physician were not in the role of an advice-giver. And I suppose that consumers should be able to manifest at least as much compassion toward their physicians, some of whom are genuinely in need of it, as they expect for themselves. Certainly, if there is any justice in this world, consumers should be able to understand the pressures on the physician—pressures that begin in pre-med education, accelerate during medical school, expand during internship and residency, and multiply during practice. These pressures, unremitting, brutal, and often inhuman, sometimes predispose physicians toward personal indulgences and harmful life-styles. Unfortunately, these mitigating circumstances don't bulk very large in the minds of patients, who come to physicians to get relief from their own health problems.

Another aspect of the consumer revolution is that people no longer feel deprived or undertreated if they leave the physician's office without a prescription. At one time, the prescription was a standard part of the treatment ritual; doctors understood the tendency of patients to associate full value with a piece of paper containing mysterious markings. Today, however, many consumers are not unaware of the limitations and, indeed, the hazards of medications. There is a tendency, of course, to go to the other extreme, but at least the modern physician need not feel that patients regard it as an article of faith that they cannot recover without pills. Nor does the physician need to feel that the lack of a prescription slip will cause the patient to go running off in search of another doctor.

In the minds of at least some physicians, the most specific expression of the new spirit of consumerism is to be found in the proliferation of malpractice suits. Obviously, physicians do not wish to expose themselves and their families to random attack in the courts. And so, they are forced, in effect, to pay inordinate amounts for protection, with no real assurance that even these defensive measures can fully anticipate the entire range of punitive approaches available to patients.

In considering the general problems of malpractice suits, however, physicians may find it helpful to consider studies showing that the chances of being sued increase in direct proportion to the physician's distance from the patient. That is, the physician who has the closest relationship to the patient is least likely to be sued. Family physicians are very rarely faced by patients in legal actions. Surgeons who have little or no direct contact with the patient are at high risk.

The conclusion seems clear: doctors who spend more time with their patients may have to spend less money on malpractice protection. My own interviews with patients strongly support these conclusions. When I talk to patients whose personal physicians may have made mistakes in diagnoses, or patients who have otherwise been subject to physician error, I am struck by the fact that very few of them would dream of taking the family doctor to court. They generally say that they would find it inappropriate and embarrassing to subject a friend to punitive action.

It is difficult for me to believe that the patient should be kept at a distance, no matter what the circumstance. Any medical encounter is an extremely private matter for the patient. If that person is left with a depersonalized feeling as the result of the encounter, the exchange has failed in a vital respect, because the treatment of illness, especially serious illness, requires a favorable environment, in which the will to live and recover is the central element. If that will is demolished or even impaired, the entire course of treatment may be complicated and impaired.

A good relationship with the physician contributes to the quality of life of the patient even as it contributes to the security of the physician. A good example is to be found in the reaction of the patients to supposedly irreversible situations. Consider the use of Laetrile. Researchers at the University of Arizona made a study of patients who deviated from the recommendations of the physicians and took Laetrile for their malignancies, whether by going to Mexico or by other means. The researchers were primarily interested in finding out whether there were any common characteristics among such patients. Did they belong to any particular sector of the community? Did they tend to come from any one ethnic background? What about their level of education? What about their occupations or professions? What about income?

What the University of Arizona researchers discovered was that none of these factors was a common denominator. The people who were reaching out for the magic cure came from all backgrounds, were widely diversified in their occupations, belonged to no income group, were both poorly educated and well educated. What, then, did they have in common? They had in common, the researchers discovered, an unsatisfactory relationship with their primary physicians. They felt that their total needs were not being met. That fact in some way reduced the influence of the physician and figured in the decision to pursue an alternative.

Dr. Fred Robbins, former dean of the School of Medicine at Case Western Reserve University, was asked by a medical student what he should say to a patient who was determined to use Laetrile.

"Whatever you do, don't burn your bridges," the dean replied. "Say you understand why she wants to reach out for anything that has the remotest chance of success. But also say, as gently as you can, that you have seen no evidence that Laetrile has specific anticancer capabilities. If the patient, despite everything you say, is determined to go to Mexico anyway, don't make her feel stupid or guilty. Say that you want her to continue to regard you as her physician and that your door is always open to her, whatever happens. Wish her all the luck in the world. And if, as is likely, her experiment should backfire, be sure she knows she can come back to you without shame or penalty. Tell her your concern for her will always be there."

Another aspect of consumer concern calls for positive understanding. I refer to the entire question of nutrition. It is quite possible, in fact, that developing public attitudes in regard to nutrition may represent the main thrust of consumerism today in the medical field. How to explain it? One answer, perhaps, is that the general level of education in this country has risen impressively in the past half century. This forward thrust has embraced the entire field of health. If the marijuana cigarette and the "trip" were the symbols of the 60's, the jogging track and the health-food rack have become the symbols of the 80's. And an interest in nutrition is one of the specific and emphatic aspects of that new surge. At least seven major American foundations are now embarked on extensive programs to increase the public's knowledge of nutrition. One such program, for example, is designed to provide children of "Sesame Street" age with some awareness of the food connection, and uses the most advanced television techniques to lead children away from over-sugared foods and beverages. Another program, at Stanford University, is designed especially for medical students—not just for the purpose of helping them as physicians but for the purpose of enhancing their own well-being. Medical researchers at the University of Minnesota have pointed to the strong probability that eating habits have a strong bearing on the incidence of cancer. The American people may be the best fed in the world, but they may be among the most poorly nourished.

I have no way of knowing whether the conclusion of the White House Conference on Nutrition some years ago figures to any extent in the current growth of consumer interest in nutrition. The report of that conference called attention to the fact that many students of medicine do not have the same expertise in nutrition as they do in other matters related to health. To be sure, that report is more than a decade old. Many medical schools have incorporated high-level courses on nutrition since the report was issued. But the public perception is that many physicians tend to be not as well informed about the importance of good nutrition in maintaining health as they are about clinical medicine in treating disease.

The new consumerism need not be regarded as a threat to medicine or as anything alien. It can be an important source of the physician's support and growth, for what it is actually doing is seeking the best in the physician, even as the physician seeks to bring out the best in a patient.

CHAPTER XIII

The Basic Nature of Emotional Needs

The term "denial," when used clinically, is applied to patients who, consciously or unconsciously, try to relieve their anxiety by pretending that the serious situation described to them by their physicians is either exaggerated or non-existent. I write here about three cases in which the term was used. The basic facts in each case, however, indicate that the term may have been misapplied. It should be pointed out that the patients, while understandably anxious and apprehensive, were not considered to be neurotic or psychotic. My knowledge of the cases was based on interviews with the patients and their physicians.

Patient #1 was a 43-year-old woman who was an ambulance driver and paramedic. A mammogram and a biopsy specimen of a small lump in her breast led to the recommendation of a radical mastectomy. The patient declined to accept surgery. The physician, disturbed by her apparent denial of her condition, suggested she see a psychiatrist. Again the patient rejected the advice.

Patient #2 was a 32-year-old woman who was an administrative assistant in a large corporation. The patient's symptoms led to comprehensive tests and the diagnosis of cervical cancer. Despite this diagnosis, she remained in excellent spirits, interpreted by her physician as a denial of her underlying condition. He spoke to her sternly, saying he did not think she fully understood the severity of her illness. He also impressed on the family his concern over what he regarded as a neurotic failure to accept reality. The patient accepted the prescribed therapy, but the physician was convinced, because of her cheerfulness, that she never really believed him.

Patient #3 was a 45-year-old man who was a dispatcher for a radio cab company. An annual company medical checkup indicated evidence of a slight coronary. The patient had no recollection of chest pains. His blood pressure was 158 over 90. A treadmill test result was equivocal. Antihypertensive medication was prescribed, along with diuretics and a salt-free diet. The patient was asked to return for an angiogram. He failed to keep the appointment. It was also ascertained that he was not taking the prescribed medication.

In each of these three cases, the term "denial" was used to describe the patient's behavior. Closer scrutiny, however, showed that the term was inappropriate and misleading to varying degrees.

Patient #1: It turned out that the patient, after the recommendation of surgery, sought a second opinion but did so without informing her primary physician. She was reluctant, she later said, to hurt his feelings. Nor did she inform the consultant about the previous diagnosis and recommendation. He kept the patient under close observation for three weeks, during which time there was some shrinkage in the size of the tumor. A lumpectomy was performed. One year later, there was neither recurrence nor further symptoms.

It is obvious that what appeared to be a clear-cut case of denial was actually a reflection of the patient's desire to exercise due diligence. She was at fault for failing to inform her primary physician that she was seeking a second opinion, whatever her concern about his sensitivity. Since the second physician had no way of knowing he was providing a second opinion, he cannot be faulted for not consulting with the primary physician. This case illustrates the fact that "denial" can sometimes be a subjective determination by the physician. The second physician had no reason to believe his patient was anything but cooperative and responsible.

Patient #2: The patient did not deny to herself or anyone else the fact of a malignant neoplasm. What she denied was the inevitable outcome generally associated with the diagnosis. Her basic personality was upbeat; she would not allow herself to be steered into a mood of futility and resignation. She did not resist the chemotherapy and radiation prescribed by her physician, but she believed that such treatment would have a better chance if augmented by a continuing life-style of confidence and high spirits. She joined We Can Do and was able to share experiences with those who had just received the diagnosis of a malignant neoplasm.

Patient #3: Strictly speaking, this case comes closer to noncompliance than to conventional denial. Even when viewing it as noncompliance, however, one must take into account the fact that the patient was not refusing any treatment. He was seeking a broader informational base on which to act. Proceeding on his own initiative, he developed a program emphasizing diet, exercise, and a compatible life-style. He rigorously reduced salt, fats, and sugars and increased his intake of fresh vegetables. He took up a daily program of walking; within a month he was up to a mile a day; within two months, four to five miles a day. He quit his job as a dispatcher, with its intense pressure, and found work instead as a supervisor for telephone-book sales solicitations. He learned about the biofeedback exercises used at the Menninger Foundation, in Topeka, Kansas, for the reduction of high blood pressure and was able to bring his down to 140 over 82. At the end of six months, an examination showed that his cholesterol level had dropped from 315 to 175, with substantial reduction of triglycerides and low-density lipoproteins. He was given another treadmill test; there was no ST-segment depression or drop in blood pressure. Putting this case in the category of denial or noncompliance would appear to be a mistake.

These three cases have several things in common. First, they illustrate the hazards of imprecise categorization. What appeared to be a denial of serious medical problems—or even noncompliance with the prescribed treatment—was more like an effort to explore other options. To the extent that a positive or hopeful attitude was behind these efforts, treatment may actually have been enhanced by them.

It is not necessary here to review the abundant literature on the therapeutic value of affirmative attitudes by patients. The editorials and special articles in the *Journal of the American Medical Association* and in the *New England Journal of Medicine* over the years and in various books and articles serve as reminders that patients tend to move in the direction of their expectations. What may appear to be unreasonably optimistic behavior under circumstances that would seem to dictate acquiescence and surrender can actually work to augment the effectiveness of the physician's ministrations. Indeed, few things a physician can do in combating a serious illness can be more salubrious than providing full support for a patient's determination to give his "best shot" to the challenge confronting him. This is not a matter of superimposing; there is something in the human spirit, as William James reminded us, that makes us want to fight back. Hope is seldom out of season.

It is difficult to define and even more difficult to mandate patient behavior that will be considered "acceptable" or "normal." As E. M. Cooperman pointed out, it should not be surprising that a catastrophic diagnosis will often produce irrational patient responses. Many physicians themselves, when ill, exhibit the same emotional tendencies.

A second quality that the three cases discussed may have in common involves possibly faulty communication between physician and patient. One wonders whether the young woman who did not inform her physician that she had obtained a second opinion would have been so secretive if the relationship between patient and primary physician had been better developed. The wise physician takes pains to encourage a patient to seek other opinions. This is done not in a spirit of legalistic self-protection but as a reflection of professionalism and concern for the patient. Certainly, the ability of a physician to provide support for a patient's emotional needs is not irrelevant in any consideration of the patient's response to the fact of critical illness. W. W. Weddington, Jr., considering the implications of four physically ill patients who "used denial, rationalization, and displacement to avoid recognizing the physical nature of their disorders," concludes that "it is best not to discard patients' use of defense mechanisms as unconscious or malicious behavior."

Large numbers of patients hesitate far less than they did only a few years ago to participate in vital decision-making concerning their own health and to move toward greater control over their own situations. Increasingly, in private and public discussion, one encounters a new desire on the part of many people to seek as much information as possible about medical matters, especially if they themselves happen to be directly involved. Along with this trend toward increased patient responsibility are other contributing factors: the prominent coverage of medical news and health matters in the news media; the eruption in recent years of malpractice suits and the appeal they have for laymen as conversation pieces; and the mounting costs of medical care.

All these factors are reflected in the enlarged expectations patients carry with them into the medical encounter. They attach hardly less importance to the exchange of ideas with the physician than to their exposure to the new technology. Such a mood need not be regarded as inimical or extraneous. Treatment tends to be more efficacious not just when the patient feels free in talking about the things that are troubling him but when the physician feels comfortable in listening to matters that are not strictly "medical" in nature.

At this point, someone is certain to invoke Sir William Osler's *Aequanimitas* as authority for the view that physicians should not allow themselves to become emotionally involved with their patients. Yet Sir William was not advocating cold or remote relationships with patients. What concerned him was the shattering effect, especially on young physicians, of defeat. He knew that, in the war against illness, defeat all too often is inevitable. The best medical skills in the world are not always able to stem nature's powerful downward pulls. However, Sir William also recognized that a good relationship between patient and physician is something of a victory in itself. That victory is made possible because the physician attaches as much importance to the patient's psychobiological needs as he does to the patient's physiological needs.

In a sense, the physician who treats a terminally ill patient is himself practicing a form of denial. He battles malignancy against heavy odds, employing his special knowledge and a wide array of methods and techniques. Just as the patient clings to life with whatever tenacity his instincts and millions of years of evolution have made possible, so the physician believes that his own obligation is to put all his science and art fully to work in that cause. It is natural that both physician and patient should refuse to go down without a fight, and defeat is deferred or deflected often enough to give a quality of realism to the encounter.

The wise physician will not rub the patient's nose in the fact of incurable illness. He will encourage feelings of hopefulness and confidence for the same reason that he himself prescribes chemotherapy, radiation, or surgery— or a combination of all three. In the act of applying all the resources at his command, he is challenging the odds. For the same reason, he does everything possible to encourage the patient to mobilize a strong will to live and all the positive forces that go with it. The more robust the patient's attitude, the greater the likelihood that the physician's own program will have a better chance. Denial can sometimes be channeled into a higher level of cooperation.

CHAPTER XIV

Changing Fashions
in Disease

The report of the U.S. Surgeon General for 1980 begins with the auspicious statement that the American people have never been healthier. As prime evidence, the report cites the fact that life expectancy for both sexes is now in the mid-70's. Four diseases that at the turn of the century were major killers—diphtheria, tuberculosis, gastroenteritis, and poliomyelitis—have been brought under control. In 1980, the combined death toll in the United States from those four diseases was 10,000. If the death rate in 1900 had persisted, the death toll in 1978 would have been 875,000. Even some forms of cancer are now on the decrease—cancer of the stomach, for example. The rising curve in the incidence of heart disease has flattened out.

This improvement in the nation's health is attributable to many factors, not least among them the continuing development of advanced medical technology. Within little more than two decades, new techniques have been devised both to diagnose otherwise elusive cases and to treat cases of extraordinary complexity. The usefulness of transistors in detecting subtle changes in internal chemistry, or to regulate heartbeat; the efficiency of laser beams in intricate surgery without the hazards of blood loss; the help furnished by computers in dealing with shock; the remarkable contributions made by science and technology to organ transplants; the prodigious forward leap represented by computerized tomography; the availability not just of radioactive tracers but of sound and echoes to provide basic information; cardiopulmonary bypass machines; high-voltage radiation; kidney-dialysis devices; blood-gas analyses—all these are only a few examples of the rapidly enlarging role of machines and chemistry in the war against disease.

But inevitable questions arise. What effect does advanced medical technology have on the physician-patient relationship? Indeed, how do the new techniques affect the practice of medicine? And how does the public at large react to its own new role, one created for it by the rapid progress made by medical technology?

Perhaps the most tangible impact of the new developments is the emergence of a new breed of physicians who are uncomfortable with the notion that medicine can be practiced out of a little black bag. Indeed, the reluctance to make house calls may be a reflection more of the dependence on headquartered high technology than of time limitations alone. No one can doubt the vast extension of the physician's competence represented by scientific instrumentation. The doubt rather is whether science has cut into the physician's art—a vital ingredient in the treatment of humans. The practice of medicine, as it has been emphasized over the centuries by almost every great medical teacher—from Hippocrates to Holmes, from Galen to Cannon, from Castiglione to Osler—calls first of all for a deeply human response by the physician to the cry of the patient for help. In the overwhelming majority of cases, as Franz Ingelfinger, the late and much-loved editor of the *New England Journal of Medicine* pointed out, what patients need most of all is assurance that their own healing systems are beautifully designed to handle most of their complaints. The physician who understands the importance of sitting at a bedside, even though his presence may actually be in the nature of a placebo, is tending to a prevalent and therefore quintessential need.

If the critical-care specialist, writes James J. Strain in *Critical Care Medicine,* for January–February 1978, "is to provide adequate medical and psychological care for his patient, he must understand the nature of the psychological stresses the patient is experiencing, and be able to enhance the patient's ability to adapt to his situation."

"Technological knowledge," wrote Malcolm C. Todd in *Medical Instrumentation,* May–June 1977, "must be supplemented by a broad unaerstanding of man's nature, lest limited points of view generate an oversimplified formula of action." It should be no surprise, therefore, that resistance by many patients to medical technology is becoming increasingly widespread. This resistance is not unnatural and ought not be regarded by the reasonable physician as a challenge to his authority. Such a situation offers the physician an opportunity for adroit and compassionate negotiations.

It is likely that the chances of a patient's opposing or resenting medical technology are in direct proportion to the physician's distance from the scene. People feel secure in the presence of their doctors. It is only when the patients are dispatched to other places and are deprived of direct contact with or access to their own physician that they tend to become uneasy. And the more removed they are from the main source of their security, the more apprehensive they become.

The wise physician, therefore, makes a careful estimate of the mind-set and emotional needs of the patient. He creates a mood of confidence for the encounter with modern technology. He explains that he will not attach sovereign importance to the results. He doesn't abandon the patient to a device if he can possibly help it. The wise physician understands, too, that the results of the test do not necessarily forecast the response of the patient under normal conditions. My own experience, as related earlier in this book, may indicate that a patient's biochemistry may respond differently to challenge according to emotional and physical circumstances.

The more exotic and sophisticated the technology, the greater the likelihood that patients will feel diminished or apprehensive. The physician who cannot afford the time to stay close to the patient during this experience had better find effective equivalents, for the ultimate impact of those tests can be harmful psychologically and therefore physiologically. Patients cannot be blamed for retreating from encounters they find distasteful or upsetting. The argument that the procedures are necessary for the patient's own good misses the point, for the source of the patient's disquiet may not be the procedure itself so much as the climate or the context in which it occurs. The absence of human warmth during those experiences can figure larger in the reactions of patients than the vaunted value of the tests.

In recent years, patients have become far more knowledgeable than they used to be about diagnostic procedures. The steady rise in the educational level of the general population is reflected in a higher level of awareness about the hazards of medical technology. The press coverage of material appearing in medical journals is certainly a factor in the reluctance of many people to accept uncritically a wide number of technological diagnostic procedures. By this time, for example, people are generally aware that the use of X-ray examinations in the past was far too promiscuous. The testimony of medical experts themselves on this matter has registered in the public mind. People compare the reassuring statements made by physicians about X-ray examinations only a decade or two ago with what is now known about the hazards of radiology. They have become aware that the effects of such exposures are cumulative; and they tend to lose confidence in physicians who routinely recommend such tests without first ascertaining the extent of previous exposures.

The value of the new technology is not absolute. It has to be measured alongside its inherent dangers. For example, the barium that is not completely eliminated from the X-ray GI series can lead to intestinal obstruction. Mammograms can carry the risk of provoking the very irregularity of cell growth they seek to detect.

The routine use of such medical technology in regular checkups calls for serious reconsideration. It is manifestly true that the equipment can often pick up indications long before they announce themselves in symptoms. But it is equally true that the hazards associated with such tests can create health problems of their own.

The serious question arising from the comprehensive use of medical technology in regular checkups is whether we have gone too far in persuading people to see their physicians at yearly intervals. It would be interesting to compare the number of persons who have become seriously ill in the absence of such regular examinations with the number of those who have been disadvantaged by the widespread use of medical technology as a standard feature of the annual checkups.

There is also the matter of expense. Someone has to pay for the lavish and almost routinized use of exotic technology. The fact that the bills can be passed on in many cases to health-insurance plans does not make the practice more acceptable. Now that consumerism has reached medicine, it is to be expected that this general area will come in for increasing scrutiny.

Obviously, it would not be in the patient's own interest to forgo whatever aids technology has to offer in those cases in which such use may be absolutely necessary. Here, once again, the physician has the opportunity to make such distinctions and to explain them to patients.

Finally we come to the concentrated triumph of modern medical technology. I refer, of course, to the intensive-care unit. This is where we find the grand assembly of medical invention. Technically, it does everything expected of it. It monitors the patient and picks up even the most obscure hint of biological failure. Yet the crisis atmosphere it produces contributes very little to the patient's peace of mind at a critical time. Every blip and click reminds the patient that he or she is in a precarious condition. If panic is to be avoided at all costs, the ICU can hardly be considered a bargain. It is as omnipresent as it is efficient, as forbidding as it is ingenious. Patients who are brought to the ICU are in critical condition, and they are not permitted to forget it for a single instant. Arnold Relman, in the *New England Journal of Medicine,* has written the most com-

pelling article I have seen anywhere on the limitations and
penalties of the scientific marvels of the ICU.

J. C. Holland, S. Sgroi, S. Marwit, and others reported
in *Psychiatry in Medicine* in 1973 that 12.5 percent of the
patients in ICU's were observed to have delirium symptoms. While it is true that delirium in varying degrees is
common in patients with serious illness, the specific danger of delirium in an ICU setting is that, if the experience
is prolonged, cerebral metabolism can be affected. A related
study, by P. J. Tomlin, makes the point that some ICU
patients exhibit the symptoms of "shell shock" victims in
warfare. "To the patients, their relatives, and to their
uninitiated clinicians, however, these psychological breakdowns appear devastating."

Does this mean that the ICU should be scuttled? Certainly not. What it means is that the patient should not be
sent into this particular battleground unaccompanied and
unbriefed. The presence of the primary physician at the
time of arrival, his hand on the patient's shoulder, is the
proper introduction to this experience. This reassuring
physical and psychological precaution provides the essential backdrop for the patient's understanding of the electronic wizardry that surrounds him. The very fact that the
patient's own doctor is present imparts an emotional cushioning.

In general, what applies to the ICU applies to all the
other encounters with medical technology discussed in this
chapter. The physician who remains close to the patient
during the exercise stress test or the other diagnostic procedures deprives that technology of its intimidating qualities, for it is not the technology itself but the
impersonalization that frequently accompanies it that is the
basis of much public resistance and apprehension.

The role of the nurse, whether with respect to the intensive-care unit or any other aspect of medical treatment, is basic and indispensable. In my own experience, I can testify that the technical knowledge of my nurses dissolved much of the forbidding and arcane nature of the technology I encountered. Nurses are generally associated in the public mind with the need for compassionate attention. Important though this function is, it is certainly not less essential than the information a nurse is frequently able to give a patient pertaining to complicated procedures and the mysterious indicators in diagnostic technology.

Medical technology has clearly justified its existence on any balance sheet of performance and problems. But the problems it presents are not minor. They affect the health and well-being of the patient. What is most significant about these problems is that they need not be unmanageable.

CHAPTER XV

Increasing the Sense of Control

Sometime early in 1979 I received a telephone call from Robert Kaufman, a Unitarian minister in Pasadena.

"You really ought to meet Harry Brink," he said. "He's able to control pain and bleeding to a phenomenal degree. I know that UCLA has been doing a great deal in pain research. Brink may have something to offer."

I asked what Brink proposed to do.

"He will subject himself to pain that doctors believe is far beyond tolerable limits," Bob Kaufman replied. "He'd like to put on a demonstration."

I told Dr. Kaufman that I did not regard myself as an authority on pain; but I would be glad to get a group of UCLA physicians and pain researchers together to witness the demonstration.

Two weeks later, Dr. Kaufman escorted Harry Brink to UCLA's Pain Control Center. Brink was about 55, tall, well-built, white-haired, ruddy-faced, and looked like a

Hollywood casting director's idea of an old-time locomotive engineer. He said he would exhibit his ability to control pain and bleeding by resting on a bed of nails. He wanted to prove that this accomplishment was not confined to yogis.

As an observer, I was not entirely new to the spectacle. Some years earlier, I had visited India's leading training center for yogis. The institute was located in Aligarh, not far from New Delhi. In witnessing the various feats at Aligarh, I became aware that not all the performances were genuine examples of the ability of human beings to preside over their autonomic nervous systems. Some of the demonstrations seemed to me to be more in the nature of manufactured illusions or vaudeville tricks. Some were a combination of the two. In the latter category, one of the yogis had demonstrated his ability to "stop" his heartbeat. I held my finger on his pulse while he drew a deep breath and caused the beating in his pulse to cease. His face lost normal color and, indeed, turned slightly blue.

I asked an American physician who was in our group whether he happened to have his stethoscope with him. He did. I asked whether the demonstration could be repeated. This time, I put the stethoscope to the yogi's heart. The yogi drew a deep breath and indicated he had "stopped" his heart. The heart sounds became fainter and the heartbeat slowed to perhaps 30 a minute—but the heart did not stop. The pulse in the wrist became imperceptible to the touch, but the heart sounds were audible through the stethoscope. The stated claim of the demonstration was incorrect.

This does not mean that the actual demonstration was not extraordinary and indeed phenomenal. To be able to slow cardiac activity to the extent exhibited was a remarkable illustration of the mind's ability to affect functions that are supposed to be beyond conscious intervention. It was only because the claim was excessive that its impact was sharply reduced.

I had also witnessed a demonstration of a yogi's ability to lie down on a bed of nails without apparent pain. After the demonstration, I went forward and examined the nail board. Two things were instantly evident. One was that the nails were so heavily forested that the pressure of weight at any single point was minimal. The other was that the nails were blunt, a fact I easily established by pressing the palm of my hand on the points.

Nevertheless, the act of reclining even on blunted nails could hardly be regarded as a soothing experience. What detracted from the cogency of the demonstration was the fact that it did not meet the claims that had been made for it.

When, therefore, the white-haired gentleman who had come to UCLA to display his abilities as a sort of American yogi began his act, I thought of the exhibitions I had seen in India. I asked whether I might see the "bed" of nails. Harry produced his board from out of a dirty burlap bag. The board was about two feet by three feet. It contained about 40 to 50 nails, irregularly spaced and extending perhaps an inch and three-quarters above the board. I pressed the palm of my hand against the nails and winced; they were sharp enough to cut.

Another difference between the demonstration we were about to see and the one I had seen in Aligarh was that the announced purpose of this demonstration was not to lie on top of the nails but actually to have the nails penetrate the flesh. Harry also wanted to display his ability to control bleeding.

Just as Harry was about to lie down on the nails, I had a terrifying vision. I could visualize a front-page article in the *Los Angeles Times* under some such headline as:

UCLA MEDICOS STAND AROUND
WHILE MAN COMMITS SUICIDE

And I could imagine the story going on to say that several members of the medical faculty were gulled into believing that a man could lie down on nails without having them penetrate his vital organs. The story would no doubt emphasize that the doctors permitted a 55-year-old citizen to go through with his plan to end his own life in a way that made fools of physicians.

I placed a restraining hand on Harry's shoulder as he started to kneel. I told him it was not necessary for him to go through the actual demonstration. We all knew he could do it. Why didn't he just tell us how he did it?

"But *you* don't know that I can do it," he said to me sharply. He asked for complete silence, then proceeded to lie down on the board. We could hear the sickening pop of the flesh as the nails penetrated the skin. I bent down and could see very little daylight between Harry's back and the board.

Harry lay on the nails for perhaps three or four minutes without apparent pain or discomfort. His eyes were closed and he was breathing deeply and rhythmically. Then he rolled off the board. When he sat up we could see that his back was heavily peppered with red puncture sites. No bleeding—except for one spot on the shoulder where the blood was spurting. We called this fact to Harry's attention. He thanked us and shut it off.

The world of medicine is a world of cause and effect in which clear predictions can be made as the result of accumulated experience involving many thousands of cases. Physicians don't need William Shakespeare to inform them that, if human beings are pricked, they bleed. Yet here was a human being who was stuck in 50 places or more and was not bleeding except in one place. What was even more startling was that he arrested the flow once he learned of its existence.

What about the pain itself? How did Harry make himself impervious to the penetration of sensitive tissue and even organs? Even more pertinent, perhaps, what about the possibility of infection? The nails had not been sterilized. They had been in contact with a soiled burlap bag. They also carried whatever bacteriological organisms we had on our own hands when we tested the sharpness of the nails.

What Harry had done, as the yogis in India had done, was to enable the mind to exert control over the body's autonomic nervous system. This is the system that governs the various functions that occur for the most part without our conscious knowledge or control. The reproduction and circulation of the blood cells; the manufacture of hormones and their flow; the conversion of chemical energy into electrical energy and the delivery system along which this power moves to different parts of the body, including the heart; the breakdown by the body's chemicals of different foods into nutrients that supply the body with basic energy and the materials of maintenance and growth; the storage of information by billions of brain cells; the interaction of enzymes throughout the body—this is only a partial list of the functions that are performed by the human body without our awareness.

Each of these functions is something of a miracle in itself. The fact that they are carried out without our knowledge is a prime example of nature's wisdom, for if we did have a complete and constant sense of all the interacting wonders that make our lives possible we would probably spend all our time in jubilant celebration and have no time for anything else.

The very absence of an awareness of the life processes, however, gives rise to the notion that we are totally deprived of any control over them. Yet some measure of control is well within our capacity. Very early in life, a child's toilet training is an exercise in transferring basic bodily functions from the autonomic to the voluntary nervous system. The feats performed by yogis in India and by Harry Brink are made possible by systematic training. Harry Brink was not able to control pain and bleeding the moment he decided he would like to demonstrate this ability. He had to develop it by connecting his deep purpose to systematic training.

What was basic in Harry's feat was that he began with the conviction that it was possible. He began with the knowledge that extraordinary acts of seemingly superhuman control were being demonstrated by other human beings—in this case, the yogis—and he was convinced that what others could do he could do. His first such experience came in a dentist's chair when he was told he would be given anesthesia for gum surgery. He didn't want the nausea and discomfort that usually accompanied anesthesia, and he informed the dentist that he was capable of controlling the pain himself. The dentist acquiesced. Through concentration and the conviction that it was possible, Harry made it through the gum surgery. What was even more significant was that he was also able to moderate the bleeding. After that experience, Harry decided to extend his control over himself.

One of the best places in the United States for observing systematic training in exercising control over the autonomic nervous system is at the Biofeedback and Psychophysiology Center, founded by Elmer and Alyce Green at the Menninger Foundation, in Topeka, Kansas. As a trustee of the Menninger Foundation, I received reports from time to time about the work of the Greens. Also, I met Elmer Green in New York and was delighted to have his invitation to visit the laboratory in Topeka.

The occasion for the visit was furnished by a meeting of the Menninger trustees. I came a day early and received a thorough introduction to the operations of the Biofeedback Center. The first demonstration concerned the use of biofeedback in relieving migraine. Migraine is much more than a severe headache; it can be accompanied by nausea, vomiting, and even seizures. Over the centuries, countless treatments have been tried and discarded. Drugs that work for some patients do not work for others. Estimates of the number of migraine sufferers go into the millions.

One of the nation's leading experts on migraine, Dr. H. G. Wolff, has written that migraine generally starts with constriction of arteries inside the brain, followed by extreme dilation of arteries in the scalp. This dilation of blood vessels in the scalp causes the pain, even though it seems to come from deep inside the head. Dr. Green enlarges this view with the finding that emotional and psychological stress has an adverse physiological spillover effect on the body's various organs, the brain not excluded.

Serendipity figured in the use of biofeedback hand warming for relieving migraine. A woman who participated in Elmer and Alyce Green's 1966 research on "hand warming through autogenic training" (self-regulation training) happened to recover from a migraine while she was being tested in the lab. Elmer noticed that the paper chart record showed a remarkably large increase of blood volume in her hands with an increase in hand temperature of 10 degrees. This all happened in two minutes. Later, at the end of the research session, when he asked what had happened to her, she said, "How did you know my migraine suddenly went away?"

Elmer Green followed this trail. He discovered that it was not unusual for migraine sufferers to complain of cold extremities, caused by excessive activation of the sympathetic nervous system. He reasoned that self-correction of the condition of cold hands would necessarily involve relaxation of the sympathetic nervous system. Thus, hand warming might have a corrective effect on associated abnormalities. With this idea in mind, and using simple temperature feedback machines of his own design, he successfully "trained" two patients out of their migraines and off of their pain-control drugs. This development fascinated Dr. Joseph Sargent, director of internal medicine at the Menninger Foundation. After learning the autogenic feedback training procedure himself, he had some additional temperature machines built and taught 75 headache patients to increase blood flow to the hands. Results showed a verifiable connection between warm hands and migraine relief.

Since those earlier experiments, many hundreds of migraine sufferers at the Menninger Foundation, as well as thousands of others throughout the country, have been successfully treated. An additional benefit is that the majority of patients no longer have to use medications that sometimes have unfavorable side effects.

When I went through the biofeedback laboratory, I was invited to participate in the hand-warming program. I readily accepted. I was brought to a room that was softly lit and comfortably furnished. About a dozen other people, members of an introductory biofeedback seminar, were sitting in recliner chairs with tall backs and headrests.

The instructions were simple. We were told to sit back and to free our minds of all concerns. We were to breathe slowly and deeply.

A thermometer was taped to the middle finger of my right hand; it showed that my skin temperature was 76 degrees. I was told that it was within my power, as an act of visualization coupled with will, to increase the surface temperature of my hands by more than 10 degrees.

The person in charge of the exercise spoke to us slowly, putting us in a relaxed state. For 15 minutes, we repeated after him, silently in our minds, autogenic phrases such as "I feel quite quiet. My feet are heavy and comfortable. My whole body is comfortable, heavy, and relaxed. Warmth is flowing down my arms into my hands. My hands are heavy, comfortable, and warm."

It was all phrased to emphasize that I was saying this, I was doing this, I was the one who had control. This notion of individual responsibility inside our skins is the core of self-regulation training, rather than the idea's coming from outside: "*You* feel heavy, *you* are comfortable, *you* are relaxed."

Just as we had the power to transmit our own orders to the nervous system and move our fingers, we imagined the feeling of warmth in our hands, and told our hands to get warm. It was an exercise of quiet willpower. The Greens call it "passive volition."

I breathed slowly and deeply. It was a kind of self-hypnosis. Or, more accurately, it was visualization and self-regulation training. I relaxed and thought of nothing except the feeling of warmth in my hands.

I looked at the other persons sharing the experience. Their eyes were still closed; their heads were still leaning against the backs of their chairs. They seemed far off.

After about three more minutes, we were asked to open our eyes and look at the temperature readings. Mine was at 93 degrees. It put me next to the bottom of the class; one patient was at 91 degrees. The others ranged up to 97 degrees. The increases were as great as 18 degrees.

The effect was electric. Just to see the evidence that I had the ability to affect bodily processes that were supposedly beyond my control was a mind-stretching experience.

Seven biofeedback trainees whom I met at the Menninger Foundation had been migraine patients; all reported unmistakable relief. Three patients had suffered from high blood pressure. Autogenic feedback and visualization exercises had enabled them over a period of weeks to reduce the average daily systolic reading by from 20 to 30 points, and gradually to stop using medications, under their doctors' guidance. Two persons were at the clinic because of asthma. Both reported improved respiration.

What was there about this particular kind of exercise in warmth control (which means blood-flow control) that provided help for persons whose ailments· were so disparate?

Dr. Green believes that the process involved is related to the restoration of the body's own balancing mechanisms. Illness is an interruption of the body's vital balances. Dr. Green refers to the early work of Dr. Johannes Schultz, in Germany, the founder of autogenic training. Dr. Schultz believed that in the very act of relaxing and asserting self-control over circulatory flow, the brain also activates natural forces in the body connected with correct nervous balance and with a correctly working immune system. The result is a "self-regulatory normalization."

If I understand it correctly, this explanation says that disorders such as migraine or asthma are disturbances of the body's own corrective or balancing mechanisms. These mechanisms have become unbalanced, usually because of stress, but when the brain is able to extend its authority into areas that are generally outside conscious control, the effect is not just particular but general. In a state of balance, the body is in a good position to meet its needs. By entering into the normally unconscious autonomic nervous system, the conscious brain helps to restore those chemical balances.

In addition to the hand-warming exercises, I participated in an experiment to test my ability to control the electricity produced by my brain. It was explained to me that a wide range of electrical rhythms go on within the brain. For example, in its most active state, the brain produces beta waves, manifested by 13 to 25 cycles per second. Alpha waves run from 8 to 13 per second. In a state of sleep or near sleep, the brain produces theta waves, 4 to 8 cycles per second. And in deep sleep the frequency usually drops below 4 cycles per second.

The test was simple. Electrodes were attached to my head. An attendant said he would intermittently say "beta" or "alpha." I would then direct my brain to produce one or the other. The results would be recorded on a printout. It was explained to me that the small, fast waves were associated with beta. I was then hooked up to a brain-wave feedback machine that produced a high tone for beta and a low tone for alpha, and was told to experiment, with my eyes shut, with mental states that produced those tones.

Since beta waves can be produced by highly directed intellectual activity, and alpha waves by quiet, non-directed activity, I hit on a plan of action. When I wanted to produce beta, I would try to do two things simultaneously. I would try to recite the Gettysburg Address to myself, and I would also try to set the words to Bach's Fugue in D Minor. And to produce alpha, I would simply turn off the effort and let my mind relax, and react in a totally non-focused way to whatever stimuli might be present in the room.

I confess that setting the Gettysburg Address to a Bach fugue called for all the concentration I could muster. I therefore welcomed the respite afforded by the signal "alpha."

After it was over, I was handed a printout showing the results of the test. I was pleased to see the evidence that I could be in command of the type of electricity manufactured by my brain. This capacity took on added significance when I learned of the different roles played by the brain's electricity in maintaining or restoring the vital balances of the body.

What was most encouraging about these experiments—not just to me but to all the others who took part in them—was the evidence that we need not feel that we are non-participants in all the life processes that go on inside the human body. A certain measure of control *is* possible; this control can often be exercised, as Elmer and Alyce Green have demonstrated, for the body's own good.

Dr. Green has sent me a generous supply of skin thermometers, which I put to use with patients who are referred to me by physicians for a morale boost. Few things are more gratifying to me than to see the way the patients respond to the evidence that they can preside over some functions generally thought to be locked within the autonomic nervous system.

In working with these patients, I try to combine the central features of Dr. Green's methods with the key elements of the "relaxation response" techniques developed by Dr. Herbert Benson, mentioned earlier in these pages. The techniques he espouses require no monitoring equipment. His relaxation-response methods seek a comprehensive effect. For example, a single individual may have high blood pressure, elevated cholesterol readings, and abnormally high triglycerides, may be addicted to smoking or drugs, and may be unable to handle the stress produced by his job or family. Through the "relaxation response," such an individual may be able to achieve improvement over the full range of his symptoms and problems.

Four features are central to Dr. Benson's relaxation response:

(1) *Quiet environment.* Distractions and extraneous sound should be eliminated to the fullest possible extent.

(2) *Restful conditions.* The individual should be made as comfortable as possible. The chair should be conducive to restfulness. Head and arms should be supported. It is useful to remove the shoes and prop up the feet a few inches.

(3) *Progressive relaxation and passive attitude.* Eyes should be closed. Breathing should be deep and regular. Muscles should be relaxed, beginning with the feet and working up through calves, thighs, hips, midsection, chest, shoulders, neck, and head.

(4) *Mind control.* An effort should be made to free oneself of distracting thoughts or concerns. A single word or syllable should be made dominant in the mind and repeated slowly and consistently. A shift is necessary from external stimuli to internal focus. The repetition at regular intervals of the word "one," because of its simplicity and symbolism, is a helpful device.

The routine takes about 20 minutes and can be employed

twice a day. Dr. Benson reports a number of controlled experiments in which striking results have been achieved. For example, patients with heart disorders who have had difficulty in bringing down cholesterol levels through dietary regimens or use of medications have experienced significant reductions in the fatty content of their blood. The implications of this fact for atherosclerosis should not be minimized.

The relationship of these techniques to transcendental meditation is apparent. What is important in all such efforts, including the one I have tried to use, is that one empties body and mind of tensions, apprehensions, and forebodings in order to free the healing system or the immune system of all impediments. The term "homeostasis," given currency through the writings of Dr. Walter Cannon, is descriptive of the human mind and body in a condition of balance in which all the regulatory mechanisms are able to do their job. What these systematic relaxation efforts seek to do is remove all obstacles to those natural processes.

As I mentioned earlier, in working with patients referred to me by their physicians for a morale boost, I borrow heavily from both Dr. Green and Dr. Benson. I try to give as much emphasis as possible to the need to block subconscious tensions and apprehensions. This is generally done by bringing positive thoughts into play.

The patients are seated in reclining chairs with headrests. Eyes are closed. Breathing is deep and rhythmic. The bulb of the thermometer is held between thumb and forefinger. The patient is asked to dwell on his or her fondest memories. These summoned memories should be made as real and close as possible. The longer the patient stays with them, the better.

Then the patient is asked to "go exploring" inside his or

her head. The instructions follow along these general lines: "Try to imagine that your consciousness is like a blackboard pointer. You can move the pointer from place to place inside your head; all your energies are focused at the spot where the pointer comes to rest. Now, the pointer stops inside your head toward the front of your face, just behind your nose. Your entire consciousness is now focused at this point. Now, concentrate on the tip of your nose. By riveting all your energies at this point, you seem almost to be touching your nose with your consciousness.

"Now, elevate that concentrated consciousness until it comes to rest just behind your eyes. Bear down at this point. After a while, you will feel a slight pulsing inside your head.

"Next, elevate that focal point of concentration until it comes to rest just under your scalp in the middle of your head. After a moment or two you will feel a slight sensation on the top of your head, a sort of tingling.

"You have now succeeded, as an act of will, in moving your focus of sensation to different parts of your head. You are able to extend this process and, by quiet concentration, to increase the flow of warmth into your hands. Just as you can order your fingertips to move, so you can use a different part of your capacities to move blood into your hands.

"Concentrate on it. Breathe slowly and deeply.

"Now, look at the thermometer. Any rise above your starting point is the result of your own will and the power of imagination, visualization."

Generally, as I said earlier, the thermometer registers in the low or mid-90's, representing an increase of 10 or 15 degrees above the baseline, even allowing for the heat caused by compression.

When the patients see that they are able to direct a vital activity of their bodies that they had thought was beyond reach, they are eager to repeat the experiment and, indeed, to go even further. The specific benefit here is that they now regard a measure of control over their own bodies as a practical reality. They are also able to create a psychological environment that is congenial to the physician's ministrations.

Perhaps the most dramatic example of the practical use of this procedure is furnished by patients who have been taught to use this kind of visualization to increase their tolerance to essential drugs. For example, not all patients afflicted by cancer are able to tolerate the side effects of chemotherapy, which can be harsh in the extreme. By "programming" themselves to concentrate on the action of the chemotherapy in destroying the cancer cells, as well as to "contain" the punitive action of the drug beyond that point, some patients are able to derive benefits of therapy that might otherwise be excluded from their treatment, and at the same time diminish unpleasant side effects.

Obviously, the benefits of biofeedback-aided training vary from patient to patient. Even where, however, there may be resistance to the procedure, some benefit can be experienced. I have heard some medical researchers speculate that the process has the effect of releasing painkilling endorphins into the bloodstream, as well as enabling the brain to exercise its larger apothecary functions. Whether that is so, I cannot say. I do know that most of the patients who have been given such exercises report increased confidence in themselves and in their ability to make the most of the treatment being given them.

When Dr. Hitzig visited me in California several months after the heart-attack episode, I was able to demonstrate

THE HEALING HEART

for him some specific examples of the ability of the mind to exercise a degree of governance over autonomic functions. When he took my pulse, I was able to "think" my way into a minor arrhythmia, as well as to make it disappear. Also, when he took my blood pressure, I was able to move it up and down within a certain range.

These capacities, obviously, can be used for aiding the natural regenerative drive of the body. The will to live is not just a frame of mind but a specific biochemical force. For all we know, the will to live may be one of the connecting links between the belief system and the healing system.

CHAPTER XVI

Panic:
The Ultimate Enemy

Recent medical studies of joggers and runners show that many of them enjoy a "high" during their exertion. The reason, according to these researchers, is that at a certain stage of intensity of effort, endorphins are released by the brain into the bloodstream. Endorphins, as stated earlier, contain morphine-like molecules. Their effect, therefore, is similar to the one produced by opiates. Once the blood vessels are also widened, the full circulatory flow enhances the sense of narcotized pleasure.

A graphic description of this process was provided by Dr. Walter Bortz, of the Stanford University Hospital, in Palo Alto, California, in a communication to the *New England Journal of Medicine* for August 20, 1981. Dr. Bortz, himself a marathon runner, was inspired by his own experience to undertake the study that served as the basis for the article.

One of the points made by Dr. Bortz is that some jog-

gers are addicted, in effect, to the body's benevolent nar-
cotics. Conversely, if the same joggers were to flee from
danger, the biochemical effect could be in the opposite
extreme. Instead of being widened, the blood vessels would
be narrowed. Instead of hormones containing natural
opiates, the body would produce large amounts of epinephrine and other hormones that would have the effect
of stimulating or overstimulating the heart, with consequent danger of destabilization. The severity of the physical exertion may be secondary to the emotional ambience
in which it takes place.

The medical literature on the physiological effects of
psychological or emotional causes is as abundant as it is
fascinating. Once again, I call attention to the writings of
Claude Bernard, Walter Cannon, Hans Selye, Bernard
Lown, George Engel, S. Wolf, Robert Eliot, Herbert Benson, and Henry Beecher. Their findings are of prime value
to anyone interested in the harsh effects on the human body
of emotional shock.

A good introduction to this entire subject was published
in the *Annals of Internal Medicine* 74:777 (1971). Under the
title "Sudden and Rapid Death during Psychological
Stress," George Engel reported the results of a study of
people who died in response to shattering news.

The largest single category of death from emotional
shock, Dr. Engel found, consisted of those who were suddenly confronted with grave personal danger (27 percent).
Next came those who collapsed and expired on learning of
the death or catastrophic injury of a loved one (21 percent).
Acute grief following the death of a close relative produced death within 10 days (20 percent). Severe humilia-
tion or recognition of the loss of personal status accounted
for 6 percent. Interestingly enough, this latter reaction was

experienced mostly by men. Women, apparently, were far better able than men to sustain blows to the ego.

Dr. Engel referred to the wife of the owner of the motel in which Martin Luther King was assassinated in Memphis in 1968. On hearing the news of the murder, the woman collapsed; she died the next day. He also quoted the prediction of the 18th-century surgeon John Hunter: "My life is at the mercy of any scoundrel who chooses to put me in a passion." Dr. Hunter foretold his own death.

Sometimes good news can have a devastating effect. A letter in the *British Medical Journal* in 1965 told of one man who was so overjoyed on learning from his physician that there was nothing wrong with his heart, after all, that he died on the spot. Fortunately, instances of people perishing because they couldn't take glad tiding are so rare that one need not take precautions against the experience.

Dr. Engel quoted from the book *Scared to Death*, by J. C. Barker, published in London in 1968. The author described the experiences of 42 persons who died abruptly after being frightened for one reason or another.

Dr. Lown has written frequently about this phenomenon. He has observed that folklore and medical science come together in accepting the reality of sudden death through emotional causes. Folklore makes note of the fact; medical science understands what happens inside the body to bring it about. In an article written for *Science* (November 1973), of which Dr. Lown was one of several authors, the process is carefully defined. Sudden emotional shock touches off what Dr. Lown terms an "electrical accident," resulting in violently rapid and erratic heartbeat, technically known as fibrillation.

Following publication of *Anatomy of an Illness*, some critics contended there was insufficient evidence to support the notion that laughter had specific and significant therapeutic value. Laughter may or may not activate the endorphins or enhance respiration, as some medical researchers contend. What seems clear, however, is that laughter is an antidote to apprehension and panic. As such, its value is not less than that of the fire extinguisher that puts out the flame.

I return here to the main theme of this book: Nothing is more essential in the treatment of serious disease than liberating the patient from panic and foreboding. I was tremendously gratified when physicians or directors at several hospitals around the country wrote to tell me that they had instituted programs to replace the usual somber atmosphere that prevails in the care of the ill. At St. Joseph Hospital in Houston, Dr. John S. Stehlin, Jr., has redesigned the cancer floor in order to accommodate a new "Living Room" in which patients are encouraged to take part in recreational activities. Video cassettes of comedy films and stand-up comics are readily available, as, indeed, are similar materials relating to other areas of creativity—music, poetry, drawing and painting, the dance.

Hospitals in Houston, Atlanta, St. Louis, St. Paul, and Miami—to mention only those cities that have come to my attention—have instituted similar programs making use of laughter and the other positive emotions as a means of creating an emotional environment not dominated by panic. Those in charge of those facilities all tell the same story: The brighter mood of the patients not only creates a more pleasant environment for all concerned but actually enhances treatment in many cases.

Unfortunately, this aspect of health care tends to be under-emphasized. As I wrote earlier, the campaign to educate the public in cardio-pulmonary resuscitation (CPR) procedures, puts the accent on technical procedures—how to apply mouth-to-mouth resuscitation, and so forth. Such emergency measures, however, can actually deepen the panic of the patient. Similarly, being in a speeding ambulance with the siren in full cry can be harmful and even devastating in itself. This is not to ignore or minimize the need for prompt care; it is only to emphasize the need to give at least as much attention to the patient's emotional needs as to his or her physical condition.

Let me cite a specific instance. In the fall of 1982, I saw an ambulance in front of the clubhouse of one of the golf courses in West Los Angeles. I went over to the ambulance and saw a man on a stretcher alongside the vehicle. He had suffered a heart attack while playing golf. The paramedics, working systematically and methodically, were attending to their duties, connecting him to a portable cardiograph monitor, which they placed at the foot of the stretcher, hooking him up to an oxygen tank, inserting a plug in his arm to facilitate intravenous ministrations.

No one was talking to the man. He was ashen and trembling. I looked at the cardiograph monitor. It revealed what is termed a tachycardia—a runaway heart rate. The intervals on the monitor were irregular. I also looked at the paramedics, who, true to their training, were efficiently attending to the various emergency procedures. But no one was attending to the patient's panic, which was potentially lethal.

I put my hand on his shoulder. "Sir," I said, "you've got a great heart."

He opened his eyes and turned toward me. "Why do you say that?" he asked in a low voice.

In Oliver Wendell Holmes's phrase, I "rounded the sharp corners of the truth" with my reply.

"Sir," I said, "I've been looking at your cardiograph and I can see that you're going to be all right. You're in very good hands. In a few minutes, you'll be in one of the world's best hospitals. You're going to be just fine."

"Are you sure?" he asked.

"Certainly. It's a very hot day and you are probably dehydrated. The electrical impulses to the heart can be disrupted when that happens. Don't worry. You'll be all right."

In less than a minute, the cardiograph showed unmistakable evidence of a slowing down of the heartbeat. The gaps between the tall lines began to widen; the rhythm began to be less irregular. I looked at the man's face; the color began to return. He propped up his head with his arms and looked around; he was taking an interest in what was happening.

I felt no remorse at having skirted around the truth. What he needed—as much as the oxygen—was reassurance. He needed to be lifted out of his panic. As I said earlier, panic can trigger a whole series of adverse events, forcing an unstable heart to work harder at a critical time. The effect of the catecholamines on the heart under these circumstances could even tear its muscle fibers. Moreover, it was probably true that heat and dehydration had played a part in the man's heart attack. In any event, he needed to be calmed, to be given confidence in himself and in the medical attention he would shortly receive.

Depression follows panic just as surely as a hangover follows excessive drinking. When the human body suffers profound endocrinal disruptions as a result of pervasive, crushing fear or other profound emotional disturbances, depression is an almost automatic aftermath. And depression is an intensifying cause of illness. The mood of the patient, therefore, is hardly of less concern to the physician than the disease he is called upon to treat.

I speak here not just of heart attacks but of any serious illness. Since 1978, I have met with some 260 persons who were suffering from cancer. As I mentioned earlier, what was most startling about their cases was that many of them experienced a sudden and sharp worsening in their condition coincident with the diagnosis. Why was it, I had to ask myself, that the cancer should take on such added fury just after the patient learned the bad news? Was it because the patient had neglected his or her symptoms so long that their effects were due to become explosive? No doubt this was true in some cases; but there were many others where this explanation didn't apply. What seemed more likely—and this hypothesis was strengthened in my talks with the patients—was that they were emotionally unhinged when they were confronted with the fact that they had cancer and had no way to cope with the devastating news. Moreover, the internal chemistry was so disturbed by the effects of the panic that the physiological environment was far from ideal for treatment.

My speculations along these lines were stimulated by a news item appearing in the *Los Angeles Times* on October 23, 1982. The item, which appeared on the front page, concerned an episode that occurred at a Monterey Park, California, football game.

What had happened was that four persons had to leave their seats during the game because of severe nausea and dizziness. Questioning on the spot by school officials established the fact that the ill persons had consumed soft drinks from a dispensing machine under the stands. Syrup had been mixed with water out of the local piping system. Was the culprit the syrup or the water? In the latter case, had copper sulfate from the pipes infiltrated the water? If the former, had bacteriological organisms contaminated the syrup?

The football stadium lacked loudspeaker facilities. The cheerleaders were therefore directed to make a public announcement requesting that no one consume any soft drinks from the beverage-dispensing machines until the precise cause of the sudden illness affecting several persons could be ascertained. The immediate effect of the announcement was that the stadium became an arena of fainting and retching people. One hundred and ninety-one persons had to be hospitalized. Local ambulances and private cars plied back and forth between the stadium and five hospitals in the area. Emergency-room physicians reported that the symptoms of food poisoning were genuine. No one knows how many persons at the game went to their own physicians.

Laboratory analysis showed there was nothing wrong with the water or the syrup. This fact no doubt figured in the subsequent and sudden improvement of all those who had become ill during the game.

The episode was only one of a long series of historical incidents attesting to the connection between suggestion and physical illness.

Mass hysteria was a prominent feature of the Middle Ages. Thousands of persons, foaming at the mouth, engaged in wild "Saint Vitus" dancing orgies. The "dance" spread through much of Europe. In Italy, other thousands were caught up in an hysterical epidemic of "tarantism"; they were obsessed with the idea they had been bitten by poisonous spiders. Similarly there was the mass affliction called "Black Death," involving seizures and other epileptic symptoms. These illnesses were none the less real for having their origins in hysteria or mass delusion.

Modern medicine now knows that the success of Franz Anton Mesmer's "cures" in the late 18th century was not the result, as Mesmer thought, of his "animal magnetism" but of the power of suggestion. Many of his patients were in the grip of what Charcot later termed "conversion hysteria." Human beings can "think" or "imagine" their way into illness, with organic manifestations.

The implications of these facts on a negative diagnosis are worth pondering. If people can become physically ill just as the result of words, as happened at Monterey Park, consider the effect of a catastrophic diagnosis on patients who already have serious symptoms. What is the physiological impact on a person when the word "cancer" is pronounced? At such a time, what biochemical changes take place that can result in an intensification of the underlying condition, even as they serve to impair essential treatment?

Medical research has identified the connection between panic and adverse physiological events. As mentioned earlier, sudden catecholamine flooding can precipitate a wide range of negative reactions, not excluding cardiac destabilization and constriction of blood vessels. An internal environment is created that not only can accelerate the negative underlying forces but can be hostile to the prescribed treatment.

Whether the disease is cancer or cardiac insufficiency or muscle or joint disabilities, the way the diagnosis is communicated can often have a significant effect on the efficacy of treatment and, indeed, on the course of the disease. The dilemma confronting the physician is self-evident. He cannot deceive the patient yet he wants to avoid the devastating effect of the truth.

I have no criticism to make of Dr. Shine because he told me, at the time I was admitted to the hospital, that my condition was "desperate," as he had informed Dr. Hitzig.

There was no point in disabling me emotionally or putting additional weight on my subconscious apprehensions. The actions he took and the recommendations he made were consistent with his findings, which is why he was trying to steer me in the direction of an angiogram and surgery. He knew far better than I what the risks were in that course, but he measured those risks against what he considered to be the larger risk that was inherent in my condition. Once I was out of the hospital, he stepped up the rhetoric of concern, but he was able very skillfully to tread the line between reasonable truth and unreasonable alarmism.

Hans Zinsser, in his book *As I Remember Him,* disagreed with one of his Harvard colleagues who held that "absolute, uncompromising truthfulness is the only justifiable position, however cruel." Zinsser believed that no rules could be set that could fit every patient. One principle, however, he believed was unvariable. "One must pick one's situations, and adjust the truth to the judgment of wise kindness."

Artistry and kindness go together. In a large number of cases where stabilization has occurred, which I happen to know about, the physician has paid at least as much attention to the emotional needs of the patient as to the disease itself. The patients in this category unfailingly reported that they were able to leave their physicians' offices not in a mood of defeat or panic but in a mood of challenge. However ominous the diagnosis, they felt they had a chance.

In making such a reaction possible, the physician was not tilting the facts. He was recognizing that unexpected remissions are being reported in the medical journals all the time and that this possibility must never be dismissed.

The entire subject of psychological effects on health raises questions abut the emphasis given to certain aspects of public-health education. One wonders whether the effect of this education is to push the public in the direction of hypochondria, thus predisposing people to emotional collapse at a time of minor or major symptoms. As mentioned earlier, the heavy emphasis on annual or even semiannual checkups may have the effect of clogging clinics and physicians' offices with many people who have no business being there. People have been made so pain-conscious that they have become terrified of the pain. The dominant trend in advertising, especially over television, is to promote self-medication—with respect for the hazards involved in such quixotic undertakings.

The net effect of all these public campaigns, to repeat, may be pushing people in the wrong direction. What is most needed is to give people confidence in their bodies, to let them know that not every pain is a harbinger of disaster, to get them to think about those things that promote good health and about a personal life-style that reduces negative stress to the fullest possible extent. People today tend to think about health on the level of symptoms. They tend to define good health as the absence of symptoms, bad health as their assertion. The fact that symptoms are frequently the product of poor health habits has yet to become predominant in the public view.

The difficulties confronting physicians in communicating a serious diagnosis to patients may be a little less complicated if the public is made to feel less intimidated by pain and its portents.

The diagnosis of a malignancy or a serious heart problem need not be the occasion for a sudden worsening. Houston oncologist Dr. John Stehlin, mentioned earlier in this chapter, is only one of a large number of physicians who have been able to help patients avert a plunge when the news of cancer has to be communicated. I had heard about Dr. Stehlin from a patient whose condition had been diagnosed as being "terminal" by local specialists but whose cancer had been arrested after he was treated by Dr. Stehlin. For my purposes here, I shall call the patient Gordon Russell.

Russell had been told his liver cancer was inoperable. He was also told he had approximately 90 days to live. Russell turned over his business to his employees and put his estate in order in anticipation of an early demise. He also went to a library and did his own research on cancer of the liver. This was how he learned about Dr. Stehlin in Houston.

Russell went to Houston. He, his wife, and Dr. Stehlin had a lengthy discussion about his illness, his attitude toward his cancer, and his feeling about the possibility of surgical re-exploration. Dr. Stehlin made it clear to Russell that the chances of removing the cancer from his liver were very small. He asked Russell if he was able to cope with high odds against success. His answer: "It is obvious I have no chance at all without surgery. Let's go."

Dr. Stehlin accepted the challenge. He told Russell that the patient's ability to exercise the full range of the positive emotions—confidence, will to live, hope, love, purpose, joyousness—could have a significant bearing on the outcome.

Indeed, Dr. Stehlin is severely reluctant to accept any cancer sufferer for treatment if the patient is unable to accept a strong share of responsibility—by which Dr. Stehlin means a partnership in which the patient has confidence in himself and in the persons who are going to treat him.

Gordon Russell met all of Dr. Stehlin's conditions. Though only 20 per cent of his liver was still functional the surgery and treatment at St. Joseph have enabled Russell to resume a normal life. Four years later, Russell is in excellent health.

By an interesting coincidence, only a few weeks after meeting Gordon Russell, I received an invitation from Dr. Stehlin to come to Houston to take part in the dedication ceremonies of the "Living Room" of St. Joseph Hospital. Dr. Stehlin had read *Anatomy of an Illness,* the central theme of which corresponded to his own philosophy of medical care. Some of the specific approaches I had taken in my own illness, he said, were being employed in his new unit. He had designed and built a section of a floor at St. Joseph which was utterly unlike the conventional hospital. The large area called the Living Room had been set aside for cancer patients. Reproductions of famous paintings adorned the walls. One section of the room was generously supplied with books, magazines, and a reading table. One end of the room contained several videocassette recorders and stereo players. Dr. Stehlin was able to get entertainment companies in Hollywood to donate a large number of cassettes of comedies, stand-up comic routines, and a wide assortment of music tapes. The patients were encouraged to entertain themselves. The nurses at St. Joseph Hospital helped to create an upbeat mood among the patients.

When I stepped off the elevator on Dr. Stehlin's floor, the atmosphere was not somber or foreboding. A number of wheelchair patients greeted me with warm smiles. Dr. Stehlin came up to me and began to brief me about the dedication ceremonies. He interrupted himself to introduce me to Sister Mary Romana, who emerged from one of the patient's rooms. She was a trim, delicate woman in her 70's.

"Dr. Stehlin expects us to tell our patients a funny story each day," she said.

"And what is your story today?" he asked.

"I'm ready for you," she said with a trace of an Irish accent. "A lady and a man were sitting at a table in a corner of a nightclub. Suddenly, the man fell off his seat and slipped under the table. The headwaiter rushed over. 'Madam,' he said, 'your husband has just slipped under the table.'

" 'That's where you're wrong,' she replied. 'My husband has just walked into the room.' "

Dr. Stehlin howled with laughter and told Sister Mary he was going to steal her story for his own talk at the dedication ceremonies of the Living Room in a few minutes.

We walked down the hall. I peeked into some of the rooms. Several patients' arms or legs were fully encased in oversized bandages. Many of them had been referred from other hospitals where, in the ordinary course of events, their limbs would have been amputated in order to stop the spreading cancers. Dr. Stehlin has refined a technique for saving arms and legs which is called hyperthermic (heat) perfusion. Here, a heart-lung machine is used to circulate blood in and out of an arm or leg. A tourniquet is applied high in the groin or around the shoulder to cut off the blood flow and to prevent the powerful anticancer drugs from escaping into the body. The blood is circulated through a heat exchanger. When the limb gets warm enough, anticancer drugs are injected into the circuit. (At St. Joseph Hospital Cancer Research Lab, Dr. B. C. Giovanella, a cancer researcher, discovered that heat would kill cancer cells faster than normal noncancerous cells.) Thus, heated blood and anticancer drugs are circulated through the involved extremity without leaking back into the body. The cancer in the extremity is exposed to high concentrations of anticancer drugs without exposing the patient to dangerous, untoward and unpleasant side-effects of these poisonous anticancer agents. During this operation, the temperature of the limb is carefully monitored in the operating room in order to prevent serious damage to the arm or leg.

In this way, hundreds of patients have been spared amputations and many patients are alive who might not have survived conventional treatment. People come from all over the United States to St. Joseph Hospital because of the remarkable record achieved by Dr. Stehlin and his staff—not just in saving limbs but for the treatment of patients with various types of cancer.

Dr. Stehlin is proud of this record but is eager to share credit with his patients. Their confidence in him and in themselves and their will to live are as much a part of the treatment as his own science. I could readily understand why. Dr. Stehlin is a supreme artist in human relationships. When patients meet with him, they quickly overcome their feeling that they are in a courtroom where the judge is getting ready to pronounce sentence and where it is forbidden to talk back. Not that Dr. Stehlin hides the truth from his patients. He knows he is obligated to report his findings honestly. But he never does so in a way that devastates a patient. He recognizes that the patient's hope is a powerful force of medication in itself.

Dr. Stehlin works with the materials of hope as carefully and consistently as he does with his surgical instruments. He knows that an atmosphere of genuine hopefulness, faith, and confidence helps the patient to optimize his prospects. Indeed, medical and surgical measures have a far better chance of achieving their purposes when the patient is free of foreboding and despair.

(Louis Jolyon West, who, as I mentioned earlier, is my

boss in the Department of Psychiatry and Biobehavioral Sciences in the School of Medicine at UCLA, told me of a study made of some 175 patients who were about to undergo comparable surgery. The patients could be divided into two groups—those who dreaded the surgery, regarding it as mutilation, and who wanted to do everything possible to defer going into the operating room, and those who looked forward to the impending surgery, regarding it as an opportunity to liberate their bodies from a terrible scourge. Studies made of these patients showed that those in the second group had a far more rapid and auspicious postoperative experience than those in the first group. The body has a way of following the mind's expectations.)

Dr. Stehlin spends considerable time with his patients in the period preceding surgery. He provides a realistic underpinning for their hopes by reviewing with them actual cases as severe as or more severe than their own. By talking about those patients who were able to live useful and productive lives following the surgery, he is able to provide the genuine materials of confidence and purpose. He underlines the most important truth about cancer today, namely, that it is a profound mistake to equate the diagnosis of cancer with death. But he also dramatizes the fact that the medical scientist's skills are not enough. He believes that a patient's deep commitment to live is a vital part of the total process.

He emphasizes to his patients that he can offer no guarantee of success. What he does do, however, is to persuade the patient that he or she has a real chance—so long as both patient and physician give it their best effort. As in my own experience with Dr. Cannom, the patients leave his office in a mood not of defeat but of genuine challenge.

I accompanied Dr. Stehlin to the dedication ceremonies

in the Living Room. Some 200 people were crowded into the room—patients, nurses, physicians, civic leaders. After the invocation, Dr. Stehlin spoke, describing the completion of the Living Room as being no less important than the work going on in cancer-research laboratories. For the ability of patients to get the most out of life, whatever the circumstances, is integral to their treatment.

On the flight home to Los Angeles the next day, I thought about John Stehlin and his creative innovations. He was taking the sting out of the hospital environment. Like Dr. Albert Schweitzer, who built a jungle "hospital" that was actually an African village with a clinic attached to it, Dr. Stehlin was attempting to make the hospital into an extension of the patient's own home, thus freeing the body at a difficult time from the need to cope with an alien experience.

My purpose in these digressions is to underline the fact that all serious illnesses—and not just heart attacks—call for dual treatment. It is not enough for the physician to be a scientist and a technician. He must deal with a combination of apprehensions and despair, which, left unattended, can retard effective treatment. If these needs are unmet, even the most expert treatment in the world may fall short of its mark.

Human beings are unique not solely because millions of years of evolution have enabled them to stand upright but because of their sensibilities and sensitivities, their ability to feel the pain of others as their own, their ability to comprehend and respond to moral values, their ability to ponder the experience of the race, and their ability to convert not just their food but also their hopes into vital energy. Providing medical care for such a species, therefore, calls for an exquisite respect for those things that may defy measurements but that put an individual in motion and that have something to do with individual destiny.

There is a tendency in medicine to believe that, if two patients have identical symptoms, they are to be treated identically. This tendency is not always free of error. There is always a vital intangible that lies beyond the instruments of diagnosis, and that has a bearing on the course of disease and a design for treatment. The intangibles have to do with the innermost sources of a person's strength—how an individual goes about responding to crisis and transcending assumed or assigned limitations.

People sometimes discover within themselves capacities they never knew existed. No greater mystery exists than how this happens—or why these capacities should be more highly developed in some persons than in others. But it is the powerful but invisible potion in the physician's little black bag, the one ingredient that can give added value to all others and that sometimes will work when all else fails. Whether this ingredient goes by the name of the patient's own hopefulness or determination or faith or confidence or will to live—or all of them combined—is not as important as the fact that the positive emotions and attitudes are potent factors in recovery.

Physicians have always believed in the usefulness and, indeed, the necessity of attitudes as aids in the healing process, but the way attitudes made their registrations on the body was a matter more of philosophy than of physiology. Today, however, at brain-research centers in America and abroad, the biochemistry of the emotions is regarded as a tangible and classifiable process.

One such center is located at the University of Nebraska in Omaha. I had the good fortune to visit the university and to observe at first hand the work of the Department of Preventive and Stress Medicine and Cardiovascular Center. Here the role of the emotions in bringing on disease is carefully studied and researched. Attempts are made to analyze the personality of patients in order to fend off serious illness.

Chairman of the Center is Dr. Robert S. Eliot who has devised ways of measuring the physiological effects of tension, frustration, competitiveness, and other stressful emotions. Through these tests he is able to set up warning signals. The net effect of the tests can be life-saving, for Dr. Eliot has been able to help patients to create new patterns of behavior that can reduce the danger of heart attacks or strokes or other disorders.

Like Dr. Ray H. Rosenman and Dr. M. Friedman, who developed the concept of Type A and Type B personalities, Dr. Eliot believes that the way people behave is a powerful predictor of breakdown. He does not minimize the importance of low-fat diet and exercise but he feels that human response to challenge is a major factor in any equation involving risk of serious disease. Basic to this theory is his belief that illness-causing behavior can be corrected.

"Since harmful reactions to stress arise largely from learned reactions," he told a Senate Committee in July 1981, "these reactions can be unlearned. Needless stress and its harmful side effects, including cardiovascular disease, can be prevented, ameliorated, or postponed."

Dr. Eliot, who has had a myocardial infarction himself and has been able to think about heart disease from the standpoint of the patient, has long believed that not enough attention was being paid to personality and emotional factors as carriers of heart disease. This conviction went into the making of his laboratory at the University of Nebraska.

My visit to his laboratory took place two years after my

own heart attack. I had come to Omaha for a lecture but took advantage of my stay in that city in order to visit Dr. Eliot in the Prevention and Stress Medicine Center. Even before coming to Omaha, I had some familiarity with Dr. Eliot's work thanks to the medical papers he had written over the years. The dominant theme of these papers was on the role of emotional stress in the development of heart disease. I found a great deal of material in these papers to support my own notions about the possibility that cardiac testing results could be skewed by emotional factors. Earlier in these pages, I have written about my personal experience on the treadmill and the way psychological factors may have affected the result.

Dr. Eliot has designed a series of tests based on situations analogous to these encountered in real life. These tests seek to identify "hot reactor types," by which Dr. Eliot means those persons who, because of the way they respond to everyday situations, can be in cardiac jeopardy.

Extreme competitiveness, fear that one may not be performing well, inability to handle sudden shock—these are the factors that often figure in the onset of heart attacks, according to Dr. Eliot. His tests seek to measure the effects of such stress and tension on the human heart and on the vascular system.

I offered myself as an experimental guinea pig. The first thing Dr. Eliot did was to give me a thorough examination. Pertinent cardiac data was taken—blood pressure, heart rate, cardiograph, etc. This information served as a baseline against which the data from the tests could be compared.

Next, several electro-magnetic bands were connected to various parts of my anatomy. An automated blood-pressure measuring device was attached to my left arm.

I was then seated in a comfortable armchair in front of a television set. One of the physicians on Dr. Eliot's staff appeared on the screen. His manner was cordial and direct but distinctly low-key; there was nothing autocratic or urgent in his voice. He explained that I would be given three separate tests and that my response would be measured by equipment in the adjoining room.

The first test was a TV game in which I was to operate the controls of a moving "bat" and intercept as many little white balls as possible. There was a time limit, unstated.

The second test involved a simple arithmetical quiz. Beginning with the number 777, I was asked to subtract 7 and keep on going until directed to stop—770, 763, 756, 749, 742, 735, 728 etc.

In the next test, I was directed to put my right hand, up to the wrist, in a bucket filled with ice cubes and to keep it there for 90 seconds.

During all these tests, the blood pressure cuff on my left arm was taking measurements. Meanwhile, too, all sorts of other measurements were being electronically calculated. These measurements registered the effectiveness of the heart pump; the flow of blood through the chambers of the heart; the rigidity of the walls of the blood vessels, and so forth.

In the first test—the TV bouncing ball game—the purpose was to assess my competitive drive and its effect on my heart. The second test sought to measure my response to an intellectual challenge. The third test measured my response to physiological stress.

When the tests were completed, Dr. Eliot returned to the room. He held a sheaf of papers on which literally hundreds of numbers had been computerized. Interpreting the results, he said I had very little rise in blood pressure or other adverse indications during the first two tests, showing that I could handle competitive situations or intellectual challenges without untoward effects. My reaction to the ice bucket test, however, had caused a jump of about 35 points in my systolic blood pressure and 10 points in my diastolic.

This meant that I was a "hot reactor" and that my heart would be under strain for certain experiences. I thought back to my response during the test. The sensation of having my hand in a bucket stuffed with ice cubes had been so unpleasant, indeed painful, that I wanted to withdraw my hand immediately. But I had been told I was expected to keep going for 90 seconds. I started counting the seconds, feeling trapped. The analogy that came to mind was being delayed in a car on a congested highway en route to an airport. Extrication was necessary but extrication was deferred. The ice bucket test confirmed what I already knew: Stay out of situations you don't want to be in. In this respect, I was a star member of Dr. Rosenman's Type A club.

Dr. Eliot encouraged me to believe that my reactions in this respect need not be permanent. He spoke about the experience of patients who were "hot reactors" to all three tests but who, with systematic behavorial reconditioning, were able to reduce their vulnerability to heart-attack episodes.

One of the special values of this type of testing, of course, is that it is not "invasive," as is the angiogram or other procedures that require dyes to be put into the blood for X-ray purposes or catheters threaded through the veins into the heart.

Most valuable to me personally, of course, was the knowledge that I need not be imprisoned by habits of thought or behavior that, as Dr. Hitzig had told me just after my heart attack, could be time bombs ticking away inside me. Indeed, in the two years since that heart attack, I have systematically changed a great deal of my life-style, so that, even if my response to certain situations hasn't changed completely, I had fewer of those situations to deal with.

CHAPTER XVII

Beyond Invalidism

The sense of being locked into a body that is inadequate for its needs, the sense of living under a lowering ceiling, the sense of having to separate oneself from vital prospects, the sense of coming to terms with bleakness—all these are the stuff of invalidism. The person who is put on notice by the physician that he or she has a "bad heart" tends to live a life of reduced expectations, to take slower and fewer steps, and to move more tentatively in the outside world.

How does one avoid the feeling of being an invalid when underlying conditions create and indeed seem to dictate it? When a physician tells you that your heart is weak and must be spared the strains that other people routinely and joyously bear, how do you go through life without flinching when you approach stairs or hilly streets or children reaching out to be lifted?

Perhaps the best way to answer these questions is to

begin by reflecting on the way the human body works. A weak body becomes weaker in a mood of total surrender. The mechanisms of repair and rehabilitation that are built into the human system have a natural drive to assert themselves under conditions of illness, but that natural tendency is deferred or deflected by an erosion of the will to live, or by the absence of confidence in one's physician or in one's own ability to play a vital part in the attack on disease.

Obviously, it is absurd to suppose that there is no illness or somber circumstance that can't be reversed. But it is also true that under conditions of extreme illness we need all the help we can get. For the same reason it is necessary to put all our own powers to work in our own behalf. We want to get the most out of whatever is possible. An integral part of this process is respect for the human body—an organism of astounding tenacity, resiliency, and recuperative capability. And, since the human body tends to move in the direction of its expectations—plus or minus—it is important to know that attitudes of confidence and determination are no less a part of the treatment program than medical science and technology.

The day after I came home from the hospital, I arranged with a building contractor to construct a new study and storage facility for all the *Saturday Review* files and other books and records that had been moved out from the East. The only place available for the new construction was above a steep hill in back of the house. This meant I would have to climb the equivalent of four flights of stairs every time I wanted to go to the study.

The building was completed in about three months. I have never felt the slightest hesitation in making the ascent, which I have done at least twice daily. The sense of pleasurable anticipation is enough to allow me to endure any strain.

I do know this, however: if I had any distasteful expectations or reactions, my body would supply all the signs of chest pressure to accommodate that distaste. More and more, I am inclined to accept the notion that the body produces its own poisons under circumstances of apprehension or emotional strain and that this factor is intimately involved in serious illness, whether it takes the form of cardiac disease, joint disabilities, or even cancer. The title of Kenneth Pelletier's book *Mind as Healer, Mind as Slayer* may say it all.

Nothing is more amazing or heartening to me than to see the way in which many persons with severe afflictions or handicaps nonetheless manage to affirm life. Just in the act of mobilizing their emotional resources they help to potentiate themselves physically. I am not saying here that no one ever need feel disadvantaged; all I am doing is making a distinction between being an invalid and thinking and acting like one.

I know that I am still at risk. I know that, without warning, my heart could suddenly fail. If that should happen, I will have no complaints. As I told Dr. Shine, I have nothing but gratitude for a heart that has seen me through an eventful life and several medical ordeals, beginning in childhood.

Death is not the enemy; living in constant fear of it is. I have no intention of swathing myself in cotton to soften a possibly fatal episode. I will continue to live and think as actively and creatively as it is physically possible for me to do, knowing that longevity by itself can be sterile but that vital feelings and thoughts give meaning and depth to life and provide a true sense of the possibilities of human existence.

I have already lived more than an average lifetime, but I want to continue to live long enough to see the establishment of a world under law and a planet made safe and fit for human habitation. I hope, too, to live long enough to see the conquest of human squalor. What stands in the way is not insufficiency of natural resources but the way people choose to think about their problems and opportunities. In any event, I am grateful that I am able to continue working for those causes that seek to free our age from gross indignities and the fear of nuclear devastation.

What seems especially important to me in retrospect is that I am the beneficiary of the best that modern medical science has to offer. For many years, deaths from heart attacks have outnumbered fatalities from all other diseases. That number is now on the decline and will, I believe, decline further still with the full recognition, not just by the profession but by the general public, that a comprehensive program of treatment involves both the full utilization of medical science and the full development of the human healing system. The fact that the belief system can be a vital activator of the healing system may open the door to an auspicious future in medical research and practice.

I look up at the calendar as I put down these final notes and see that it is two years and five months since the heart attack of December 22, 1980. Dr. Shine has gone out of his way to congratulate me, using the word "magnificent" to describe my progress, even though he feels I may still be at substantial risk. Dr. Cannom does not refute the fact of ongoing risk but sees no evidence that my heart is not getting all the blood and oxygen my life-style requires. The portion of the heart muscle that was destroyed during the heart attack will not regenerate, but the rest of the heart muscle has been strengthened and has adapted itself to my needs. Dr. Cannom says it is difficult to believe that bypass surgery could have achieved a better functional result than has been achieved without it. The original treadmill results that produced the finding of severe coronary insufficiency have been reversed.

I manage to set aside time each week for the sports I enjoy—doubles or singles in tennis, and golf with old friends. Golf does not really qualify as exercise, but it is a game that offers tangible and tantalizing possibilities for measurable improvement of one's skill. Besides, it provides an arena for banter and the rewards of companionship in an outdoor setting. I maintain a full working schedule, and I pay visits to the hospital at the request of physicians to see ill persons in need of a morale boost. The difference between what I did before the heart attack and what I am doing now is that I now maintain some semblance of control. I try to run my schedule instead of letting the schedule run me.

What is to me most fascinating of all in retrospect about the entire episode is the evidence that it is possible for the heart to create its own bypass. A surgical bypass would have removed portions of veins from my leg and substituted them for the clogged portions of arteries going into the heart. The way nature accomplishes the same purpose is twofold. In response to the systematic regimen of careful diet, regular exercise, control of stress, and a philosophy of life that provides ample nourishment for the generous appetite of the spirit, the body slowly creates a rich network of new blood vessels across the heart, bypassing the deficient arteries with new conduits of its own, carrying the life-giving blood and oxygen.

The second way the damaged heart tries to meet its needs

is through increased arterial flow. Not all medical opinion holds that arteries, once clogged, can never become unclogged. Scientific research has not yet established beyond question that the clogging substances will dissolve naturally. But what has been established is that even a little widening or clearing will accommodate a disproportionately larger blood flow. Some cardiologists believe that a course of action that does not add to the clogging will produce some shrinkage—enough, at least, to make possible such enhanced circulation.

Neither of those two processes is automatic. The ability of the heart to function in these ways does not become manifest under ordinary circumstances. Sometimes, indeed, the effects of blockage are so pervasive that surgical bypass is absolutely required to save a life. But a stern and unyielding regimen combining diet, exercise, and positive attitudes with the natural drive of the body to heal and regenerate can sometimes produce amazing results. So long as progress in this direction is discernible, it is reasonable to try to extend it as far as it will go. It is like the case of the stalled car that needs a push to give it enough momentum so that the gears, when engaged, can start the engine.

As I said earlier, I was extremely reluctant to undergo heart surgery; I wanted to see whether significant improvement was possible without it. If such improvement had not taken place, I would have accepted the option of surgery. The course I pursued was not an easy one; it should not be adopted by anyone who is not prepared to accept its highly disciplined requirements. Nor does my experience mean that what I did would necessarily work just as well for others.

The belief that illness is something that comes into us from the outside—a sort of hostile organism or substance that gains entry—is so firmly ingrained in us that we naturally look to available outside forces to do battle with it and evict it. Since we are attacked from without we tend to believe we can be rescued only from without. We have little knowledge of, and therefore little confidence in, the numberless ways the human body goes about righting itself. The absence of such knowledge leads not only to excessive dependence on external agencies but also to undue fears and even panic, which interfere with the proper functioning of the restorative mechanisms.

The role of the physician needs to be properly understood. The physician is best qualified to determine what is wrong and to intervene to whatever extent is necessary. In doing so, however, he combines his resources with the resources of the patient.

Dr. Ingelfinger, the late editor of the *New England Journal of Medicine,* wrote that about 85 percent of the patients the physician is called upon to treat have self-limiting illnesses. That is, the human body is equipped to meet most of its own health problems. The doctor's job is to distinguish between the 85 percent that don't really need his ministrations and the 15 percent that do. The physician must then decide exactly what is required to reassure the 85 percent and to mobilize his knowledge and skills in dealing with the 15 percent.

In any case, a distinction must be made between the treating process and the healing process. The treating process seeks to do that which the body itself may be incapable of doing, but at the same time attempts, to the fullest possible extent, to restore the body's own healing capabilities. The notion that the center of the healing process is lodged with the physician is incorrect. It is lodged within the individual, and the wise physician knows how to summon and release it. The individual cannot expect to be relieved of all responsibility in the recovery effort. If he looks completely outside himself for help, he places an unreasonably large part of the burden on the physician and may retard his own recovery to that extent.

What can the individual do? First of all, it is important to be aware of the body's natural drive to heal itself, once freed of the provocations that played a part in bringing on the illness. If a person has a heart attack, for example, the first order of business is to attempt to perceive possible connections between that heart attack and the precipitating causes. If, as in my case, I was engaged in a losing war against congested highways, airport mazes, delayed check-ins, overbooked planes, lost luggage, and late lecture arrivals, it was up to me to tame the schedule and make the necessary adjustments. Also, if my body craved exercise it was not receiving, only I was in a position to satisfy that want. And if my physical nourishment had to be augmented with nutrients for the mind, including joyous thoughts and experiences, I could not expect others to meet those needs for me.

Each individual presides over the totality of himself or herself. Assuming life is worth living—and the act of reaching out for medical help is proof positive that we think it is—it is imperative that we take on that part of the battle that is uniquely ours. It is a serious error to think of medical treatment as a total answer to all the problems of illness. In the end, the war against serious illness calls not only for expert medical attention but also for a summoning of values. Victory may not always be possible—if it were, we would all live forever—but it is sometimes within reach even in cases when the conventional wisdom holds the opposite.

It is in this sense that we retain control—recognizing the existence of resources represented by the healing system and the belief system that activates it. And the belief system is not just a collection of mechanical parts but a confluence of values and attitudes—hope, faith, confidence, purpose, will to live, and a capacity for joyous living.

Few of us will pass through this lifetime without the challenge of one or more serious illnesses. We need not feel angry or guilty when that illness occurs, nor is it reasonable to expect that recovery is always within easy reach. But we have the obligation to ourselves and those we love not to invite defeat by being defeatist.

If it is true that nothing is more striking about how the human body functions than its regenerative drive, it is also true that the regenerative drive works better under some circumstances than others. What we think, what we believe, what we eat, and what we do with our bodies are all involved in the circumstances of regeneration.

If it is important to avoid a sense of defeat, it is equally important to avoid a sense of guilt when progress or recovery may not be possible. Although we want to be able to mobilize all the resources inside us and make the fullest use of the resources outside us, there are times when disease cannot be reversed. We need not feel, at such times, that we have somehow failed, or that our faith and hope were insufficient to our requirements. Nor need we feel that personal adequacy or character is measured only by the ability to prevail.

The ultimate truth about life is that it is transient. We have a certain margin for the pursuit of our aims; we have powerful natural assets in the form of the will to live and a joyous response to life. These assets serve us well and help us to make the most out of ourselves; but they are not eternal elixirs. To feel despair or guilt because we may not always be successful in overcoming illness is to put ourselves above the basic laws of life.

We are not capable of banishing death. The final triumph is beyond us. But we are entitled to the fullest measure of help the world has to offer, just as those who are close to us are entitled to feel that we ourselves have offered the best within us. Death becomes tragic only when we have allowed things to die inside us that give meaning to life.

Even when the verdict is certain, we are not barred from the exercise of powers that rarely come into play at other times. I think of Hans Zinsser, the physician-philosopher, stricken with incurable illness, writing about the wide range of new perceptions that enabled him to sense and see things he had never sensed or seen before. His book *As I Remember Him* is a tribute not just to the man but to the uniqueness of human life.

"My mind is more alive and vivid than ever before," he wrote during his illness in a passage remarkably similar to L. E. Trombley's observations quoted earlier in this book. "My sensitivities are keener; my affections stronger. I seem for the first time to see the world in clear perspective. I love people more deeply and comprehensively. I seem to be just beginning to learn my business and see my work in its proper relationship to science as a whole. I seem to myself to have entered into a period of stronger feelings and saner understanding."

Zinsser made an important discovery about life—the way time can be transformed into energy. Time is the most important capital we own. We can lose great fortunes, and, if we are lucky, we may be able to regain them. But time is the only source of wealth which, once spent, can never be regained. There is only a finite amount of it for every person. "Ask me for anything," Napoleon is supposed to have said at the height of his power, "and I will be able to give it to you. Anything, that is, except time."

The way we choose to live and the depth of our feelings, our ability to love and be loved and to take in all the colors of the world around us—these determine the worth and true extent of whatever time we have. The clock keeps ticking away. Our job is to put as much meaning as possible into the intervals between the ticks. A minute can open out into a vast realm in which all our senses, finely attuned, can come into full and splendid play—or those same senses can be shut down, imparting nothing to our years except numbers.

What makes time so valuable is that it is convertible into nourishing memory. Memory is where the proof of life is stored. It offers material for stock-taking and provides clues about where our lives are going. Serious illness can be redemptive if it opens the sluices of vital memory, sharpens the focus, transforms the improbable into the possible, and imparts a quality of high art to the gift of time.

Summary

One of my main purposes in joining the faculty of a medical school was to try to find an answer to a question that had arisen out of an illness some years earlier: Is there any scientific basis for the belief that the positive emotions—hope, faith, love, laughter, will to live—have salutary effects on the body's chemistry and functions?

Within two years, a second and related question arose as the result of a heart attack: Is the human body capable of more than one titanic regenerative effort in one lifetime?

These two questions are related in my case because the positive emotions were a central feature of the recovery program following both a collagen disease in 1964 and a heart attack in 1980.

I believe there are affirmative answers to both questions.

As for the first question: as sometimes happens, the answer was right under my nose. I had been looking for it in the wrong place—in laboratory experiments involving elaborate studies of biochemical changes under varying emotional states. Such studies offered interesting clues, but they were not definitive, because of the difficulty in finding subjects whose individual differences would not skew the results in double-blind studies, and because of the wide range of emotional intensities. A key part of the answer was to be found in what was already known about the biochemical effects of the negative emotions. The medical literature was replete with data showing that panic, fear, suppressed rage, exasperation, frustration, and depression all levied a fearsome toll on human physiology. People became ill as the result of such negative forces. Hormonal flow would be affected. Heart functions would be altered. Blood vessels would be constricted.

The self-evident answer was to be found in the fact that positive emotions can block the panic, foreboding, and depression that do such damage, inviting illness or intensifying it. Any antidotes to these emotional states have biochemical and physiological significance and value. The positive emotions, therefore, serve a specific and definite purpose in protecting the human body both in illness and in health.

Blocking agents play a major role in medications. Some are designed to protect the heart against biochemical activity that may produce erratic rhythms. Others are designed to intercept severe pain in joints and muscles. Still others seek to modify the chemistry of the brain in mental illness. Such blocking medications are considered to have a therapeutic effect. The same is true of the positive emotions in their blocking actions against the effects of panic, foreboding, or depression. It is the bullet-proof vest that protects us against the effects of emotional assaults.

With respect to the second question: Essentially the same

strategy was used in overcoming a heart attack as was used years earlier in combating a collagen illness. More than two years after the attack, there is no evidence of abnormal rhythm or cardiac insufficiency.

Obviously, the regenerative capacities of human beings are limited. If they were not, we would probably discover the secret of immortality. Fortunately, no one knows enough to identify those limits. Since this is so, we are justified in putting the regenerative principles to the test time and again.

Several times, during the course of writing this book, I have tried to emphasize that I am not attempting to propose or suggest universal prescriptions. What worked for me might not work for others. But I must not push that caveat too far. Some things I have experienced may be of general value. In particular:

First, conquest of panic is an essential part of any recovery program from a serious disease. There is the tendency, especially if illness if prolonged, to expect the worst. Confidence, deep purpose, joyousness, laughter, and the will to live are good conditioning agents and their value should never be underestimated. At the very least, they increase the value of the medical treatment we receive.

Second, the body's drive to recuperate may not work under all circumstances but it works often enough to warrant one's confidence and special effort.

Third, a sharing of responsibility with one's physician is in the best interests of both physician and patient. The physician brings his or her trained knowledge; the patient brings a healing system that needs to be freed to do its job.

Fourth, there are times when intervention in the form of medicine or surgery is absolutely necessary but there is never a time when the nourishment one puts into one's body or one's mind are not essential to health.

Fifth, as it concerns heart attacks or coronary disease in general: Surgical bypass procedures may sometimes be required to save one's life, but a second or third opinion on this point need not be regarded as lack of confidence in the physician who made the original recommendation. The heart is capable in many cases of making its own bypass. Whether it can function in this manner in a specific case calls for the greatest wisdom accessible.

Sixth, medical treatment should seek not just to repair damage and restore vital balances but to enhance the quality of life and to help the patient overcome feelings of hopelessness and helplessness. If the physician is to be fully effective in these directions, the patient must be a responsive and appreciative partner.

Epilogue

Irony and Anomaly

In reflecting on my experiences inside the medical
community, I have pondered the irony that we have health
institutions and research centers for every purpose except
the well-being of society itself. On a personal level, I take
note of the fact that I have written a dozen or so books
over the years on the ills of nations. All of them combined
did not get the response that the account of a personal bout
with illness received.

I am not complaining, nor do I mean to suggest that
individual health is not as important as we make it out to
be. What concerns me is that everyone's health—including
that of the next generation—may depend more on the
health of society and the healing of nations than on the
conquest of disease.

Let me digress.

When I was 11 or 12, I had a friend whose father was a
physician. Sometimes, when the doctor was off making

house calls, we would steal into his library and go rummaging through medical books. As you might imagine, the volumes with the greatest appeal for us were the ones with the most explicit anatomical illustrations. The most memorable of these books was entitled *Anomalies and Curiosities of Medicine*. More than half a century later, I still have vivid recollections of this bulging brown book in its frayed binding. It was copiously illustrated with line drawings of nature's mistakes—a catalogue of freakish biological events that P. T. Barnum might have found useful in recruiting for his sideshows.

Those illustrations stick in the mind. Among them, I recall a two-headed infant, a young woman with three breasts, a boy of 10 who weighed 275 pounds, a man with six toes on one foot and four on the other, a nude female dwarf with a beard that stretched below the waist, and a man with teeth protruding from his chin. And so the ghastly gallery went. It was just the sort of display to kindle the macabre imagination of young boys.

Today, the most serious anomalies of medicine are chargeable to society itself. I refer to hazards and threats to human health and safety to which society is indifferent or acquiescent. These hazards are the result of policies and practices that may not produce actual freaks but have a freakish effect on lives and values. And the effect on the medical profession may be the most anomalous of all, for the physician is expected to preside over human junk heaps created by society's aberrant notions and failures. It is difficult enough to attend to the ravages of disease that occur in the natural processes of living without having to contend with society's own misdeeds or defaults.

Perhaps the most obvious, but by no means most severe, example of such failures is the permission that society gives to those who manufacture and sell handguns and other killing devices. This grim indulgence results in death or serious injury each year to thousands of persons. The physician is not involved in the authorization to make or distribute these weapons but is obligated to provide medical care for the casualties they produce.

An equally obvious anomaly is society's attitude toward automobile and highway safety. The physician is given no major role in setting standards for automobiles or highways, but he becomes society's main recourse when those policies result in human wreckage. The hospital emergency room, just in terms of twisted human forms extricated from crumpled automobiles, looks like an appendix to the drawings in *Anomalies and Curiosities of Medicine*.

At the turn of the 20th century, the principal causes of death for American children were tuberculosis, diphtheria, smallpox, and poliomyelitis. These diseases have been largely conquered by medical science. They have been replaced, however, by man-made agents of death and disability in the form of handguns and motor vehicles. The causes are known. The effects are clearly visible and just as clearly felt. But society has yet to act on the connection between cause and effect in a major area of its responsibility.

In the catalogue of contemporary medical anomalies, consider also society's stamp of approval on legal brain battering, publicly deodorized by the name "prizefighting." The human brain is the most exquisitely fashioned, fragile, and complex mechanism in the universe. Nature has encased this delicate mechanism in a thick protective covering. But nature's design is easily foiled. Any hard instrument—whether a club or a metal rod or a human fist—can produce enough force to damage the tender tissues inside the shell. In prizefighting, the human fist is taped and padded, a procedure that offers more protection to the hand of the attacker than to the head of the attacked.

The people who derive pleasure from witnessing these legalized assaults experience their peak of satisfaction when one of the participants is battered into unconsciousness, generally the result of burst blood vessels inside the brain. Society pays a penny to the civilized conscience by engaging physicians to sit in attendance during these human combats, but the physician has no way of preventing or reversing the brain hemorrhages that provide the supreme moment of public excitement and elation. If the word "anomaly" does not fit here, any other term will do, but it will not restore damaged brain tissue or bring Mr. Duk Koo Kim back to life.

We climb the ladder of anomalies where even greater defaults of society come into view. Begin with the subsidies given by government to those who grow poisonous plants that cause serious disease. The same government that announces that cigarette smoking and cancer are closely related gives money to encourage farmers to produce the crops that produce the cancer. Even more bizarre is the appropriation of taxpayers' money to promote the sale of American cigarettes throughout the world. Thus American citizens are put by their government in the position of underwriting the spread of malignancies within and without their borders. To be sure, the process is filtered, like the nicotine itself, through slogans of self-interest.

In the same category, we can ponder the fact that manufacturers of lethal sprays and insecticides who are not licensed to sell these poisonous chemicals within the United States have no difficulty in receiving a license from the U.S. government to sell their products to peoples in other countries. Questions of responsibility and morality apparently decrease in validity and vitality with distance.

At the top rung of the ladder, we can observe the anomalous and combustible way nations conduct their affairs with one another. Within their borders, nations have legislative bodies, courts, and enforcement facilities—all based on defined standards of behavior for the citizens. Laws exist for the purpose of setting limits to misconduct or evil, with penalties for violations. Yet, in the international arena, each nation acts on its own. The principal instruments of force are in the hands not of law-enforcement agencies but of the military. Thus we share with all the other people in the world not just a common humanity but a common anarchy.

Nothing in history or human experience is more terrifying than the fact that breakdowns among nations produce more death and disease than any other combination of causes on earth. The conclusion is inescapable that the main threat today to the health of the human population on this planet is the foreign policies of the governments. Those policies in the aggregate are anarchic, unworkable, primitive, volatile, and pathological. They represent the ultimate betrayal of the people the nations are supposed to protect. Indeed, the most important fact of life in the 20th century is that nations are no longer capable of performing their historic functions. The nation was invented for the purpose of protecting the lives, values, and property of its citizens. But no nation is able today to carry out that function. Total power leads to total vulnerability. When the means of warfare reach their zenith, war becomes an exercise in mutual annihilation, a sort of national Jonestown, a forced parade of entire populations to the edge of the cliff and beyond.

As evidence, consider what society is doing to counteract the efforts of medical researchers who are searching for
new and more efficient ways of combating disease. The
governments operate laboratories in which scientists are
working to create new strains of disease organisms, far
beyond the reach of any known antibiotics or other medical defense. The fact that these bacteriological organisms
would be used only against an enemy is supposed to sanc-
tify the process.

If individuals were to involve themselves in the attempt
to invent new epidemics, they would be regarded as mon-
sters and would be put away. But governments may engage
in this madness and all is quiet.

Perhaps the quintessential symbol of society's anomalies
is the neutron bomb. The distinctive feature of this weapon
is that it will expunge life but spare property. It does,
however, have this virtue: it is an open autobiographical
statement. It is a confession of values. It identifies the hierarchy of things society believes are worth saving: the inan-
imate ahead of the animate, property ahead of people. The
MX missile presents the same melancholy prospect. The
MX missiles will be theoretically secure from destruction,
but people in the cities will be exposed and vulnerable.

In the same order of destructive efficiency and horror is
EMP—the electromagnetic pulse. Very little has been said
about this particular weapons development, a fact that in
itself should be of major concern. What is of primary significance is that it has been described in the magazine *Science 83,* published by the American Association for the
Advancement of Science, as potentially the most awesome
weapon of all.

Weapons technology not only enjoys survival priority
over humans; it is also clothed in semantic splendor. Words

like "smart," "brilliant," and "sophisticated" are now attached to computerized electronic devices that can penetrate the most ingenious defenses and deliver their apocalyptic cargoes. Marvs, mirvs, lasers, and cruise missiles all belong to the same elaborate and redundant inventory. Alongside these devices, human beings become puny, irrelevant, and incidental. The rationale for the development of these weapons is that the enemy is making them. And if the enemy is not already making them, it is said, he soon will.

The strongest argument in behalf of massive military spending is that the other side is spending at least as much or more. No one stops to inquire whether the other side may be spending its money wisely or whether, indeed, our own spending has anything to do with genuine safety. It is almost as though we can preserve our "manhood" only by superior foolishness.

Thus the greatest anomaly of all in our time is the imitation of madness. Society has devised a phrase that stifles the moral indignation, paralyzes the rational intelligence, and produces unreasoning acquiescence. The phrase is "national security." It is not necessary for those who invoke this magical phrase to demonstrate exactly how the national security will be served by any of the cataclysmic terrors that now inhabit the arsenals. All that is necessary is to point to the Russians. And, in this world of mirror images, all that is necessary for the Russians is to point to the Americans. The madness is reciprocal, inexorable, inexcusable.

By making sheer force the ultimate value, we have become its prisoner. By equating the national security with total power, we have become more insecure than ever before. By tying our freedom and historical values to the accumulation of cataclysmic explosives, we have ignored the need to develop the world institutions that alone can deal with basic problems of war and peace. By putting a large part of our natural resources at the disposal of the military, we have made the weapons industry the architect and arbiter of much of our foreign policy.

We have in fact become a welfare state, but the beneficiaries are not the poor or the dispossessed or the sick; the prime beneficiaries are the makers and sellers of the weapons, those who, to paraphrase President Eisenhower, are becoming a controlling factor in the society. Very little attention is paid to the reports of the Government Accounting Office documenting the waste, mismanagement, misspending, and fraud in the military budget. Meanwhile, in the name of economy and efficiency, the sums of money spent for education and for the care of the ill and the elderly have been heavily reduced.

Of all the anomalies, of course, none is more bizarre than the government's reassurance that the American people could survive a nuclear war. In offering this assurance, the government does not identify its assumptions. It does not tell us how many bombs the enemy will drop on what cities, or what the power of each bomb will be. Is it talking about kilotons or megatons? Is it talking about a token attack or about radioactive firestorms that will devour the cities and convert the air-raid shelters into human incinerators? The military spokesmen who seek to provide the reassurances have not answered those questions. The truth is that they do not know. The only thing we know is that those who give the appearance of being least concerned about the use of ultimate force are the ones who have access to the triggers. We have not announced to the Russians how many atomic warheads we will drop on their cities. Are the Russians going to tell us? We need drop only a small fraction of the bombs we now possess in order to achieve not just total destruction but total pulverization.

Is the same species of reasoning behind the further assurance that the cities can be evacuated and that the people in the large population centers can be moved to zones of safety 50 or 100 miles away? Are we to assume that, despite a nuclear attack, the routes to the highways and the highways themselves will be undamaged, accessible, and traversable; that accidents and breakdowns will not cause tie-ups; that gasoline-station operators will remain sacrificially at their posts in order to accommodate those whose cars are low on fuel; that people will know exactly where to go and what to do, if they should get there; and that other people will be waiting to serve them when they arrive?

Inevitably, anomaly culminates in irony, for the massive buildup of weaponry and the elaborate planning behind it rest not on military but on psychological strategy. The rationale for our vast military program, costing trillions of dollars, is that it will have a deterrent effect on decision making by the Soviet Union. It is not claimed that we can intercept attacking missiles with thermonuclear warheads; what is contended is that we can make the Soviet Union think one way rather than another.

This means that all our military planning and preparations rest on a psychological base. But a fundamental rule of psychology is not to attempt to persuade others with arguments that are not persuasive to ourselves. The policymakers in the United States are not impressed by statements made by Soviet strategists pointing to their possession of obliterative force. Quite the contrary; any pronouncements by Soviet leaders calling attention to their military power serve only to spur us on to even higher buildups of our own.

Another fundamental rule in psychology is to avoid confusion. At the same time that we are trying to get the Soviet leaders to think it would be unprofitable for them to strike first, in view of our own overwhelming and certain retaliatory capacity, we are renouncing any policy based on not hitting first ourselves. The reason previous American presidents emphasized that we would not be the first to start a nuclear war was that the failure to do so could produce nervous nuclear trigger fingers elsewhere. In reversing the policy that rejected a first strike, the government now undermines the very sense of restraint we say we want to foster in Moscow. If the Soviet Union were to announce that it would not consider itself bound by a no-first-strike pledge, we would probably feel we had no choice except to hit first ourselves, whatever the risk or the consequences. Do not, said Aristotle in his essay on logic, do not expect the next person to be influenced by an argument you would reject yourself.

If the defense of the American people is going to be tied to psychological strategies, then the least we should do is bring in professional psychologists instead of committing the national future to men who talk and act like hunch players. Quite possibly, professional psychologists would advise us that our most effective approach would be to pursue a policy toward the Soviet Union based on common dangers and common needs rather than on castigation and ultimatum. The only thing we know for certain about the Russians is that they will be governed by their self-interest. This is what the American people and the Russian people have most in common.

The overriding issue confronting both peoples is the need

to avoid a mutual nuclear convulsion. Good sense tells us that this will not be accomplished by mutual threats or by increasing the horrors that would inevitably produce the convulsion. Good sense should tell us that this common danger will be reduced only by our moving resolutely toward three objectives. First, control of the weapons. Second, control of tensions that could set the stage for their use. Third, the creation of world institutions that can define the obligations of nations to one another and create the legal mechanisms for dealing with basic causes of war.

The question is not whether the Russians will accept. It is whether we are prepared to propose. The advocacy of ideas that serve the human condition may in fact be the only true source of our own security, for what we need is not just the concurrence of the Soviet Union but a world consensus based on a plan for making our planet safe and fit for human habitation.

We cannot expect to dispose of armaments until we have a plan for the common safety. Such a plan is not shrouded in mystery. It must seek to end world anarchy and to develop instruments of law. The only ideology that is favored under that course is one that respects and understands the right of each nation to its own institutions and values, and that understands the need of nations to accept a clearly defined code of obligations to one another under constituted law.

The language of power, especially nuclear power, is no longer consonant with the meaning of freedom, for power not only corrupts, as Lord Acton observed; it also devours. It devours resources, both physical and human. The only thing that stands against it is the free mind.

In the end, our freedom and safety are tied to the fullest possible exercise of the free mind. We have to explore, as

Madison and Hamilton were able to explore, the principles that make governance and peace possible among large collective units.

The health and well-being not just of Americans but of the human race are incompatible with war and preparations for war. The conquest of war, therefore, must become our grand preoccupation and magnificent obsession.

Afterwords

1. By K. I. Shine, M.D.

Norman Cousins has made important contributions to our notions of the patient's role in health and disease. Central to these is a reaffirmation of the pivotal responsibility that the patient should and must take in the partnership with his physician. During hospitalization for his heart attack, Norman commented that, if it requires 20 points to win the game, the physician should bring 10 and the patient should bring 10 in order to achieve victory. The number of points each player contributes may vary, but the principle is a sound one. Norman emphasizes an integrated approach to the well-being of the patient. This holistic attitude is not new to medicine, but it requires cultivation and nourishment if it is to achieve its ultimate fruition in health care today. Finally, Norman describes the ways in which to deal with anxiety, uncertainty, doctors, and data. He recognizes that these coping mechanisms may be quite appropriate for him, but not necessarily for all other patients or their physicians.

The concept of a therapeutic alliance has long been understood by psychiatry as an essential element in the successful confrontation of psychiatric or psychological disorders. Much less emphasis has been placed in other branches of medicine on the unique contribution that the patient can make to his own care. The ability to enlist a patient in a program of proper nutrition, exercise, cessation of smoking, and related healthful activities necessitates this kind of commitment from the patient. It also requires that the physician be skillful enough to accommodate the physiological goals of a program to the particular interest of the patient. In many forms of chronic health maintenance the patient can play a practical as well as symbolic role. For example, the effective management of high blood pressure is facilitated when the patient records his or her own blood pressure. Exercise can be effectively monitored when the patient determines the heart rate.

During acute illness, the experienced clinician attempts to adapt his management to the particular needs of the patient. Unfortunately, this is not always done nor does the organization of health care itself facilitate it. Until the late 1960's the treatment of heart attacks included an obligatory three-week hospitalization during which the patient spent a week or 10 days in bed, completely immobile, fed by nurses and family, and afraid that any movement, activity, or emotion was likely to precipitate his death. Such a program of immobilization was physiologically not sensible, and, equally important, it removed from the patient any sense of control over his body or his environment, thereby producing enormous stress and anxiety. Fortunately, the care of heart-attack victims has improved so that now efforts are made to mobilize patients earlier. The patient is encouraged to assert more control over his person and increasingly to adapt the technology to personal needs. It should be emphasized, however, that there are also patients who wish to delegate to nurses and physicians all of the duties related to their health during acute illness. Successful management requires a gradual education of the patient and his family so that the patient's role in his own care can evolve and mature during the hospitalization and after discharge from the hospital.

The wise physician must know the patient and individualize care. I once participated in the care of the president of a South American country who reigned there almost as a complete dictator. He could deal with complex political, social, and economic problems, including an occasional rattling of sabers by the military, without bringing on chest pain from his coronary disease, whereas confronting his son over the latter's career predictably produced chest pain. Medical management required that this patient know how to use nitroglycerin prophylactically before any confrontation with his son.

Physicians generalize from their own experience and the medical literature to the case of the individual patient. Learning the lessons taught by the last 100 patients should improve the chances of recovery for the next 100 patients. The difficulty arises, however, when one realizes that this is a numbers game. Consider Norman's experience on the treadmill after his acute myocardial infarction. Among groups of patients described in a number of major medical centers throughout the country, those patients who developed significant EKG changes, chest pain, and blood-pressure declines during exercise had a 35 to 40 percent risk of a serious catastrophe in the first year after the heart attack. Catastrophes included sudden death and recurrent heart

attacks. Among these abnormal responders one can further sharpen the prognosis by doing a coronary angiogram. The angiogram will then reveal certain individuals
among those with abnormal responses who are at very low
risk for a serious problem. There will also be patients who
are at a very high risk and for whom cardiac surgery may
be appropriate.

I first learned about Norman Cousins's heart attack when
the paramedics were bringing him into the emergency
room at UCLA Hospital. It was an interesting encounter.
He was quite short of breath, sweaty, and obviously
uncomfortable, but he was also remarkably in control of
the situation. As soon as he had been put into a bed, he
accepted oxygen, and the EKG monitors were hooked up
to him so that one could follow his heart rhythm. His blood
pressure was taken. But as soon as the question of medication came up, Norman suddenly started asking questions. I was really rather concerned about him. He had
fluid in his lungs and looked very ill. One of the principal
medications prescribed under those circumstances is morphine. Norman refused to let the nurse administer the drug.
I asked him about it. His immediate response was that he
felt that his own endorphins could probably do the job. I
told him that I had to do something to improve his circulation and that I wanted to administer nitroglycerin. This
he accepted. I first gave it to him under the tongue, in
increasing doses. It appeared to have a beneficial effect.
Then he took it as a paste on the skin. It was interesting
that the nitroglycerin seemed to be very helpful in controlling the congestion. It remained to be seen, whether
his own endorphins also helped, but his situation improved
significantly.

I must admit that it was an unusual experience for me to

confront someone who, although severely ill, was clearly determined to control the kind of medication he received.

There was a great deal of concern about Norman. We couldn't give the kind of treatment we usually give in such cases. As with the morphine, Norman was hesitant when we wanted to give him a diuretic. He preferred to discuss this matter with me directly rather than with the medical interns or residents. There is no question that it was time-consuming and to a certain extent frustrating, but at the same time he taught us a great deal. As the staff watched his case evolve, and as they developed a closer relationship with him, they began to get insights they would not have gotten otherwise.

Norman's heart attack was fairly severe. Not everyone with a heart attack has heart failure (or fluid in the lungs). The electrocardiographic and enzyme changes all indicated a very significant heart attack. Before he left the hospital, we did an exercise test on him, and that made us very concerned, because instead of having an increase in blood pressure, which one would expect from exercise, he had had a decrease. That was a finding of considerable seriousness, and I so informed him. In fact, I recommended to him that he take an angiogram, an X ray of the blood vessels supplying the heart. I felt that he was still in jeopardy and that there were risks associated with future damage. That has been the source of a continuing dialogue between us ever since.

Norman rejected a coronary angiogram. Fortunately, the result so far has been satisfactory, but the implications of this decision should still be considered. First, it deprived his physicians and Norman of knowing relatively early in his course whether he was in a very high risk group for serious complications after his heart attack. As a result both he and his physicians proceeded with a degree of uncertainty which was not necessary. Does it make sense to try to beat the odds in this kind of situation, if the odds include a high possibility of sudden death? Moreover, since we do not know the details of Norman's coronary anatomy, it is impossible to generalize to other patients from his experience. Norman was willing to live with a high degree of uncertainty and to carry out a progressive and comprehensive program so that he could improve his cardiac function. He did so with the help and support of many of his friends and physicians. The longer he continues to do well, the better the prognosis for the future.

Complicating the matter, however, is the extent to which Norman's involvement in his own care limits the physician's ability to apply data obtained from his situation to those derived from other patients. For example, his concern about an exercise test was such that he requested control of the treadmill and background music. This was a very reasonable request and one that did not compromise the test, except to the degree that Norman individualized the test so as to limit its comparability to that of other patients. Indeed, Norman has never had a full-fledged exercise test done according to a protocol and to a level of activity that would allow one to draw inferences about prognosis in comparison to other coronary patients. This approach has been useful in Norman's management, but it would be difficult to develop similar data in 100 patients. This presents a dilemma for the physician. He must respect the patient's interest and desire to understand and participate in his or her care, and recognize that the patient has a great many personal resources to bring to the maintenance of health and the re-establishment of well-being. However, medical knowledge is advanced by the observation of how groups of patients respond to certain problems and therapies. On the basis of those results, therapies are discounted when they prove ineffective and extended when they appear to benefit a group. There are so many variables in biology that the conclusions arise from a group and not from a single patient. Yet each patient is an individual and must be treated as such. The physician must somehow work with the patient to balance these conflicting forces.

In Norman's case, I have agreed to live with a degree of medical uncertainty which makes me uncomfortable. I will feel deeply responsible if anything arising out of a cardiovascular cause should happen to Norman. But I cannot logically espouse the cause of patient involvement in his own care and then be unwilling to accept partial responsibility when the patient makes a decision in which I do not concur. The physician's responsibility is not truly fulfilled if he merely separates himself from the patient who disagrees with him.

It has not been easy for the physicians, interns, residents, and other medical staff to care for Norman Cousins during and after his illness. He forced many of us to do things in a way that differed from the previous way. This was sometimes irritating, time-consuming, and anxiety provoking. But we all learned something from the encounter. To the extent that Norman Cousins challenges the status quo, shakes our self-satisfaction, and gets both physicians and patients to examine their relationships to each other and to illness, we all gain.

Norman has done much reading and thinking about heart disease and its medical and surgical treatment. He knows a good deal about it. I think our biggest disagreements have arisen out of the notion that, from my point of view—

from the cardiologist's point of view—it would be preferable to proceed from a position where he and I both have a maximum amount of information about his risks and prognosis. Norman's position, as I understand it, is that he has enough personal faith in the healing capacity of his body and his mind to be convinced that, for him as an individual, time will allow that process to continue. I think, too, that he has great reservations about surgery. Norman has focused on the notion of control of his own self, of his being, and an angiogram and surgery represent for him the uncontrollable intrusion of medicine and technology into his body. That's not an unusual or unreasonable concern, provided it doesn't go against good judgment. Norman and I agree, emphatically so, that what worked for him will not necessarily work well for others. We also agree that the patient should take an increased measure of responsibility for a recovery program.

2. By David S. Cannom, M.D.

It is "much more important to know what sort of patient has a disease than to know what sort of disease a patient has." When Sir William Osler, the father of bedside medicine, made this comment, he anticipated the author of this book. I was called in to treat Norman Cousins early in 1981, following his heart attack. From the very start, I realized that the treatment had to fit a particular patient and not a particular disease.

Norman Cousins came to me for a second opinion and continuing care after he had been advised that he had substantial arterial blockage and that an angiogram was necessary. He was aware that the angiogram was an essential and probably inevitable prelude to bypass surgery. Since he had decided against the surgery, he felt there was little point in his taking the angiogram. His purpose in seeking a second opinion was to ascertain whether he was acting responsibly in substituting a rigorous program of rehabilitation for the surgery.

I looked at the hospital records and the findings of Dr. Kenneth Shine, one of the most eminent cardiologists in the nation and one of my colleagues at the UCLA School of Medicine. In view of the clinical evidence, I could readily understand Dr. Shine's apprehensions. The indications for arteriography were unequivocal. Yet, knowing something of Cousins's history and personal background, I could readily understand why the angiogram-surgery route was being resisted. I had to take into account not just the condition of his heart but his philosophy and personality. Having read his *Anatomy of an Illness,* I was aware that I was dealing with someone who could think objectively and clearly about his own case. He knew how to consult the relevant medical literature. He had been through other life-threatening situations and had come out of them physically and intellectually strengthened.

I supported him, therefore, in the decision not to take the angiogram. Yes, it would have furnished valuable information, but I was convinced that the price that might have to be paid for it was too high. An angiogram is a fairly innocuous procedure for those patients who put themselves completely in the hands of their physicians and exist in something akin to a state of suspended animation. But for some patients who have a keen sense of the integrity of their own bodies, an angiogram can be a serious and even precarious undertaking. In short, the risk factor varies with the patient.

In the angiogram, a tiny extension of an X-ray machine

is threaded through the veins directly into the heart. The patient is fully conscious; in fact, his active cooperation is an essential part of the procedure. The knowledge that one's heart is being penetrated can be not merely unsettling but potentially dangerous for sensitive persons who, as I said a moment ago, react to invasive medical procedures. Since the effect of a treadmill experience on Norman was psychologically adverse, I had to take into account the impact of a mechanical entry into his heart while he was fully conscious. That is why I was not disposed to press an angiogram on him, whatever the value of the information to be gained.

Dr. Shine tried to convince Norman of the need for an angiogram, but he dropped the matter when he realized that Norman's reasons, however subjective, deserved to be respected. I don't want to give the impression that Norman was trying to "run his own case." The main point of his *Anatomy of an Illness* was his belief that a working partnership between physician and patient was an essential element in any recovery program. The partnership concept as he saw it meant he would combine his deep respect for medical authority with his determination not to be the passive recipient of medical care. Applying this concept to our relationship, he wanted to see whether significant progress was possible without major surgery.

I couldn't blame him or anyone for wanting to make a careful decision in such matters. The fact of arterial blockage was incontestable. The prevailing view among cardiologists is that reversibility is very rare. Dr. Shine's recommendation therefore had the support of dominant medical experience. Yet I had in front of me not just the hospital charts but a human being who had a clear-cut plan of action designed to put his heart back in working order.

All he asked was that I monitor his progress under that plan. I could systematically check his progress or lack of it. If the plan didn't work, we still had the option of surgery.

As I listened, I realized that his program would take all the physical, intellectual, and spiritual resources any human being could muster. I didn't want to encourage anyone to run counter to established medical knowledge, but I quickly became aware that this patient probably knew his own body better than I did. His thoughtful reactions to the treadmill test; his initiative with respect to the Holter cardiograph test; his absence of panic at the time of the heart attack and since; his ability to ferret out solid information that had a bearing on his own case—all this seemed to me to be as significant as any of the clinical findings.

It is not necessary for me here to itemize all the elements of the program he put into effect. This book provides ample material on that subject. What I can say is that his progress, from the very start, was dramatic and measurable. After the first month or so, he received no medications. He came to see me regularly throughout 1981 and, less often, in 1982. As early as the second visit, his improvement was significant and verifiable.

During these visits, we spent at least as much time in exchanging views as in actual clinical examinations. I realized that what I had to offer was a philosophical ambience that was just as essential for this patient as any scientific ministrations. His interest in the workings of the heart became an integral part of the treatment.

I also came to recognize a strong interaction between the intellectual support I tried to give him and the main features of his program—long daily walks, good nutrition with a diet low in animal fats, life-style change away from

stress, high resolve, and robust good spirits. All these features are fully described in these pages.

When I say that his heart became demonstrably stronger
month by month, I don't want to give the impression that
he no longer has to be careful about it. His symptoms have
steadily diminished, but they have not disappeared altogether. Given the severity of the heart attack, it would
indeed be surprising if they had. Clinically, these symptoms take the form of what are known as "anginal equivalents." He does not have the typical pressure-like chest
pains. At times, he has a heaviness in the heart region
or a very uncomfortable and thick feeling in the throat.

It is interesting that these symptoms are not usually produced by his physical exertion but by anxiety and frustration. As he writes in this book, he is able to play hard
tennis singles. It is probably just as well that I am not there
to see it, for I should probably risk a heart attack myself
just to observe someone running at top speed who had
congestive heart failure only recently. Dr. Omar Fareed,
who sometimes plays with him, reports that Norman's
blood pressure during and following such strenuous exercise behaves beautifully and that his pulse rate returns to
normal reasonably soon after he leaves the tennis court.

What I find especially fascinating is his low tolerance for
exasperation or emotional tension and his high tolerance
for vigorous sports. These contrasting facts provide genuine substance for the ideas he has been expounding about
the glandular activity of the brain and the biochemistry of
the emotions. Since joining the medical faculty at UCLA,
he has occupied himself with studies on the brain's ability
to prescribe for the body under varying emotional states,
and also with the negative or inhibiting effects of stress on
this glandular activity.

Two examples from his own experience in the months following his heart attack come to mind. He was trapped in a taxicab by heavy traffic for more than an hour en route to the JFK airport in New York City. When he arrived at the terminal, he had only two or three minutes in which to rush from the curb to the gate, carrying his bags. The actual amount of physical exertion expended was probably only a fraction of what he would put into a set of singles at tennis, yet for several hours after the episode his heart made known its protest in the manner I described earlier.

On another occasion, as he writes in these pages, he had to give an evening lecture in Laguna Hills, California. It took place in a large auditorium, and the house was packed. Just as he started to speak, the electricity went off. The microphone and amplifying system went dead. The house was in total darkness except for a small emergency flashlight. He went ahead with the lecture for a full hour. On the way home, and for the rest of the night, he experienced symptoms. The next morning he went out on the tennis court.

The natural tendency for any patient, under those circumstances, would be to retreat, take to bed, become fearful, and summon a physician. I would not for a moment want to disparage such a rational response. In his case, however, I have to respect his insistence on "getting right back on the horse." Physical activity may actually be helpful for him. His entire being seems to flourish under circumstances of enjoyable exercise like tennis or golf. Such activity can actually be an antidote for symptoms produced by emotional stress.

In the absence of an angiogram picture of his heart and arteries, I cannot say whether a vasospasm had an important part in causing his heart attack. He himself was the first to raise this question about his own case. The phenomenon of coronary-artery spasm—actual phasic tightening or constriction of the coronary artery—has been discussed in the periodical literature on cardiology for a quarter of a century. The causal relationship between the emotions and spasm is not known. Norman's speculations on spasm, I must say, would be difficult to disprove. Certainly they do not contradict anything that is familiar to me in the literature. In this light, his rationale for avoiding bypass surgery cannot be dismissed out of hand.

In his 1982 commencement talk at the Baylor College of Medicine, he said that "one's confidence, or lack of it, in one's physician has a marked effect on the prospects for recovery." He spoke about the connection between the belief system and the healing system. He pointed to the fact that secretions controlled by the brain—for example, norepinephrine or prostaglandins—could have a constricting effect on the coronary arteries, causing heart symptoms or even a heart attack. Then he asked whether the positive emotions, by blocking the panic, might be therapeutic. There is strong supportive medical literature for such views.

Six months after his heart attack, he asked to return to the UCLA treadmill, with Dr. Shine present, to demonstrate not just his physical progress but the extent to which emotional factors could affect treadmill testing. He wanted to go on my treadmill as a sort of warmup. He proposed that he operate the treadmill controls himself. He came early to the laboratory with a tape recording machine and two cassettes—one containing a lovely Vivaldi composition: the other, a Woody Allen monologue. The results of the treadmill test showed a complete reversal from the treadmill experience at UCLA half a year earlier. The ominous changes on the cardiograph were now absent. There was no drop in blood pressure. An indisputable change had occured after half a year of the rehabilitation program.

Not all patients would benefit from running the tread-mill controls themselves. Some of them derive comfort from being completely in the hands of their physicians. But for certain patients—those who want to be deeply involved in the recovery program—I believe that Nor-man's protocol for treadmill testing might be highly use-ful. Just changing the atmosphere in the treadmill room—whether by transferring the controls to the patient or by using congenial music or comedy—may put the patient in a relaxed emotional state and thus offset the misleading effects of psychological factors.

As for his well-known emphasis on laughter and good spirits, I can testify that the impact on the physician is hardly less auspicious than that on the patient. Our time together has been an alliance emphasizing communication and optimism. I shared his concerns, exalted in his triumphs, warmed at his good humor, roared at his jokes, and mourned his losses. I was made to feel that he respected my counsel and encouragement—while I, in turn, mar-veled at the intelligence and high spirits he brought to his fight against serious heart disease.

No cardiologist can say, given the massiveness of the heart attack, that he is no longer at risk from another attack or even sudden death. What I do know is that he functions superbly in every way that is vital to him and that, to quote one of the key lines in his book, he is getting the most and the best out of whatever may be possible.

I have profited from this experience and shared it with patients who need to believe that their spiritual resources may be as important as anything my special knowledge has to offer. His story proves that the individual heart patient need not be psychologically crippled and that the patient's own attitudes and life-style can be integral and powerful parts of a recovery program.

3. By Omar Fareed, M.D.

Imagine the scene in the emergency room of the UCLA Hospital. Dean Sherman Mellinkoff, of the UCLA School of Medicine, and several of the school's top cardiologists are awaiting the arrival by ambulance of a patient who has just had a heart attack. The telephoned report from the paramedics is alarming; it says that the patient is coughing up blood, an ominous indication of congestive heart failure.

The swinging doors to the emergency room open wide and a rolling stretcher comes through. The patient sits up, waves, grins, and says, "Gentlemen, I want you to know that you're looking at the darnedest healing machine that's ever been wheeled into this hospital."

This incident does more to epitomize Norman Cousins than anything else I might say. In that one scene you have the essence of the man's personality, philosophy of life, and approach to illness and healing. First of all, there is the absence of panic despite grave danger. Second, there is the confidence in the ability of the human body to fight back even under extreme circumstances of illness or injury. Third, there is the irrepressible good humor that creates an auspicious environment for both healing and treatment.

Concerning this last point: a patient's upbeat mood, when picked up by physicians and hospital personnel, works to the advantage of the patient. I don't think I am giving away any secrets of the medical profession when I say that many doctors, being human, find themselves, consciously or otherwise, drawn to those hospital rooms where patients are confident of their chances and are able to maintain their good spirits and good humor. Cheerfulness under difficult conditions is not easy to achieve. But, as this book vividly demonstrates, it can be a powerful factor in the healing process.

Both as physician and as personal friend, I have learned a great deal from the author. He has emphasized for me the importance of making patients feel that I take their own perceptions seriously. It is always possible that the physician may reach a wrong diagnosis or prescribe prematurely if the patient isn't given adequate opportunity to talk about his or her ideas of what is wrong and why. With respect to medications, I find that if I take the time to explain to patients that their illness is self-limiting (when such is the case, and it frequently is), they don't feel insecure or neglected if they leave without a prescription slip. They develop more confidence in themselves and are not disposed to believe the worst about their symptoms.

Norman has also reinforced for me the fact that one of the best investments a physician can make in the treatment of patients is to give them a share in the responsibility for getting well and staying well. Once patients understand that they possess a superb mechanism for combating illness, they have less of a tendency to look to the physician to monitor every aspect of their lives.

At this point, it may be useful to comment on the nature of my relationship with the author. We met in 1957 at the hospital of Dr. Albert Schweitzer in Lambaréné, in what was then French Equatorial Africa. I was there as a visiting physician in residence; each year I would serve at the hospital for varying lengths of time. Norman came at the invitation of Dr. Schweitzer, who wanted to talk to him about philosophical and political issues.

Out of those early meetings developed a close relationship with Norman that was strengthened as the result of various medical projects he helped to launch and direct. The project with which I had the closest connection was called ABC—Aid to Biafran Children. Stories in the news from Africa told of starvation conditions in the Biafran civil war. Norman arranged for on-the-spot medical treatment and distribution of food and medical supplies. He brought together a team of physicians and assistants. From the Los Angeles area, Dr. Davida Taylor Cody, Dr. Frank Catchpool, my wife Martha, my son George (himself a physician), and I participated in the program. We would go there in relays. We would drive the ABC jeep into the war-ravaged areas and set up our field clinic. Altogether, I suppose more than 150,000 children were treated for kwashiorkor (extreme debility produced by lack of protein). Norman, like the rest of us, flew into Biafra in the airlift, which was under fire much of the time.

Many times, in the course of carrying out this and other medical projects abroad, all sorts of obstacles developed that seriously threatened the program and filled some of us with despair. Having to cope with officialdom was probably the most onerous of these difficulties. But Norman's certainty of purpose, calm confidence, innovativeness, and robust good spirits were powerful factors in bringing those projects to successful conclusions. He informed himself fully about the medical problems involved in those projects. It was no surprise to me, therefore, that those same characteristics and approaches should have been in evidence during his own bouts with serious illness. I have no doubt that these qualities, and not just the expert medical treatment he received, were prime factors in his ability to overcome grave health problems.

It may be asked why I encouraged Norman in his belief that he could recover from his serious heart attack without surgery, even though all the indications supported a decision in its favor. The accuracy of the diagnosis was beyond question. The difference, perhaps, between Dr. Shine's position and mine was that I had the advantage over the years of having been close to Norman through other supposedly irreversible health situations. For example, in the years following a bout with collagen disease, when his hands, wrists, knees, and shoulders couldn't function properly, he would get out on the tennis court and make his body work for him. Being aware of the severe pain he must have been experiencing, I would suggest that he stop. He assured me that the pain was tolerable so long as he was enjoying himself. We didn't know it at the time, but his brain was probably releasing endorphins, the body's own painkilling secretions. It is interesting, as I look at it now, that he should have been the beneficiary of those secretions that later served as the basis of his work and studies at UCLA.

As recently as 1980, he was still serving underhand in tennis because he couldn't raise his arm above his shoulder. But he stayed with it, and the profound pleasure he experiences in vigorous competitive sports was an important factor in correcting that condition. Today, he is fully mobile and is as agile, swift, and physically well coordinated as a person half his age.

Dr. Shine has used the word "reconditioned" to describe what happened to Norman's heart by the end of the first year of his self-designed rehabilitation program. What to me is most interesting about that program is that he converted it into an intellectual adventure, a time of fun and fulfillment. Dr. Cannom, in his comments in this section, refers to the stern and spartan requirements of the program Norman set for himself. That observation is objectively correct, but I doubt that Norman regarded his program as harsh or even demanding. He had a wonderful time through it all. Our outings together on the track or golf course or tennis court were pure pleasure.

During this period of his recuperation he was able to pursue his photography, keep up with writing and reading, and have his friends sing around the piano or organ while he played. My main worry about him now is not that he is following too disciplined a program but that the fun part of his life is shrinking as the demands on his time increase. He turns down no request to see a patient. I doubt that any patient he has seen has not experienced a profound boost in determination and morale. He maintains a schedule that, while sharply reduced from what it was before his heart attack, is still staggering. Dr. Shine and Dr. Cannom are as concerned as I am that even his reconditioned heart may be inadequate to the burdens he now carries. But he has a philosophy of life I must respect. He wants to be able to use himself to the fullest. This helps to explain his commitment of many years to a healthy national and world society.

Inevitably, people who have heart problems will want to know what aspects of Norman's experience have meaning for them. They may contend that his work in medical fields for such a long time and his special access to medical knowledge give him an advantage most patients do not possess. Yet Norman's main ideas transcend that special station. All patients will find vital meaning in his message that serious illness tends to produce, quite naturally, attitudes of panic and defeat, which in themselves intensify disease. He contends, however, that the human brain, under circumstances of high determination and a powerful will to live, can produce secretions that enhance the body's immunological and recovery capabilities and provide an auspicious environment for the physician's treatments. He has articulated—and I know of no one who has done it better—the connection between the belief system and the healing system and their combined role in giving sub-stance to the patient-physician relationship.

I would certainly not recommend to anyone who is recovering from a heart attack that he or she plunge into violent athletics soon after leaving the hospital. But it is true, as the Canadian physician Terence Kavanagh has demonstrated, that people who have had heart attacks can be systematically trained to sustain exercise and take on physical work loads that are beyond the reach of people in average conditions. Norman's own experience supports this theory. It is important to correct the notion that any physical activity is bad for damaged hearts.

If I had to single out any one idea from this book that needs to be widely accepted, it is his belief that serious illness should be regarded as a challenge and not as a pro-nouncement of doom. It is a challenge that calls not just for the best medical care obtainable but for the best that the patient himself or herself has to offer. Confidence, the ability to be joyously involved in the world around oneself and to savor the good things in life, can be as important as medical treatment and can actually enhance the value of that treatment.

4. By William M. Hitzig, M.D.

After the publication of *Anatomy of an Illness,* some of the commentary appearing in the medical press was to the effect that Norman couldn't possibly have been as ill as the book indicated, for recovery in such cases is not supposed to be as complete as he has experienced. I have no doubt that similar comments will be voiced about his heart attack, from which he has made an even more remarkable recovery.

I confess that I myself find it difficult to believe that anyone who has been hit by a myocardial infarction and congestive heart failure could have come through the experience as he has done.

Early in the evening of December 22, 1980, I received a telephone call from Dr. Kenneth Shine in Los Angeles. He said he was calling me because he had been informed I had been Norman's family doctor for many years in the East. He said that Norman had been brought by ambulance to the UCLA Hospital and was in intensive care because of congestive heart failure and a myocardial infarction. The term "desperate" was used to describe his condition. I began to make plans to fly to Los Angeles. Norman was more to me than a patient; he was the closest of friends.

The next morning, I put through a call to the hospital. I spoke to the floor nurse, who said she would transfer my call to his bedside. In a few seconds, Norman was on the phone, his voice strong and cheery. Given the clinical findings, I thought it inconceivable that anyone in his condition would be strong enough to pick up the phone, let alone sound as coherent as he did. Over the years, I had treated hundreds of patients with heart attacks. Never had

I heard anyone sound so poised the morning after having been ambulanced into a hospital with congestive heart failure and lungs filled with fluid.

Let me try to reproduce the conversation as I remember it.

"Norman, are you sure it's all right for you to speak on the phone?"

"Of course, Bill. How are you?"

"Norman, I don't know what to say. Dr. Shine called me last night. I didn't think they would let you talk. Norman, you've got to take it easy. Do everything Dr. Shine tells you to do. Do you hear me?"

"Of course I hear you. You didn't tell me how you are."

"You shouldn't even be talking now," I said sternly. "For God's sake, don't do anything. No laughing, no spoofing. Don't even try to brush your own teeth. I'll talk to you tomorrow."

The next morning, I spoke to the resident physician, who brought me up to date. The enzyme count, measuring the amount of heart-muscle destruction, was very high. So was the MB fraction, another important indicator. There was confirmation of fluid in his lungs. He was coughing up blood. I could understand why I had been told his condition was "touch and go."

Shortly after I hung up, the phone rang. It was Norman.

"Just wanted you to know I made it through the night," he was saying. "Stop worrying."

"Norman, you really shouldn't be putting through any calls. Are you obeying Dr. Shine's orders? You've really got to do what he says. You can't run your own case this time. We know exactly what's wrong. You've had a heart attack and you need a complete rest. Let Dr. Shine run the case. Remember, you're no longer a general; you're only a buck private and you've got to take orders. Do you hear me?"

"Sure, Bill; now cheer up."

After we rang off, I tried to reconcile the strong, confident voice with his condition. Even now, more than two years later, I find it difficult to believe that anyone who was that ill could have sounded the way he did or could have made such a rapid improvement in those early days.

When I visited him at the UCLA Hospital a week or so after the heart attack, his room looked more like an editorial office than a hospital facility. He had a typewriter on a stand near his bedside. A table was littered with books and papers.

Norman was propped up in bed. He had lost weight and was pale. But when he began to talk, there was the old vibrancy in his voice. Just hearing him speak made me feel better. Again, I wondered how anyone who had suffered the kind of heart attack he experienced could be so strong and confident in manner. And again I thought back on my own long experience as a cardiologist and internist; I could find no parallel.

Five months later, I returned to Los Angeles for another visit. I came to the house and found him working with two patients whose physician felt they needed to be encouraged to believe they had a chance.

I listened to Norman as he spoke to the patients about their own role in the fight against disease and about the ability of the mind to create a congenial environment for the treatment by their physicians. He told them about biofeedback exercises he had learned at the Menninger Foundation. I had more than passing interest as I watched him lead the patients through autogenic exercises in which they increased the skin temperature of their hands. They were amazed to discover that they had this kind of control over their own bodies. He asked them to use these powers to fortify their confidence and to program themselves to get the most out of the treatment by their physicians.

He then extended the biofeedback to himself. I took his pulse and blood pressure. He was able through biofeedback to increase his pulse rate by at least 15 beats and then slow it down again as an act of will. I picked up a slight arrhythmia on my stethoscope; in two minutes he returned the rhythm to normal.

These abilities are remarkable, but they are not phenomenal. It is well known that people who have had autogenic training are able to control their pulse and blood pressure within a certain range. Norman believes these abilities can be put to good use in combating certain kinds of illness. He also deeply believes that willpower and human development are closely allied. He has strong feelings about human uniqueness and the way it can be put to work in health and illness.

Norman is convinced that the way one thinks about life has a great deal to do with one's capacities. The same philosophy in overcoming the illness he described in *Anatomy of an Illness* has worked for him again. His 1980 heart attack was even more serious than the illness from which he recovered in 1964, and his present recovery, I believe, is even more remarkable than the recovery from his previous illness. I have no doubt that qualities of mind and spirit were no less important than medical treatment in his extraordinary recuperation from the heart attack. And, as I said at the beginning of this commentary, I have no doubt that some of my colleagues will question whether the myocardial infarction and congestive heart failure really took place, in view of his excellent present condition.

His ideas about the importance of laughter and the other positive emotions are well known. What is not known is that these qualities in him go back many years and are not solely the product of the experience he wrote about in *Anatomy of an Illness*. I remember how, more than 20 years ago, he would accompany me on my rounds and cheer up my patients, getting them laughing with his stories. How they looked forward to his coming! I would join him in his laughter routines and think to myself that we would probably make a good vaudeville team.

At the *Saturday Review,* too, he infused the journal with his own spirit of responsible optimism and intelligent purpose. Under him, the *Saturday Review* was one of the most positive forces in our society. He left the magazine at the height of its powers and started a "new" career in medicine. I use quotation marks because he had always been deeply interested in medicine. I remember his urging me, some years before the scientific evidence came into general view, to cut down sharply on my use of my X-ray and fluoroscope machines and to shield myself properly.

Norman organized the project to bring to the United States for medical and surgical treatment a group of young women who had been disfigured or crippled by the atomic bombing of Hiroshima. I was proud to be involved in this project. The physicians and surgeons who took part in this program had no hesitation in bringing him into the medical decisions that had to be made.

Again, several years later, he organized a medical project to provide medical and surgical treatment for victims of Nazi medical experimentation. And again, I was proud to be identified with such a program. Here, too, he was able to steer the project to a successful completion despite many difficulties and complications.

When Norman moved to California in 1978, I, along with his other friends, felt a great loss. I had come to depend on the intellectual stimulation and good cheer he brought to our friendship. I enjoyed his spoofing. He had a wide range of foreign accents, and I would receive telephone calls from "visitors" to these shores who had the most bizarre array of symptoms one could imagine. I hate to admit how many times I was taken in by these amusing spoofs. But I relished them all.

The side of Norman that has commanded the most attention is his commitment to a world without war. The mayor of Hiroshima, Vatican officials, and Red Cross leaders are among those who have nominated him for a Nobel Peace Prize. Whether or not he ever receives one, he has done much good in this world.

Bibliography

In order to avoid encumbering the text with footnotes, I have attempted in some places to incorporate reference sources within the running text. In general, this book deals with the following:

varying emotional states as a cause of heart attacks and other serious illnesses;

the biochemistry of the negative emotions;

the role of the positive emotions in contributing to health and in overcoming disease;

the concept of the human brain as a gland;

life-style, exercise, and diet as factors in promoting recovery from heart disease;

factors affecting reversibility of blocked or clogged coronary arteries;

non-dietary factors affecting cholesterol levels;

atherosclerosis and coronary spasm;

problems posed by cardiac diagnostic testing;

efficacy of biofeedback techniques.

The following references are pertinent to these themes.

Ader, R., ed. *Psychoneuroimmunology.* New York: Academic Press, 1981.

Agras, W. S., M. Horne, and C. B. Taylor. "Expectations and the Blood-Pressure-Lowering Effects of Relaxation." *Psychosomatic Medicine* 44 (1982): 389–95.

Alexander, F. *Psychosomatic Medicine.* New York: W. W. Norton, 1950.

Alexander, G. H. "An Unexplained Death Coexistent with Death-Wishes." *Psychosomatic Medicine* 5 (1943): 188–94.

Barndt, R., et al. "Regression and Progression of Early Femoral Atherosclerosis in Treated Hyperlipoproteinemic Patients." *Annals of Internal Medicine* 86 (1977): 139–46.

Basta, L. L., et al. "Regression of Atherosclerotic Stenosing Lesions of the Renal Arteries and Spontaneous Cure of Systemic Hypertension through Arteries and Spontaneous Cure of Systemic Hypertension through Control of Hyperlipidemia." *American Journal of Medicine* 61 (1976): 420–23.

Bauer, J. "Sudden, Unexpected Death." *Postgraduate Medicine* 22 (1957): A34.

Beaglehole, R., et al. "Serum Cholesterol, Diet, and the Decline in Coronary Heart Disease Mortality." *Preventive Medicine* 8 (1979): 538–47.

Beisser, A. R. "Denial and Affirmation in Illness and Health." *American Journal of Psychiatry* 136 (1979): 1026–30.

Benson, H. *The Mind/Body Effect: How Behavioral Medicine Can Show You the Way to Better Health.* New York: Simon & Schuster, 1979.

Benson, H. *The Relaxation Response*. New York: Morrow, 1975.

Benson, H. "Systemic Hypertension and the Relaxation Response." *New England Journal of Medicine* (1977).

Benson, H., et al. "The Placebo Effect: A Neglected Asset in the Care of Patients." *Journal of the American Medical Association* 232 (1975): 1225–27.

Bernanos, G. *Underground grammarian,* December 1982.

Blankenhorn, D. H. "Reversibility of Latent Atherosclerosis." *Modern Concepts of Cardiovascular Disease* 47, no. 5 (1978): 79–84.

Bortz, W. Letter to *New England Journal of Medicine* 305 (1981): 466–67.

Braunwald, E. "Coronary Artery Spasm as a Cause of Myocardial Ischemia. *Journal of Laboratory Clinical Medicine* 97 (1981): 299–312.

Brod, J. "Psychological Influences on the Cardiovascular System." In *Modern Trends in Psychosomatic Medicine,* edited by O. W. Hill, p. 53. New York: Appleton-Century-Crofts, 1970.

Brown, B. B. *Stress and the Art of Biofeedback*. New York: Harper & Row, 1977.

Bruhn, J. G., et al. "Psychological Predictors of Sudden Death in Myocardial Infarction." *Journal of Psychosomatic Research* 18 (1974): 187–91.

Buell, J. C., and R. S. Eliot. "Psychosocial and Behavioral Influences in the Pathogenesis of Acquired Cardiovascular Disease." *American Heart Journal* 100 (1980): 723–40.

Buell, J. C., and R. S. Eliot. "Stress and Cardiovascular Disease." *Modern Concepts of Cardiovascular Disease* 48, no. 4 (1979): 19–24.

Burke, R. J., and T. Weir. "Marital Helping Relationships: The Moderators between Stress and Well-being." *Journal of Psychology* 95 (1977): 121–30.

Cannon, W. B. *The Wisdom of the Body*. New York: W. W. Norton, 1963.

Cassel, J. "Psychosocial Processes and 'Stress': Theoretical

Formulation." *International Journal of Health Services* 4 (1974): 471–82.

Chambers, W. N., and M. F. Reiser. "Emotional Stress in the Precipitation of Congestive Heart Failure." *Psychosomatic Medicine* 15 (1953): 38–60.

Collison, D. R. "Cardiological Applications of the Control of the Autonomic Nervous System by Hypnosis." *American Journal of Clinical Hypnosis.* 12 (1970): 150–56.

Coolidge, J. C. "Unexpected Death in a Patient Who Wished to Die." *Journal of the American Psychoanalytical Association* 17 (1969): 413–20.

Cooperman, E. M. "Coping with Cancer: Denial and the Need for a Better Bedside Manner." *Canadian Medical Association Journal* 117 (1977): 1123–24.

Cousins, N. "A Layman Looks at Truth Telling in Medicine." *Journal of the American Medical Association* 244 (1980): 1929–30.

Cousins, N. "Anatomy of an Illness (as Perceived by the Patient)." *New England Journal of Medicine* 295 (1976): 1458–63.

Cousins, N. "Denial: Are Sharper Definitions Needed?" *Journal of the American Medical Association* 248 (1982): 210–12.

Cousins, N. "The Healing Heart." *American Health* 2, nos. 3 and 4 (1983).

Cousins, N. "The Healing Heart." *International Journal of Cardiology* 3, nos. 1 and 2 (1983).

Cousins, N. "Laymen and Medical Technology." *Annual Review of Public Health* 2 (1981): 93–99.

Cousins, N. "The Physician as Communicator." *Journal of the American Medical Association* 248 (1982): 587–89.

Cousins, N. *The Physician in Literature.* Philadelphia: W. B. Saunders, 1982.

Cousins, N. "Potentiation and the Patient." *Bulletin of the American College of Surgeons,* June 1980.

Cousins, N. "Writers and Physicians: Toward a Common Culture." *Archives of Internal Medicine* 142 (1982): 2160–62.

Crawford, D. W., M. E. Sanmarco, and D. H. Blankenhorn.

"Spatial Reconstruction of Human Femoral Atheromas Showing Regression." *American Journal of Medicine* 66 (1979): 784–89.

DeBakey, M. *The Living Heart.* New York: McKay, 1977.

Dembroski, T. M., et al. "Type A, Stress, and Autonomic Reactivity: Considerations for a Study of These Factors in the Work Place." In *Myocardial Infarction and Psychosocial Risks,* edited by J. Siegrist and M. J. Halhuber, p. 89. Berlin: Springer, 1981.

Dembroski, T. M., J. M. MacDougall, and R. Lushene. "Interpersonal Interaction and Cardiovascular Response in Type A Subjects and Coronary Patients." *Journal of Human Stress* 5, no. 4 (1979): 28–36.

Dossett, S. M. "The Patient in the Intensive Therapy Unit." *Nursing Times* 74 (1978): 890–91.

Dubos, R. *Man Adapting.* New Haven: Yale University Press, 1965.

Dubos, R. *Man, Medicine, and Environment.* New York: Praeger, 1968.

Dubos, R. *Mirage of Health.* New York: Harper & Row, 1971.

Dubos, R. "The State of Health and the Quality of Life." *Western Journal of Medicine* 125 (1976): 8–9.

Duncan, C. H., I. P. Stevenson, and H. S. Ripley. "Life Situations, Emotions, and Paroxysmal Auricular Arrhythmias." *Psychosomatic Medicine* 12 (1950): 23–37.

Dwyer, T., and B. S. Hetzel. "A Comparison of Trends of Coronary Heart Disease Mortality in Australia, U.S.A. and England and Wales with Reference to Three Major Risk Factors—Hypertension, Cigarette Smoking and Diet." *International Journal of Epidemiology* 9 (1980): 65–71.

Eliot, R. S. *Stress and the Major Cardiovascular Disorders.* Mount Kisco, N.Y.: Futura, 1979.

Eliot, R. S. "What I Learned from My M.I." *Modern Medicine* 49 (1981): 62–72.

Eliot, R. S., et al. "Influences of Environmental Stress on Pathogenesis of Sudden Cardiac Death." *Federation Proceedings* 36 (1977): 1719–24.

Engel, B. T. "Comment on Self-control of Cardiac Functioning: A Promise As Yet Unfulfilled." *Psychological Bulletin* 81 (1974): 43.

Engel, G. L. *Psychological Development in Health and Disease.* Philadelphia: W. B. Saunders, 1962.

Engel, G. L. "Sudden and Rapid Death during Psychological Stress: Folklore or Folk Wisdom." *Annals of Internal Medicine* 74 (1971): 771–82.

Ernst, F. A., R. K. Korderat, and C. A. Sandman. "Learned Control of Coronary Blood Flow." *Psychosomatic Medicine* 41 (1979): 79–85.

Flynn, R. E. "Medical Technology Raises Moral and Ethical Issues." *Hospitals* 52, no. 22 (1978): 70–71.

Francis, K. T. "Psychologic Correlates of Serum Indicators of Stress in Man: A Longitudinal Study." *Psychosomatic Medicine* 41 (1979): 617–28.

Frank, J. *Persuasion and Healing: A Comparative Study of Psychotherapy.* 2d ed. Baltimore: Johns Hopkins University Press, 1973.

Frank, J. "The Faith That Heals." *Johns Hopkins Medical Journal* 137 (1975): 127–31.

Friedman, M., et al., "Plasma Catecholamine Response of Coronary-Prone Subjects (Type A) to a Specific Challenge." *Metabolism* 24 (1975): 205–10.

Friedman, M., and R. H. Rosenman. *Type A Behavior and Your Heart.* New York: Fawcett Columbine Books, 1974.

Friedman, M., R. H. Rosenman, and V. Carrol. "Changes in the Serum Cholesterol and Blood of Occupation Stress." *Circulation* 17 (1958): 825.

Friedman, M., et al. "Feasibility of Altering Type A Behavior Pattern after Myocardial Infarction." *Circulation* 66 (1982): 83–92.

Fry, W. F., Jr., et al. "Mirth and Oxygen Saturation Levels of Peripheral Blood." *Psychotherapy and Psychosomatics* 19 (1971): 76–84.

Fry, W. F., Jr. "The Respiratory Components of Mirthful Laughter." *Journal Biological Psychology* 19, no. 2 (1977): 39–50.

Glass, D. C. *Behavior Patterns, Stress, and Coronary Disease.* Hillsdale, N.J.: Lawrence Erlbaum, 1977.

Glass, D. C. et al. "Effect of Harassment and Competition upon Cardiovascular and Plasma Catecholamine Responses in Type A and B Individuals." *Psychophysiology* 17 (1980): 453–63.

Glueck, C. J., et al. "Diet and Atherosclerosis: Past, Present and Future." *Western Journal Medicine* 130 (1979): 117–22.

Gould, G. M. *Anomalies and Curiosities of Medicine.* Philadelphia: W. B. Saunders, 1897.

Green, E. and A. *Beyond Biofeedback.* New York: Delacorte Press, 1977.

Greene, W. A., S. Goldstein, and A. J. Moss. "Psychological and Social Variables Associated with Sudden Death from Apparent Coronary Heart Disease." *Psychosomatic Medicine* 35 (1973): 458–59.

Hackett, T. P., and N. H. Cassem. "Development of a Quantitative Rating Scale to Assess Denial." *Journal of Psychosomatic Research* 18 (1974): 93–100.

Haft, J. I., and Y. S. Arkel. "Effect of Emotional Stress on Platelet Aggregation in Humans." *Chest* 70 (1976): 501–5.

Harris, P. "Effects of Dietary Restriction on Myocardial Composition." *Advances in Myocardiology* 2 (1986): 31–38.

Harvey, W. P., and S. A. Levine. "Paroxysmal Ventricular Tachycardia Due to Emotion: Possible Mechanism of Death from Fright." *Journal of the American Medical Association* 160 (1952): 49.

Haynes, S. G., M. Feinleib, and W. B. Kannel. "The Relationship of Psychosocial Factors to Coronary Heart Disease in the Framingham Study: Eight-year Incidence of Coronary Heart Disease." *American Journal of Epidemiology* 111 (1980): 37–58.

Helfant, R. H. "Coronary spasm." *American Journal of Cardiology* 44 (1979): 839–41.

Hellstrom, H. R. "Coronary Artery Vasospasm: The Likely Immediate Cause of Acute Myocardial Infarction." *British Heart Journal* 41 (1979): 426–32.

Holland, J., et al. "ICU Syndrome: Fact or Fancy." *Psychiatry in Medicine* 4 (1973): 241–49.

Jenkins, C. D. "Recent Evidence Supporting Psychologic and Social Risk Factors for Coronary Disease." *New England Journal of Medicine* 294 (1967): 987, 1033.

Jenkins, C. D. "Behavioral Risk Factors in Coronary Artery Disease." *Annual Review of Medicine* 29 (1978): 543.

Katcher, A. H., et al. "Heart Rate and Blood Pressure Responses to Signaled and Unsignaled Shocks: Effects of Cardiac Sympathectomy." *Journal Comparative and Physiological Psychology* 68 (1969): 163–74.

Katz, L. N., S. S. Winton, and R. S. Megibow. "Psychosomatic Aspects of Cardiac Arrhythmias: A Physiological Dynamic Approach." *Annals of Internal Medicine* 27 (1947): 261.

Kavanagh, T. *The Healthy Heart Program*. Toronto: Van Nostrand Reinhold, 1980.

Kay, R. M., et al. "Acute Effects of the Pattern of Fat Ingestion on Plasma High Density Lipoprotein Components in Man." *Atherosclerosis* 36 (1980): 567–73.

Krehl, W. A. "The Nutritional Epidemiology of Cardiovascular Disease." *Annals of the New York Academy of Sciences* 300 (1977): 335–59.

Leren, P. "Prevention of Coronary Heart Disease by Diet." *Postgraduate Medical Journal* 51, no. 8 suppl. (1975): 44–46.

"Lipids, Platelets, and Atherosclerosis" (editorial). *Lancet,* March 1, 1980, 464–65.

"Lowering Blood Pressure without Drugs" (editorial). *Lancet,* August 30, 1980, 459–61.

Lown, B. "The Verbal Conditioning of Angina Pectoris during Exercise Testing. *American Journal of Cardiology* 40 (1977): 630–34.

Lown, B., and R. A. DeSilva. "Is Coronary Arterial Spasm a Risk Factor for Coronary Atherosclerosis?" *American Journal of Cardiology* 42 (1980): 901–3.

Lown, B., D. B. Kosowsky, and M. D. Klein. "Pathogenesis, Prevention and Treatment of Arrhythmia in Myocardial Infarction." *Circulation* 49 and 50: suppl. (1969): 261.

Lown, B., R. Verrier, and R. Corbalan. "Psychologic Stress

and Threshold for Repetitive Ventricular Response." *Science* 182 (1973): 834–36.

Lynch, J. J., et al. "Human Contact and Cardiac Arrhythmia in a Coronary Care Unit." *Psychosomatic Medicine*.

Manuck, S. B., and F. N. Garland. "Coronary-Prone Behavior Pattern, Task Incentive, and Cardiovascular Response." *Psychophysiology* 16 (1979): 136–42.

Marx, J. L. "Coronary Artery Spasms and Heart Disease." *Science* 208 (1980): 1127–30.

Maseri, A., et al. "Coronary Vasospasm as a Possible Cause of Myocardial Infarction. *New England Journal of Medicine* 299 (1978): 1271–77.

Mathis, J. L. "A Sophisticated Version of Voodoo Death: Report of a Case." *Psychosomatic Medicine* 26 (1964): 104–7.

Matthews, K. A., et al. "Competitive Drive, Pattern A, and Coronary Heart Disease: A Further Analysis of Some Data from the Western Collaborative Group Study." *Journal of Chronic Diseases* 30 (1977): 489–98.

McGrath, J. E., ed. *Social and Psychological Factors in Stress.* New York: Holt, Rinehart & Winston, 1970.

Menninger, K. A., M. Mayman, and P. Pruyser. *The Vital Balance: The Life Process in Mental Health and Illness.* New York: Viking Press, 1963.

Menninger, W. W. " 'Caring' as Part of Health Care Quality." *Journal of the American Medical Association* 234 (1975): 836–37.

Miettinen, M. "Prevention of Coronary Heart Disease by Cholesterol Lowering Diet." *Postgraduate Medical Journal* 51, no. 8 suppl. (1975): 47–51.

Murray, R. H., et al. "Blood Pressure Responses to Extremes of Sodium Intake in Normal Man." *Proceedings of the Society for Experimental Biology and Medicine* 159 (1978): 432–36.

Oliva, P. B. "What is the Evidence for and the Significance of Spasm in Acute Myocardial Infarction?" *Chest* 80 (1981): 730–35.

Ornish, D. *Stress, Diet, and Your Heart.* New York: Holt, Rinehart & Winston, 1982.

Osler, W. *Aequanimitas*. New York: McGraw-Hill, 1906.

Owen, A. *Hysteria, Hypnosis and Healing: The Work of J. M. Charcot*. New York: Garrett Publications / Helix Press, 1970.

Parfrey, P. S., et al. "Blood Pressure and Hormonal Changes following Alteration in Dietary Sodium and Potassium in Young Men with and without a Familial Predisposition to Hypertension." *Lancet*, January 17, 1981: 113–17.

Patel, C. "Reduction of Serum Cholesterol and Blood Pressure in Hypertensive Patients by Behavior Modification." *Journal of the Royal College of General Practitioners* 26 (1976): 111.

Pelletier, K. R. *Holistic Medicine: From Stress to Optimum Health*. New York: Delacorte Press / S. Lawrence, 1979.

Pelletier, K. R. *Mind as Healer, Mind as Slayer: A Holistic Approach to Preventing Stress Disorders*. New York: Delacorte Press /S. Lawrence, 1977.

Peter, L. J., and B. Dana. *The Laughter Prescription*. New York: Ballantine Books, 1982.

Pittner, N. S., and B. K. Houston. "Response to Stress, Cognitive Coping Strategies, and the Type A Behavior Pattern." *Journal of Personality and Social Psychology* 39 (1980): 147–57.

Rabkin, S. W., F. A. L. Mathewson, and R. B. Tate. "Chronobiology of Cardiac Sudden Death in Men." *Journal of the American Medical Association* 244 (1980): 1357–58.

Reich, P., et al. "Acute Psychological Disturbances Preceding Life-Threatening Ventricular Arrhythmias." *Journal of the American Medical Association* 246 (1981): 233–35.

Relman, A. S. "Technology Costs and Evaluation" (editorial). *New England Journal of Medicine*. 301 (1979): 1444–45.

Rosenman, R. H., and M. Friedman. "Neurogenic Factors in Pathogenesis of Coronary Heart Disease." *Medicine Clinics of North America* 58 (1974): 269–79.

Roth, D., and W. J. Kostuk. "Noninvasive and Invasive Demonstration of Spontaneous Regression of Coronary Artery Disease." *Circulation* 62 (1980): 888–96.

Sanders, C. A. "Medical Technology: Who's to Say When We've Had Enough." *Hospitals* 52, no. 22 (1978): 66–69, 72.

Schecter, N. "Psychological Aspects of Chronic Cardiac Dis-

286)   BIBLIOGRAPHY

ease." *Psychosomatics* 8 (1967): 166.

Scott, D. W., et al. "Diet and Coronary Heart Disease: The Statistical Analysis of Risk" (editorial). *Circulation* 63 (1981): 516–18.

Selye, H. *From Dream to Discovery.* New York: McGraw-Hill, 1964.

Selye, H. *The Stress of Life.* New York: McGraw-Hill, 1956.

Shekelle, R. B., et al. "Diet, Serum Cholesterol, and Death from Coronary Heart Disease: The Western Electric Study." *New England Journal of Medicine* 304 (1981): 65–70.

Shephard, R. J., et al. "Post-Coronary Rehabilitation and Risk Factors, with Special Reference to Diet." *Canadian Journal of Applied Sport Sciences* 5 (1980): 250–54.

Sigler, L. H. "Abnormalities in the Electrocardiogram Induced by Emotional Strain." *American Journal of Cardiology* 8 (1961): 807.

Simonton, O. C. *Getting Well Again.* Los Angeles: J. P. Tarcher, 1978.

Smith, A. *Powers of the Mind.* New York: Random House, 1975.

Stamler, J. "The Established Relationship among Diet, Serum Cholesterol and Coronary Heart Disease." *Acta Medicine Scandinavica* 207 (1980): 433–46.

Stanek, B., P. Hahn, and H. Mayer. "Biometric Findings on Cardiac Neurosis. III: Changes in ECG and Heart Rate in Cardiophobic Patients and Their Doctor During Psychoanalytical Initial Interviews." *Psychotherapy and Psychosomatics* 22 (1973): 289–99.

Stevenson, I. P., et al., "Life Situations, Emotions, and Extrasystoles." *Psychosomatic Medicine* 11 (1949): 257–72.

Stotland, E. *The Psychology of Hope.* San Francisco, Jossey-Bass, 1969.

Strain, J. J.: "Psychological Reactions to Acute Medical Illness and Critical Care." *Critical Care Medicine* 6 (1978): 39–44.

Subbiah, M. T., et al. "Dietary Restriction and the Development of Atherosclerosis." *British Journal of Nutrition* 41 (1979): 1–6.

Surawicz, F. G. "Psychological Aspects of Sudden Cardiac Death." *Heart and Lung* 2 (1973): 836.

Surgeon General, United States Army. *Annual report*. Washington, D.C.: GPO, 1980.

Theorell, T., and P. O. Webster. The Significance of Psychological Events in a Coronary Care Unit: Preliminary Report." *Acta Medica Scandinavica* 193 (1973): 207–10.

Thomas, S. A., J. J. Lynch, and M. E. Mills. "Psychosocial Influences on Heart Arrhythmia in a Coronary Care Patient." *Heart and Lung* 4 (1975): 746–50.

Todd, M. C. "Man, Medicine, and Machines." *Medical Instrumentation* 11 (1977): 185–88.

Tomlin, P. J. "Psychological Problems in Intensive Care." *British Medical Journal* August 13, 1977, 441–43.

Turpeinen, O., et al. "Dietary Prevention of Coronary Heart Disease: The Finnish Mental Hospital Study." *International Journal of Epidemiology* 8 (1979): 99–118.

Van Egeren, L. A. "Social Interactions, Communications, and the Coronary-Prone Behavior Pattern: A Psychophysiological Study." *Psychosomatic Medicine* 41 (1979): 2–18.

Van Pelt, S. J. "The Control of the Heart Rate by Hypnotic Suggestion." In *Experimental Hypnosis,* edited by L. M. LeCron, p. 268. New York: Macmillan, 1956.

Vernon, C. R., D. A. Martin, and K. L. White. "Psychophysiological Approach to Management of Patients with Congestive Heart Failure." *Journal of the American Medical Association* 171 (1959): 1947.

Weddington, W. W., Jr., "Psychogenic Explanation of Symptoms as a Denial of Physical Illness." *Psychosomatics* 21 (1980): 805–13.

Weiss, S. "Instantaneous 'physiologic' death." *New England Journal of Medicine* 223 (1940): 793.

Weiss, S. M., "Coronary Prone Behavior and Coronary Heart Disease: A Critical Review." *Circulation* 63 (1981): 1199–215.

Werkö, L. "Diets, Lipids and Heart Attacks." *Acta Medica Scandinavica* 206 (1979): 435–39.

Wolf, S. "Central Autonomic Influences on Cardiac Rate and

Rhythm." *Modern Concepts of Cardiovascular Disease* 38 (1969): 29.

Wolf, S. "Psychosocial Forces in Myocardial Infarction and Sudden Death." *Circulation* 49 and 50, suppl. (1969): 74.

Wolff, H. G. *Stress and Disease.* Revised and edited by S. Wolf and H. Goodell. Springfield, Ill.: Charles C. Thomas, 1968.

Yates, A. J. *Biofeedback and the Modification of Behavior.* New York: Plenum Press, 1980.

Young, P. J. W. "Scared to Death." *British Medical Journal* 2 (1965): 701.

Zanchetti, A., G. Bacceli, and G. Mancia. "Cardiovascular Effects of Emotional Behavior." In *Cardiovascular Regulation in Health and Disease,* edited by C. Bartorelli, p. 17. Milan: Cardiovascular Research Institute, 1971.

Zinsser, H. *As I Remember Him.* Boston: Little Brown, 1940.

Index